The
Minnesota
Almanac

Candice Gaukel Andrews

TRAILS BOOKS
Madison, Wisconsin

To Those Who Came Before.

Thanks to all of those who have written
so knowledgeably about Minnesota
and made my research within easy reach,
and to Trails Books who believed in this project
long before I came along.

Library of Congress Control Number: 2008908450
ISBN: 978-1-934553-22-0

Editor: Melissa Faliveno
Book Design: Rebecca Finkel

Printed in the United States of America

13 12 11 10 09 08   6 5 4 3 2 1

TRAILS BOOKS
a division of Big Earth Publishing
923 Williamson Street • Madison, WI 53703
(800) 258-5830 • www.trailsbooks.com

Contents

January

February

Seasonal Gardening Advice

January in the Garden:
Protecting Your Garden in Winter

February in the Garden:
Plants on Vacation; Winter Burn; The Attraction of Shrubbery

March in the Garden:
Spring in the Garden; Signs of Spring: Phenology; Average Frosts and Growing Seasons

April in the Garden:
Pruning Deciduous Trees; How to Keep Garden Pests Away; Average Frosts and Growing Seasons

May in the Garden:
I Beg Your Pardon, I Never Promised You a Rose Garden; Summer Mulching; Lawn Care; Should You Aerate and Dethatch?

June in the Garden:
A Checklist for Your Summer Garden; Be a Friend of the Earth ... worms!; You Can Be a Butterfly Gardener

March

April

December in the Garden: Feeding Birds; Peanut Butter Suet Cookies; A Living Christmas Tree;

Recipes

Pickled Fish (January)

Wild Baked Chicken (February)

Minnesota Wild Rice Creamy Chicken Soup (March)

Grandma's Scalloped Asparagus (April)

Pecan Crusted Minnesota Walleye (May)

Minnesota Blueberry Muffins (June)

Gourmet Burgers (July)

Wild Surf and Turf (August)

Minnesota Honeycrisp Apple Praline Cake (September)

May

June

**Salmon Fillets With
Morel Mushrooms**
(October)

**Indian Wild Rice Corn
Pudding** (November)

Fattigmand (December)

Gladys's
Household Tips

Pulling the Wool;
Cure a Cold (January)

Caring for Books;
Removing Musty Odors
from Books (February)

Treating Carpet Stains;
How to Clean Windows
(March)

Removing a Fishhook
from Your Skin; Signs
of Infection (April)

What to Keep in a
Medicine Cabinet;
What to Keep in a Locked
Cupboard or Closet (May)

How to Handle Injured
Animals: Dogs, Cats, Birds
(June)

July

Keep Your Straw Sun Hat Looking Its Best; What to Keep in a First Aid Kit (July)

Preventing Drains from Clogging; Cleaning a Garbage Disposal (August)

Identifying Poisonous and Nonpoisonous Snakes; How to Treat a Snake Bite (September)

Household Tips for Dust-Sensitive People; How to Thaw a Frozen Water Pipe (October)

Sharpening Knives; How to Load a Dishwasher (November)

Building a Fire in Your Indoor Fireplace; Building a Fire in Outdoor Bowls and Fireplaces (December)

August

September

October

November

December

JANUARY

"Every man should be born again

on the first day of January.

Start with a fresh page.

Take up one hole more in the buckle

if necessary, or let down one,

according to circumstances;

but on the first of January

let every man gird himself once more,

with his face to the front,

and take no interest in the things

that were and are past."

— HENRY WARD BEECHER

In Roman mythology, Janus was a god who had two faces: one of them looked into the past, and the other saw into the future. Janus, the "doorkeeper," was the god of doors and gates, of entrances and exits. Today, the month of "January" represents a new beginning, an opening into the New Year.

January is the coldest month in Minnesota, bringing subzero weather to almost everyone in the state. With typical good humor, Minnesotans cope. In 1886, when a New York reporter wrote that Minnesota was the "second Siberia" and "unfit for human habitation in winter," St. Paul residents responded with a Winter Carnival that drew thousands from throughout the United States and Canada. And farther north, Minnesotans celebrate winter by holding the annual John Beargrease Sled Dog Marathon along the North Shore. The race commemorates the mail route of Ojibwa John Beargrease during the 1800s and brings together world-class sled dog teams from across the nation and around the globe.

This month, take a look back at Minnesota winter festivities that had their beginnings more than a hundred years ago, just as you look forward to your own new beginnings this New Year.

International Falls
Average High and Low Temperatures

With typical Minnesota humor, as part of International Falls's annual "Icebox Days," the city holds a "Freeze Yer Gizzard Blizzard Run." And in the 1970s, Sears filmed a commercial for its Diehard car battery there, using the extreme winter climate to demonstrate the battery's longevity.

Despite all this, International Falls doesn't hold the title of record low temperature for the state. That honor is shared by two other cities: Leech Lake Dam, which nabbed the record on February 9, 1899, when the city reached -59 degrees Fahrenheit, and Pokegama Falls, which achieved the same low on February 6, 1903.

Month	Jan	Feb	Mar	Apr	May	Jun	Jul	Aug	Sep	Oct	Nov	Dec
Avg. high °F	14	23	35	52	67	74	79	76	65	52	33	18
Avg. low °F	-8	-1	12	27	40	49	54	51	42	32	16	-1

Source: Minnesota State Climatology Office: DNR Waters

Eveleth

The Capital of American Hockey

According to the United States Hockey Hall of Fame in Eveleth, "No community the size of Eveleth has produced as many quality players or has contributed more to the development of the sport in the United States." Hence its nickname, "The Capital of American Hockey."

As the sport of ice hockey moved south from Canada, it found a welcome reception in Minnesota. In January 1895, the first organized game in the state was played between two Minneapolis city teams. By 1906, children were playing for hours on frozen lakes and rivers or outdoor rinks. Sticks were often homemade, and siblings shared skates that were rarely out of use. In 1912, St. Paul opened the Hippodrome, and Duluth residents could play hockey at the curling club (see "Throwing Stones: The Ice Sport of Curling," December chapter).

In 1921, the small town of Eveleth built its first Hippodrome, enabling the city's teams to compete against much larger rivals from St. Paul, Duluth, and even Pittsburgh. The town became a hockey hotbed, with some of the best athletes in North America coming to play. In 1927–28, the Eveleth junior college team was invited to represent the United States at the Olympic Winter Games. Unfortunately, however, the town was unable to raise the funds for the team to make the trip.

In 1967, a group of Eveleth citizens researched ice hockey in the United States and discovered that no other town of Eveleth's size had contributed so much to the sport and no other state had contributed more than Minnesota. In fact, Minnesota has provided more Olympic and professional ice hockey athletes than any other state in the nation.

"January brings the snow,

Makes our feet and fingers glow."

— SARA COLERIDGE

St. Paul, aka Pig's Eye

Today, St. Paul is the capital of Minnesota and the state's second most populous city. (The 2007 estimate is 275,500; Minneapolis is first with 372,811.) If not for the intercession of a clergyman, however, the city might have been called "Pig's Eye."

In 1838, a small group of drifters from the Canadian Red River Settlement set up camp on Fort Snelling military reservation land, which stretched for ten miles up and down the Mississippi River. The United States Army soon evicted them, and a few families moved across the river, thinking they were safely outside the reservation limits. There they found a French Canadian named Pierre Parrant living near the steamboat landing. He had set up a saloon a few weeks earlier, selling liquor to the soldiers, riverboat crews, and Native Americans. Parrant was known as "Pig's Eye," either because he was blind in one eye or, in the words of one contemporary writer, had "a crooked, sinister, white ring glaring around the pupil which lent a kind of piggish expression to his sodden, low features." The saloon—and the settlement that grew up around it—was soon called "Pig's Eye Pandemonium," and Parrant became recognized as the first resident of what is today St. Paul.

As the town grew, however, Parrant eventually moved downstream a few miles to a backwater that became known as Pig's Eye Lake.

In 1841, Father Lucian Galtier built a little log chapel at the steamboat landing, which he consecrated to St. Paul. Rather than "Pig's Eye," the settlers chose to name the place after the saint.

The Right to Breathe

The Minnesota Clean Indoor Air Act (1975) was the first law to ban smoking except in designated areas. White Bear Lake was the first city in the United States to ban cigarette vending machines.

A Tradition of Almanacs

Known for his folksy humor, Cedric Adams, a native of Adrian, Minnesota, published *Poor Cedric's Almanac* in 1952. It is said he may have been the "hardest working journalist in the business." A workweek for Adams consisted of fifty-four radio shows, eight TV shows, and seven columns in the *Minneapolis Star* and *Sunday Tribune*.

Facts About St. Paul

- In 1849, St. Paul became the capital of the Minnesota Territory.

- James Madison Goodhue began publishing Minnesota's first newspaper, the *Minnesota Pioneer*, in St. Paul in 1849.

- In the mid-1800s, St. Paul became the busiest river port and leading commercial center in the Northwest. It was the farthest upstream a riverboat could reliably navigate, with fifteen miles of rapids and St. Anthony Falls above it. By the late 1850s, twenty or more steamboats at a time would jockey for positions at the two landings in town.

- In 1857, St. Peter almost became the state capital. Joseph Rolette, a member of the Territorial Council (the modern-day Senate) and the son of a Canadian fur trapper, took the bill that would have changed the capital's location and hid it in a St. Paul hotel room. It stayed there until the end of the legislative session, too late for the bill to be signed by the governor.

- By 1888–89, St. Paul had an elevated monorail.

- During the 1880s, the St. Paul climate was advertised as a cure for tuberculosis.

- On February 1, 1886, St. Paul residents built the city's first Ice Palace and held the first Winter Carnival. When the palace was completed, it boasted twenty thousand blocks of ice and was the tallest building in the city. The palace stood nearly fourteen stories high (106 feet) and 140 feet long. It contained Gothic archways and towers, turreted walls, and battlements.

- By 1893, railroad financier James Hill had extended the Great Northern Railway from St. Paul to Puget Sound in Washington State.

- There existed two state capitol buildings before the current one, which was dedicated in 1905.

- In 1959, the city established the first full-time, professional chamber orchestra in the United States: the St. Paul Chamber Orchestra. The orchestra continues to perform locally and on national and international tours.

Bigfoot Does Exist!

Whether you choose to call him "Bigfoot," "Sasquatch," or "Yeti," it seems the big man himself has a fondness for Minnesota. Every few years, he manages to make an appearance somewhere in the state.

In 1911, two hunters in northern Minnesota came upon a trail of "strange" footprints. They followed the tracks and reported that they found a "human giant" with long arms and covered in short, dark hair. And in 1966, Helen Westring was walking in the woods near Bemidji when she said a hairy, humanoid, pink-eyed creature attacked her. Terrified, she shot it and ran home. One of her neighbors, Frank Hansen, convinced her that she should preserve the creature in ice and charge people money to see it. For two years, she did. At the time, a few reputable scientists even called the strange beast a "missing link" in human evolution.

Another sighting happened in the early spring of 1981 when large, mysterious tracks were found in a cow pasture just outside Crookston. Little was made of the incident at the time, but on June 20, 1995, the *Crookston Daily Times* ran a story with a large headline reading "Bigfoot Sighted?"

The wire services picked up the story, and within weeks, people from the East Coast to the West wanted to know more about Bigfoot and Crookston. All the national interest seemed to jog the memories of other local people, who came forward with stories of their own Bigfoot encounters.

For a while, Crookston publicized itself as the "Bigfoot Capital of the World" in an effort to draw visitors. Things didn't turn out quite so well for Helen Westring. It was later discovered that whatever the creature she shot may have been, the one on ice was really made of rubber.

"The wild gander leads his flock through the cool night,

Ya-honk he says, and sounds it down to me like an invitation,

The pert may suppose it meaningless, but I listening close,

Find its purpose and place up there toward the wintry sky."

— WALT WHITMAN, FROM THE POEM *SONG OF MYSELF*

A Whale of a Ship

An immigrant from Scotland, Alexander McDougall moved to Duluth in the mid-nineteenth century. Working as a seaman and ship's master on the Great Lakes, he became fascinated with finding a way to build a cheap vessel to carry a maximum amount of bulk freight—such as iron ore, coal, and grain—at a minimum depth.

In 1887 and '88, McDougall built his first "whaleback" at the Robert Clark Shipyard in Duluth. At 191 feet long and 21 feet in beam, the 428-ton, cigar-shaped barge had a cargo capacity of 1,200 tons. Between 1889 and 1898, McDougall built nineteen whaleback steamers. The ships, also known as "pig boats,"

became obsolete when they proved incapable of adapting to advances in unloading equipment.

The only surviving whaleback is the S.S. *Meteor*, which was converted into a tanker in 1943 and retired from service in 1969. It was purchased by the city of Superior, Wisconsin, in 1972 and set on Barker's Island in the Superior Harbor as a museum vessel.

The Real "Snowbirds"

Dark-Eyed Juncos

For many, the term "snowbirds" means Aunt Jenny and Uncle Jim who leave Minnesota for Florida every October and don't return until April. It's a twist to imagine that for some, "snowbirds going south" means spending the winter in warmer Minnesota.

Dark-eyed juncos spend their summers in the coniferous and mixed woodland forests of Canada and arrive in the Midwest with the coming of the snows. The small sparrows flock together in winter and travel in

groups. You'll know they've arrived when you hear their clicking calls and songs, twittering trills that carry across backyards on crisp winter days.

Dark-eyed juncos are about six inches long, with slate-gray backs and white underbellies, beaks, and outer tail feathers. Males tend to be a darker gray than females.

Juncos like bird feeders, so stock yours in winter. Watch as the different groups establish a pecking order to work out who gets to eat what and when.

Mark Your
JANUARY
C A L E N D A R

John Beargrease Sled Dog Marathon, Duluth
www.beargrease.com

St. Paul Winter Carnival, St. Paul
www.winter-carnival.com

The John Beargrease Sled Dog Marathon: Ojibwa John Beargrease carried mail along Lake Superior's rugged North Shore from 1879 to 1899. He traveled by dogsled in winter and by a small boat in summer. Every January since 1984, the four hundred-mile John Beargrease Sled Dog Marathon from Duluth and through Minnesota's north woods to Poplar Lake on the Gunflint Trail—where the mushers and their teams turn around for the return leg—commemorates his legendary mail service.

The grueling race is the most challenging long-distance dogsled race in the lower forty-eight states. The mushers vie for an $8,000 first prize. The annual event also includes a mid-distance race, beginning in Duluth and ending in Tofte, that earns the winner $3,700.

A St. Paul Palace: In 1888, the St. Paul Winter Carnival ice palace was the largest ice structure ever built. It was made of fifty-five thousand blocks of ice.

Throughout its 122-year history, the St. Paul Winter Carnival has been, and continues to be, an important part of St. Paul life. From skiing and skating, snowshoeing and tobogganing, to art, music, and culture from all over the world, the festival has something for everyone—and it shows: over 350,000 visitors pour into the capitol city each year to join the wintry fun.

It's a Bird ... No, It's a Plane!

On January 12, 1913, pilot Alexander Heine flew the first airplane over Minneapolis. In subzero weather, he circled the Hennepin County Courthouse.

Shantytown

Every winter, "Arctic villages" sprout up on Minnesota lakes as passionate ice fishers pull their shanties onto their favorite fishing spots, whether their makeshift homes are one-person canvas tents or wood units that hold up to ten or more. The only requirement is a hole in the floor. Sometimes the ice hole is the only thing that marks an individual's settlement, as some prefer to ice fish while exposed to the winter-white views and elements.

The most popular species to catch in winter are walleye and panfish, such as bluegill and crappie. Gathering in schools, bluegill are usually caught during the day; crappie just before sundown. Walleye and sauger tend to bite best around dawn and dusk—and at first ice. Walleye are usually caught by jigging, though the tip-up method is also gaining popularity.

Northern and trout are not as light-sensitive as crappie, walleye, and sauger, and may be caught at any time of day. It's possible to catch muskie and bass, although they aren't as active in winter as other game fish.

As in any village, the shantytowns provide an opportunity for socializing. Ice-fishing neighbors often trade some great "northern" stories.

January Recipe Pickled Fish

The M.A. Gedney Company, located in the town of Chaska, has been making pickles since 1881.

If you can't eat all of the fish you've set aside from this season's abundant ice fishing, here's a recipe for pickling that works with almost any kind of meaty fish.

Pickled Fish

3 pounds whitefish, lake trout, or bass (almost anything)
1½ cups cider vinegar
1 teaspoon salt
½ cup sugar
1 jalapeno pepper, sliced and seeded (optional)
3 bay leaves
½ cup pickling spices

Clean and bone the fish and cut it into serving-sized pieces. Put them in a cooking pot with the vinegar, salt, sugar, and pepper. Add bay leaves and pickling spices (tied into a little cheesecloth bag). Barely cover with water, bring to a boil, and simmer for 10 to 12 minutes. Let cool, then chill in refrigerator, covered with the pickling liquid. For long-term use, place fish in sterile jars while still hot, cover with the pickling liquid, and seal.

Source: Northwoods Cottage Cookbook by Jerry Minnich

What's New—and Old—in Windchill Temperatures

In 2001, the National Weather Service implemented an updated Windchill Temperature (WCT) index. The goal was to upgrade and standardize the index for temperature extremes internationally.

The current formula uses advances in science, technology, and computer modeling to provide a more accurate, understandable, and useful formula for calculating the dangers from winter winds and freezing temperatures. The new windchill formula is now being used in Canada and the United States.

> **NOTE:** Windchill temperature is only defined for temperatures at or below 50 °F and wind speeds above 3 mph. Bright sunshine may increase the windchill temperature by 10 to 18 °F.

Specifically, the new WCT index:
- calculates wind speed at an average height of five feet (typical height of an adult human face) based on readings from the national standard height of thirty-three feet (typical height of an anemometer),

- incorporates modern heat transfer theory (heat loss from the body to its surroundings, during cold and breezy/windy days),

- lowers the calm wind threshold to 3 mph,

- uses a consistent standard for skin tissue resistance, and

- assumes no impact from the sun (i.e., clear night sky).

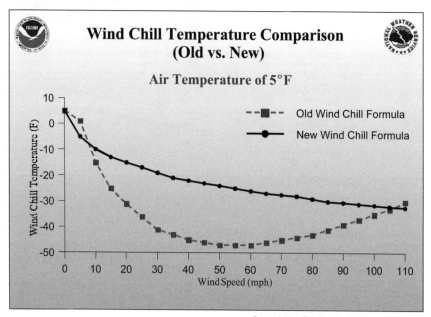

Wind Chill Temperature Comparison (Old vs. New)

Air Temperature of 5°F

Source: National Weather Service, www.nws.noaa.gov

One of the Worst *The Blizzard of 1873*

One of the worst blizzards to ever hit Minnesota began on January 7, 1873, and lasted three days. A hurricane-force wind blew for fifty-three hours, visibility was no more than three feet, and the temperature dropped almost forty degrees in one minute.

After the storm there were blizzard reports from twelve counties. Seventy people had died, cows had suffocated in the deep snows, and trains were stuck for days. It was said that a student in New Ulm had started for his home across the road, and his frozen body was found eight miles away. Another man lost in the storm stayed in a stable for two days, only to find when he emerged that he was just a few yards from his own house. Some bodies were not found until spring.

Average Precipitation High and Low Temperatures in January

Place	Avg. Precip. (Inches)	Avg. High Temp.	Avg. Low Temp.
Bemidji	0.7	12	-11
Duluth	1.2	16	-2
Int'l Falls	0.8	10	-10
Minneapolis	0.8	20	2
Moorhead	0.6	15	-3
Rochester	0.8	21	3
St. Cloud	0.7	17	-5
Windom	1.0	20	0

Source: Minnesota State Climatology Office: DNR Waters

Get the Drift?

About twelve thousand years ago, the last continental glacier passed through the Midwestern United States. When glaciers recede, they usually leave behind a mixture of debris consisting of dirt, vegetation, and rock known as "drift." A 24,000 square-mile area of southeastern Minnesota, northeastern Iowa, western Wisconsin, and northwestern Illinois was circumvented by the last Wisconsin Glacier (bounded on the north near Red Wing, on the west by St. Charles, on the east by Madison, Wisconsin, and on the south near Clinton, Iowa). The resulting lack of drift led to this region being called the "Driftless Area."

In Minnesota, the Driftless Area consists of the southeastern counties of Houston, most of Filmore, and the south part of Winona. The topography of Driftless Areas typically includes rugged terrain, spectacular bluffs, and deep valleys.

JANUARY WEATHER

January Normals for Duluth

Day	High	Low	Mean	Precip.	Snowfall
1	18	0	9	0.03	0.6
2	18	0	9	0.03	0.6
3	18	-1	8	0.03	0.6
4	18	-1	8	0.03	0.6
5	18	-1	8	0.03	0.6
6	17	-1	8	0.03	0.6
7	17	-1	8	0.03	0.6
8	17	-1	8	0.04	0.6
9	17	-2	8	0.04	0.7
10	17	-2	8	0.04	0.7
11	17	-2	8	0.04	0.7
12	17	-2	8	0.04	0.7
13	17	-2	8	0.04	0.7
14	17	-2	8	0.04	0.7
15	17	-2	8	0.04	0.7
16	17	-2	8	0.04	0.7
17	17	-2	8	0.04	0.7
18	17	-2	8	0.04	0.7
19	18	-2	8	0.04	0.7
20	18	-2	8	0.04	0.7
21	18	-2	8	0.04	0.6
22	18	-1	8	0.04	0.6
23	18	-1	8	0.04	0.6
24	18	-1	8	0.04	0.6
25	19	-1	9	0.04	0.6
26	19	-1	9	0.04	0.6
27	19	-1	9	0.03	0.6
28	19	0	9	0.03	0.6
29	20	0	10	0.03	0.6
30	20	0	10	0.03	0.5
31	20	1	10	0.03	0.5

JANUARY WEATHER

January Normals for International Falls

Day	High	Low	Mean	Precip.	Snowfall
1	14	-8	3	0.02	0.5
2	13	-8	3	0.02	0.5
3	13	-8	3	0.02	0.5
4	13	-8	2	0.02	0.5
5	13	-8	2	0.02	0.5
6	13	-9	2	0.02	0.5
7	13	-9	2	0.02	0.5
8	13	-9	2	0.03	0.5
9	13	-9	2	0.03	0.5
10	13	-9	2	0.03	0.5
11	13	-9	2	0.03	0.5
12	13	-9	2	0.03	0.5
13	13	-9	2	0.03	0.5
14	13	-9	2	0.03	0.5
15	13	-9	2	0.03	0.5
16	13	-9	2	0.03	0.5
17	13	-9	2	0.03	0.5
18	13	-9	2	0.03	0.5
19	13	-9	2	0.03	0.5
20	14	-9	2	0.03	0.5
21	14	-9	2	0.03	0.5
22	14	-9	3	0.03	0.5
23	14	-8	3	0.03	0.5
24	14	-8	3	0.03	0.5
25	15	-8	3	0.03	0.5
26	15	-8	4	0.03	0.5
27	15	-8	4	0.03	0.5
28	16	-7	4	0.03	0.5
29	16	-7	5	0.03	0.4
30	16	-7	5	0.02	0.4
31	17	-6	5	0.02	0.4

Source: National Oceanic and Atmospheric Administration (NOAA)'s National Weather Service

These climate normals are an average of thirty years of data between 1971 and 2000. Every ten years, the National Weather Service recalculates the normals using the next interval of thirty years. In 2010, the new normals will be recalculated using the period of 1981 to 2010.

JANUARY WEATHER HISTORY

On This Day in January

Day	Year	Weather
1	1864	Extreme cold in Minnesota. The Twin Cities reach a high of only -25 degrees F.
2	1941	Grand Portage gets over 4.5 inches of precipitation in 24 hours, roughly how much normally falls in the area during the entire winter (November–February).
3	1981	Arctic air visits the state. Embarrass, Wannaska, and Tower all hit -38.
4	1981	Air cold enough to freeze a mercury thermometer pours into the state. Tower hits -45.
5	1984	Warm-up across Minnesota. The Twin Cities reaches 43.
6	1942	In Pipestone, temperature rises from -32 to 41 in 24 hours.
7	2003	Record warmth across the state. Many places reach the 50s. Nine golf courses open in the Twin Cities.
8	1902	January thaw across the state. Twin Cities warm to 46 degrees.
9	1982	Both January 9 and 10 boast some of the coldest windchills ever seen in Minnesota. Temperatures of -30 and winds of 40 mph reported in northern Minnesota, translating to windchills of -71 with the new windchill formula; -100 with the old.
10	1975	"Blizzard of the Century" begins, also called the "Super Bowl Blizzard." Stranded people watch the Vikings lose on January 12. The pressure hits a low of 28.62, a record until 1998.
11	1899	An odd flash of lightning lights up the clouds around 9 p.m. at Maple Plain.
12	1888	The "Blizzard of '88" hits during a mild day when many children are heading home from school. They make up the majority of the 200 people who die in the storm.
13	1987	Warm air invades the state with a balmy high of 48.
14	1952	Glaze, sleet, and ice storms across Minnesota from St. Cloud south into Iowa. Minneapolis General Hospital treats 81 people, many of whom have fallen on icy streets and sidewalks.
15	1981	More than 24,000 Canada geese are reported at Silver Lake in Rochester.
16	1921	Winds gusting up to 59 mph create a sand blizzard across southwest Minnesota and a snowstorm across the north.
17	1982	The citizens of Tower wake up to -52 F.
18	1994	Governor Arne Carlson orders all Minnesota public schools closed due to the extreme cold and severe winter weather. Morning readings in the -30 range.
19	1994	The cold continues from the previous day with -47 at Brainerd. The Twin Cities airport hits -27.
20	1982	Just over 17 inches of snow falls in the Twin Cities, only to be outdone 2 days later.

JANUARY WEATHER HISTORY

On This Day in January

Day	Year	Weather
21	1936	Warroad falls to a bone-chilling -55.
22	1936	Perhaps the coldest windchill the Twin Cities has ever seen occurs on this day: -67 with the new windchill formula; -87 with the old formula. A number of fatalities are caused by the cold.
23	1982	One day earlier, the Twin Cities got 21.1 inches of snow. On this day, there is a total of nearly 40 inches on the ground.
24	1925	A solar eclipse is seen across northern Minnesota during the morning. The *Duluth Herald* reports that chickens were "puzzled by the dark morning" and didn't leave their roosts.
25	1968	A rare, severe thunderstorm hit the Twin Cities a day earlier and left a coating of ice an inch thick. Today, 10,000 homes are left without power.
26	1916	A severe ice storm hits Mower County, and hundreds of birds are killed.
27	1967	"Chicago's Big Snow" brings 23 inches; to clear it away, the snow is dumped into nearby rivers.
28	1914	A very rare thunderstorm is observed at Maple Plain during the evening.
29	1977	Due to the extreme cold, the St. Paul Winter Carnival is held indoors for the first time.
30	1994	Duluth reaches a record low of -35.
31	1893	The temperature drops 40 degrees in 5 hours during a blizzard at Park Rapids.

Source: Minnesota State Climatology Office: DNR Waters

Frostbite Falls

Isn't Just in the Minds of Rocky and Bullwinkle

Frostbite Falls was the fictional Minnesota hometown of TV cartoon characters Rocket J. Squirrel (Rocky) and Bullwinkle J. Moose of *The Rocky and Bullwinkle Show.* The name is a spoof of the real-life International Falls. And like its namesake, Frostbite Falls was said to be located in Koochiching County.

It turns out the moniker is apt: During the winter, International Falls tends to be the coldest city in the continental United States. Its average mean temperature of 36.4 degrees Fahrenheit has earned the city yet another nickname—the "Icebox of the Nation" (although Fraser, Colorado, also claims this title).

January in the Garden

Protecting Your Garden in Winter

Perhaps the best thing you can do for your garden in a Minnesota winter is protect it. Officially winter begins on December 21; but gardeners in this state know that the first blast of Arctic winds and juncos at the feeders are signs that winter has really begun. To protect your garden during winter:

- Rake up pine needles and leaves from the grass; if left for an extended period of time, they will kill the grass. Pine needles can be used as mulch.
- Cut annuals off just below the soil surface. You'll leave more soil in the ground and keep flowerbeds looking neat.
- Brush heavy snow off evergreens.
- Prune evergreens and use the boughs on bulb beds and perennials to help protect them from heavy snow cover.
- Build a wooden box with no top or bottom as another way to protect perennials. Place the box over the plants after the ground has frozen and fill it with leaves.
- Cover exposed roots of perennials with mulch if you notice them heaving, or being pushed out of the soil by freezing temperatures.
- Check the structure, or "bones," of your garden for visual appeal. Hedges, tall bushes, stone walls, and pathways all contribute to the underlying framework.
- Keep bird feeders full. Songbirds need to eat their weight in seeds every twelve hours.
- Scatter mothballs to discourage rabbits from your garden. Scented clothes-dryer sheets and deodorant bath soap are effective in keeping deer away from shrubs and trees.

Gladys's

January Household Tips

Slipping into and feeling the warmth of a wool sweater is just one of the season's pleasures—and one of those things that might make you feel a little better should a cold or the flu strike. Here's how to keep yours clean and in shape.

Pulling the Wool

When the cuffs or waistline of your woolen sweaters are stretched out, dip them in hot water and dry with a hot blow-dryer. They should shrink back to normal.

Hand-wash washable sweaters in your favorite cold-water detergent. Then fill the washing machine with cool water and add a little fabric softener. Swish the sweaters around by hand until they are thoroughly rinsed. Drain the tub and set it on the final spin cycle. Spread the sweaters out on towels or hang up.

To dry and block a sweater, take a framed window screen and outline the unwashed sweater in chalk on the screen. After washing the sweater, block it to the outline and set the screen on bricks or across the backs of two chairs. Air will freely circulate underneath for quick drying.

Cure a Cold

The next time a cold or the flu threatens your enjoyment of the season, try this traditional remedy: Make a tea from equal parts cinnamon, sage, and bay leaves. Add a little lemon juice just before drinking.

Tyndall Flowers

Occasionally seen through clear lake ice on bright sunny days in Minnesota, Tyndall flowers are small, water-filled, hexagonal cavities that appear inside ice masses bathed in sunlight. Named for John Tyndall, a nineteenth-century English physicist who studied the scattering of light as it passed through smoke, mist, fog, and ice, Tyndall flowers form when radiative absorption melts ice at its weak points.

Source: *Minnesota Weather Almanac* by Mark W. Seeley, Minnesota Historical Society Press, 2006

FEBRUARY

"Why, what's the matter,

That you have

such a February face,

So full of frost,

of storm and cloudiness?"

— WILLIAM SHAKESPEARE,
MUCH ADO ABOUT NOTHING

Each February, across the country, gifts of candy and flowers are exchanged between loved ones on St. Valentine's Day. Just who is this mysterious saint of love, and why do we celebrate this holiday on February 14?

One legend has it that Valentine was a priest during the third century in Rome. Emperor Claudius II, believing that single men made better soldiers, outlawed marriage for all young males. Valentine thought the decree was highly unjust, so he defied Claudius and continued to perform marriages for young lovers in secret. When the priest's actions were discovered, Claudius ordered that Valentine be put to death—on February 14, some say.

It has even been postulated that Valentine himself actually sent the first "Valentine" greeting. While he was in prison, he supposedly fell in love with the jailor's daughter, who visited him during his confinement. As legend has it, he wrote her a letter before his death that he signed "From your Valentine," giving rise to today's popular signature.

We may never be able to fully unravel the truth about the origins of Valentine's Day traditions. However, almost everyone agrees that February is the month of romance. And in Minnesota, what better month to turn up the thermostat just a degree, curl up with a good book, and enjoy a Milky Way?

A Heck of a Lot of Winter
Record Low Temperatures and Average Annual Snowfall

Place	Record Low Temp.	Avg. Annual Snowfall (Inches)
Bemidji	-50	44
Duluth	-41	79
Int'l Falls	-49	64
Minneapolis	-41	52
Moorhead	-48	38
Rochester	-42	46
St. Cloud	-40	48
Windom	-32	37

Source: Minnesota State Climatology Office: DNR Waters

Minnesota's *Official State Song*

"Hail! Minnesota" was adopted as the Minnesota state song on April 19, 1945, by Minnesota Laws 1945 Joint Resolution Number 15. It was written by two University of Minnesota students in 1904 and 1905. Truman Rickard composed the music and wrote the first verse for a play titled *The Apple of Discord*. Originally, it included a verse referring to the president of the school, Cyrus Northrop. Northrop asked another student, Arthur Upson, to take out his name, rework the song, and add a second verse. It soon became the alma mater for the university.

During the 1920s, it was suggested that the state have an official song, but no agreement was reached. In 1945, a group of Minnesotans asked that "Hail! Minnesota" be considered.

By this time, Upson had died, but the university and Rickard gave the state permission to use the song. One phrase had to be changed: "Hail to thee our college dear!" became "Hail to thee our state so dear!"

"Hail! Minnesota"

Minnesota, hail to thee!
Hail to thee, our state so dear!
Thy light shall ever be
A beacon bright and clear.
Thy sons and daughters true
Will proclaim thee near and far.
They shall guard thy fame
And adore thy name;
Thou shalt be their northern star.

Like the stream that bends to sea,
Like the pine that seeks the blue,
Minnesota, still for thee,
Thy sons are strong and true.
From thy woods and waters fair,
From thy prairies waving far,
At thy call they throng,
With their shout and song,
Hailing thee their northern star.

A Charming Personality Test

The Minnesota Multiphasic Personality Inventory (MMPI) is one of the most frequently used and researched tests in the mental health field. The original MMPI was first published in 1942 by Starke Hathaway, Ph.D., and J. C. McKinley, M.D., and copyrighted by the University of Minnesota. It was designed to help identify and diagnose personal, social, and behavioral problems in psychiatric patients.

While no assessment tool is perfect, the MMPI remains a valuable aid in evaluating and planning treatments for mental illnesses.

Minnesota *Writes*

Whether it's an inclination toward self-reflection when the winter winds blow or the irresistible draw of staring out the window as snow paints the landscape, Minnesota has a strong tradition of inspiring the creative juices. Here are a few of the state's writers, in a line that stretches back for hundreds of years:

Father Louis Hennepin, a Belgian missionary, published the book *Nouvelle Découverte d'un Tres Grand Pays Situé dans l'Amerique (New Discovery of a Very Great Region Situated in America)* in 1697. In it, he claimed credit for many of the discoveries of others, but he did manage to bring the world's attention to two great waterfalls: Niagara Falls and St. Anthony Falls, the only waterfall on the Mississippi River.

In search of the Northwest Passage to the Orient, New Englander **Jonathan Carver** was sent out by the British from Fort Mackinac to meet with the Dakota Sioux. In 1778, he published his travels in a book called *Travels through the Interior Parts of North-America in the Years 1766, 1767, and 1768,* which aroused interest in Minnesota. The book has been through fifty-three editions in nine countries.

Thorstein Veblen (1857–1929) lived in Minnesota on a farm near Northfield from his eighth year until his early twenties. He published ten works, including *The Theory of the Leisure Class* (1899) and *The Engineers and the Price System* (1921).

Ole Edvart Rölvaag (1876–1931) left Norway when he was twenty years old and became a Norwegian studies professor at St. Olaf College in Northfield. His first novel, *Giants in the Earth,* was written while he was living in a cabin near Marcell on Big Island Lake. Critics called it "the most powerful novel that has ever been written about pioneer life in America."

Laura Ingalls was born in Wisconsin near Lake Pepin in 1867. After she became a widow, she began writing stories about her childhood. Her 1873 book *On the Banks of Plum Creek* was set in Walnut Gove. It was there that Ingalls was able to go to school for the first time and her family suffered the grasshopper plague of the 1870s.

Cole Younger, a member of the Jesse James gang, wrote a book while he was an inmate of the Minnesota State Prison located in Stillwater. It was titled *The Story of Cole Younger, by Himself: Being an Autobiography of the Missouri Guerilla Captain and Outlaw, His Capture and Prison Life, and the Only Authentic Account of the Northfield Raid Ever Published.* The book was published in 1903, two years after he was released on parole at age fifty-nine.

F. Scott Fitzgerald was born in St. Paul in 1896. After his first book, *This Side of Paradise,* was published in 1920, Zelda Sayre of Alabama accepted his proposal of marriage and they moved to New York. Fitzgerald later wrote: "I no longer regard St. Paul as my home…I never did quite adjust myself to those damn Minnesota winters…though many events there will always fill me with a tremendous nostalgia." He became known as "St. Paul's first successful novelist."

Born in Sauk Center in 1903, **Harry Sinclair Lewis,** known more famously as Sinclair Lewis, graduated from Yale University in 1908. In 1920, his controversial novel *Main Street* was published. The book was a satirical treatment of the American small town modeled on Sauk Center. *Arrowsmith*, published in 1925, won the Pulitzer Prize, but Lewis turned it down. In 1930, he became the first American to win the Nobel Prize for Literature for his book *Babbitt*. Six of his twenty-two novels take place in Minnesota.

Robert Penn Warren was a professor at the University of Minnesota from 1942 to 1950. He won the Pulitzer Prize for literature in 1947 for *All the King's Men.*

If you were around in the late 1950s and early 1960s, you probably remember **Dobie Gillis** and his "beatnik" friend **Maynard G. Krebs**—who never failed to jump when the word "work" was mentioned. St. Paul novelist and playwright **Max Shulman**

created the TV program in which the two characters starred, *The Many Loves of Dobie Gillis.*

Dean of Ely Junior College from 1936 to 1947, **Sigurd Olson** wrote nine books. His best known was *The Singing Wilderness* (1956). He also spearheaded the effort to create the Boundary Waters Canoe Area Wilderness.

Poet **Robert Bly** was born in western Minnesota in 1926. He majored in pre-med at St. Olaf College before transferring to Harvard and switching over to English. He received the National Book Award in 1968 for *The Light Around the Body.*

Clifford Simak was the third writer to receive the Science Fiction Writers of America Grand Master Award (1976). He also received three Hugo Awards, regarded as the Oscar of science-fiction writing. He was inducted into the Science Fiction Hall of Fame in 1973. In his novel *The Visitors* (1980), a fifty-foot-high black box from outer space lands in Minnesota.

Author **Gary Paulsen** wrote his first novel in a rented cabin on a lake in remote, northern Minnesota. A master storyteller, he has written more than 175 books and more than two hundred articles and short stories for children and adults. Three of his novels— *Hatchet, Dogsong,* and *The Winter Room*—were Newbery Honor Books.

Hamline University Professor **Lawrence Sutin** wrote *Divine Invasions* in 1989, a biography of science fiction writer Philip K. Dick.

From Pole to Pole *The Minnesota Connection*

Born in 1943 in Richfield, Minnesota, Will Steger worked as a science teacher in Ely. His heart, however, seemed to be split between the Earth's poles. Steger had spent many summers in Alaska and the Yukon. While running a wilderness program in the Boundary Waters Canoe Area Wilderness, he decided to launch an expedition to the North Pole on foot—a feat no one had accomplished since Robert Peary did it in 1909. On March 7, 1986, Steger and his team of seven men, one woman, and fifty dogs took off from Ward Hunt Island, at the northernmost tip of North America for the pole. On May 22, they reached it, without resupply.

Following the journey to the North Pole, Steger turned his attention to the global warming crisis. He decided to cross the entire Antarctic continent, from the Pacific Ocean to the Atlantic, in an effort to bring attention to the cause. His International Trans-Antarctic Expedition was made up of six men and thirty-six dogs. The expedition took 220 days; and on March 3, 1990, the team arrived at a makeshift finish line set up by the Soviets.

In 1995, Steger earned the prestigious National Geographic John Oliver La Gorce Medal, awarded only nineteen times since the founding of National Geographic in 1888, for "accomplishments in geographic exploration, in the sciences, and for public service to advance international understanding." Other recipients of the medal include Roald Amundson, Amelia Earhart, Admiral Robert Peary, and Jacques-Yves Cousteau.

The one woman on Steger's North Pole team in 1986 was Mendota Heights-born Ann Bancroft. She was a physical and special education teacher in Minneapolis and St. Paul. When the team arrived at the North Pole, Bancroft became the first woman in history to reach the North Pole overland.

And speaking of Roald Amundsen (1872–1928), he, too, has a Minnesota connection. The only existing remains of this lost Arctic explorer are two teeth that were extracted while he was visiting Concordia College in Moorhead as a speaker. The teeth are presently preserved in the college's library collections.

Keeping Warm with Honeywell

Honeywell was founded in 1885 by Minneapolis inventor Alfred Butz to manufacture the first automatic damper controls for home furnaces, called "thermostats." By 1910, the thermostats were actually stamped "The Minneapolis" in boldface across their covers.

First in Skiing *The Aurora Ski Club in Red Wing*

Norwegian immigrants introduced ski jumping to the United States in the 1880s. By 1885, the sport had appeared in several Midwestern communities. The first-recognized North American ski-jumping distance record was set by Mikkel Hemmestvedt, who flew a distance of thirty-seven feet at Red Wing in 1887.

Red Wing's Aurora Ski Club was founded in 1886. During their inaugural decade, Aurora club members became the first to introduce Telemark ski techniques, known well into the twentieth century as "Red Wing style." Their February 8, 1887, ski competition was named by the National Ski Association as America's "first ski tournament." At the beginning of the 1890s, Aurora was the nation's top skiing group. For an 1890 tournament, Aurora was the first to formulate, print, and distribute a list of rules for ski competitions, a concept later adopted by the National Ski Association.

Dwindling membership caused the Aurora Ski Club of Red Wing to disband in 1951.

Making a Point on the Open Range

As Minnesota's grazing grasslands were disappearing and vast prairies were being turned into wheat fields, a need for effective and inexpensive fencing arose. Both farmers and cattle herders wanted a fencing material that would protect crops and allow for selective breeding, so that the new German-Dutch Holsteins could be developed for dairy and English shorthorns could be bred for beef. Cattle could easily push through and trample over ordinary wire, so inventors began experimenting with ways to add deterrents, such as pointed barbs.

In 1874 Joseph Glidden of DeKalb, Illinois, patented a system for mechanically enmeshing and fixing barbs at regular intervals on smooth wire fencing. It was almost instantly popular with both farmers and cattle herders. The invention came at just the right time: in 1874, the legislature passed an act that made it unlawful for stock to run at large.

Today, Pioneer Village, run by the Nobles County Historical Society in Worthington, includes an exhibit of 746 pieces of barbed wire.

Slip, Sliding Away

A large portion of Minnesota bears the marks of glaciers (with the exception of the Driftless Area; see "Get the Drift?" January chapter). Like gigantic bulldozers, glaciers changed the Minnesota landscape forever.

More than a million years ago, Lake Agassiz—larger than all the Great Lakes combined—was created when glaciers melted. The Warren, a glacial river, began draining the lake more than eight thousand years ago, and was responsible for carving the Minnesota River Valley. The northern end of the Warren drained into Hudson Bay, and as the ice-dam melted, it left behind the Red River Valley. The remains of Lake Agassiz can be seen in Minnesota's Lake of the Woods and in Winnipeg, Winnipegosis, and Manitoba Lakes in Canada.

The last of the glaciers in Minnesota receded about twelve thousand years ago. Today, thousands of glacial lakes fill the central part of the state in an irregular topography. The greatest concentration of these lakes runs in an arc from the Mississippi headwaters near Bemidji, southwestward through Detroit Lakes, and south and east toward the Twin Cities. Another grouping of lakes lies north of Mille Lacs Lake and Brainerd.

The area in southwestern Minnesota where glaciers left deep deposits of clay, sand, and gravel is called the "Dissected Till Plains." And the rugged northeastern region of Minnesota least affected by glacial action is known as the "Superior Uplands." Other terms for glacial features you'll find in Minnesota are:

Drumlin: a long hill made of glacial debris.

Erratic: a rock carried and deposited by a glacier.

Esker: a long, wormlike ridge formed by debris-laden meltwater. Eskers probably mark the channels of subglacial streams.

Kame: a conical hill of glacial debris deposited in contact with glacial ice, appearing like a snow cone tipped upside down.

Kettle: a depression (which usually becomes a lake or marsh) in a deposit of glacial debris that formed when a block of ice separated from a glacier and melted.

MARK YOUR CALENDAR

Mark Your
FEBRUARY
C A L E N D A R

Wilderness Trek Ski Race, Ely
www.elynordic.org

Vasaloppet Cross-Country Ski Race, Mora **www.vasaloppet.org**

International Eelpout Festival, Walker
www.eelpoutfestival.com

Johnny Appleseed Had Nothing on Them

The 1860s in Minnesota were years of great expansion in the lumber industry and in rail transportation. In 1867, Minneapolis alone had sixty-seven miles of boardwalk, representing six million board feet—not to mention what was used in the city's buildings. Towns springing up even farther west were also demanding lumber, and the railroads themselves needed a lot of wood for ties and bridges.

Luckily, the state's legislators realized that what was taken needed to be replaced. In 1871, they passed the Tree Bounty Law, which provided funding for trees planted on the prairies and on other open land. By 1876, the Minnesota State Forestry Association had been formed.

Almost one hundred years later in 1980, a young Minnesotan named Geoffrey Steiner discovered a different kind of reward for planting trees on the prairie. Steiner, a Vietnam War veteran who did a 1967–1968 tour there as a Marine, returned home to Minneapolis deeply depressed. He moved to the woods near Cushing to be alone. In the forest, he discovered the joy and purpose in life he had been missing: he decided to plant a tree for every American— about fifty-eight thousand—who had died in Vietnam.

At last count, Geoffrey Steiner had personally planted more than thirty thousand trees in his "Vietnam Veterans Memorial Forest."

February Recipe Wild Baked Chicken

Minnesota is one of the world's largest suppliers of cultivated wild rice, producing four to six million pounds annually. The Minnesota Cultivated Wild Rice Council was formed in 1974 to promote the industry and benefit the state's growers. Minnesota is also one of the world's largest producers of hand-harvested wild rice. Cultivated or wild, the paddies provide a great habitat for waterfowl and other wildlife.

Wild Baked Chicken

12 chicken thighs
3 cups cooked wild rice
1 8-ounce package herb-seasoned stuffing mix
1 cup chopped cranberries (fresh or frozen)

½ cup chopped pecans
½ cup margarine, melted
2 cups boiling water
2 teaspoons chicken flavor instant bouillon
2 tablespoons cherry preserves, heated

Preheat the oven to 400°F. Lightly grease a 9" x 13" baking pan. In a large bowl, combine the wild rice, stuffing mix, cranberries, pecans, and margarine. In a small bowl, combine the water and bouillon. Pour over stuffing; mix well. Spoon into baking pan. Top with chicken thighs, skin side up. Bake for 35 to 40 minutes, or until chicken is browned and juices run clear when pierced with a fork. Spoon cherry preserves over chicken. Bake for another 10 minutes. Makes 8 servings. Printed with permission from the Minnesota Cultivated Wild Rice Council

Minnesota's Mammals

Native Americans and European immigrants once found plenty of wild game to feast on here. According to the *WPA Guide to Minnesota,* originally published in 1938, French explorer and soldier of fortune Pierre-Esprit Radisson (ca. 1636–1710), one of the first white men to enter the region that is now the state, wrote: "We killed several other beasts as Oriniacks (moose), stagg (elk), wild cows (buffalo), Carriboucks, fallow does and bucks, Catts of the mountains, child of the Devill—in a word we lead a good life."

Bison once blanketed the Minnesota prairies. After about 1830, however, buffalo were rarely seen and soon disappeared. The settling of towns and the slaughter of thousands of bison by market hunters and the United States Army reduced the once numerous herds to a handful of captive animals.

Today, sadly, bison in Minnesota are considered extirpated in the wild; however, they have been reintroduced in some preserves and parks. Blue Mounds State Park holds the only semi-wild buffalo herd in the Upper Midwest; it began with three buffalo acquired in 1961 from the Fort Niobrara National Wildlife Refuge in Nebraska.

The only evidence you may see today of the once great herds of bison that populated the state are an occasional find of bones on the prairie, a shallow depression originally formed by wallowing buffalo, or large boulders worn smooth by thousands who once rubbed off their shaggy, winter coats.

On the next page is a list of the mammals found in Minnesota today.

Mammals of Minnesota

Badgers

Bats
Little brown myotis
(most common)

Northern myotis

Big brown bat

Eastern pipistrelle

Eastern red bat

Silver-haired bat

Hoary bat

Beavers

Bison

Black Bears
(approximately 30,000)

Bobcats

Chipmunks
Eastern (Gray)

Least chipmunk

Cougars
(The last known mountain
lion in Minnesota was killed
in Becker County in 1897.
In recent years, there have
been several reports based
on sightings and tracks,
especially north of Duluth.)

Coyotes

Fishers

Foxes
Gray fox

Red fox

Gophers
Plains pocket gopher

Plains pocket mice
(38 varieties, plus
kangaroo mice and
kangaroo rats)

Northern pocket gopher

Lynx
(Numbers of lynx in
Minnesota are likely to
fluctuate with Canadian
populations and with the
abundance of their primary
prey, the snowshoe hare.)

Mice, voles, and rats
Deer mouse

House mouse

Meadow jumping mouse

Northern grasshopper
mouse

Western harvest mouse

White-footed mouse

Woodland jumping mouse

Heather vole

Meadow vole

Pine (woodland) vole

Prairie vole

Red-backed vole

Rock vole

Norway rat

Northern bog lemming

Southern bog lemming

Minks

Moles
Eastern moles

Starnose moles

Moose
(estimated 5,000–8,000)

Muskrats

Opossums

Otters

**Pine (or American)
martens**

Porcupines

Pronghorns

Rabbits and hares
Cottontail

Snowshoe hare

White-tailed jackrabbit

Raccoons

Shrews
Arctic shrew

Least shrew

Masked shrew

Northern water shrew

Pygmy shrew

Short-tail shrew

Skunks
Spotted skunk

Striped skunk

Squirrels
Eastern fox squirrel

Eastern gray squirrel

Flying squirrel

Franklin ground squirrel

Northern flying squirrel

Red (pine) squirrel

Richardson ground
squirrel

Southern flying squirrel

Thirteen-lined ground
squirrel

Timber wolves

Weasels
Least weasel

Long-tailed weasel

Short-tailed weasel

White-tailed deer

Wolverines

Woodchucks

Source: Minnesota Department of Natural Resources

FEBRUARY WEATHER

February Normals for Duluth

Day	High	Low	Mean	Precip.	Snowfall
1	20	1	10	0.03	0.5
2	21	1	11	0.03	0.5
3	21	1	11	0.03	0.5
4	21	2	11	0.03	0.5
5	22	2	12	0.03	0.4
6	22	2	12	0.03	0.4
7	22	2	12	0.03	0.4
8	22	3	13	0.03	0.4
9	23	3	13	0.03	0.4
10	23	3	13	0.03	0.4
11	23	4	14	0.02	0.4
12	24	4	14	0.02	0.4
13	24	4	14	0.03	0.4
14	24	5	15	0.03	0.4
15	25	5	15	0.03	0.4
16	25	6	15	0.03	0.4
17	25	6	16	0.03	0.4
18	25	6	16	0.03	0.3
19	26	7	16	0.03	0.3
20	26	7	16	0.03	0.4
21	26	7	17	0.03	0.4
22	27	8	17	0.03	0.4
23	27	8	18	0.03	0.4
24	27	8	18	0.03	0.4
25	28	9	18	0.03	0.4
26	28	9	19	0.03	0.4
27	28	10	19	0.03	0.4
28	28	10	19	0.04	0.4
29	28	10	19	0.04	NA

"If a tree dies, plant another in its place."

— LINNAEUS

February Normals for International Falls

Day	High	Low	Mean	Precip.	Snowfall
1	17	-6	6	0.03	0.4
2	17	-6	6	0.03	0.4
3	18	-5	6	0.03	0.4
4	18	-5	7	0.03	0.4
5	19	-4	7	0.03	0.4
6	19	-4	8	0.02	0.4
7	19	-4	8	0.02	0.4
8	20	-3	8	0.02	0.4
9	20	-3	9	0.02	0.4
10	21	-3	9	0.02	0.4
11	21	-2	9	0.02	0.4
12	21	-2	10	0.02	0.4
13	22	-1	10	0.02	0.4
14	22	-1	11	0.02	0.4
15	23	-1	11	0.02	0.4
16	23	0	11	0.02	0.4
17	23	0	12	0.02	0.4
18	24	1	12	0.02	0.4
19	24	1	13	0.02	0.4
20	25	1	13	0.02	0.4
21	25	2	13	0.02	0.4
22	25	2	14	0.02	0.3
23	26	3	14	0.02	0.3
24	26	3	15	0.02	0.3
25	27	4	15	0.02	0.3
26	27	4	16	0.03	0.3
27	27	4	16	0.03	0.3
28	28	5	16	0.03	0.3
29	25	2	14	0.03	NA

Source: National Oceanic and Atmospheric Administration (NOAA)'s National Weather Service

These climate normals are an average of thirty years of data between 1971 and 2000. Every ten years, the National Weather Service recalculates the normals using the next interval of thirty years. In 2010, the new normals will be recalculated using the period of 1981 to 2010.

"In seed time learn, in harvest teach, in winter enjoy."

— WILLIAM BLAKE

FEBRUARY WEATHER HISTORY

On This Day in February

Day	Year	Weather
1	1931	Heat wave across the south. St. Peter hits 60.
2	1996	State record low temperature set. The low dipped to -60 degrees 3 miles south of Tower.
3	1947	Strong dust storm hits Crookston with winds near 50 mph. Visibility is cut down to 300 feet.
4	1984	A "surprise blizzard" hits Minnesota. Meteorologists are caught off guard by its rapid movement. People describe it as a "wall of white," and thousands of motorists are stranded in subzero weather. Sixteen people die.
5	1834	Warm-up at Ft. Snelling with a high of 51.
6	1994	Tower hits the national low with -41.
7	1857	Snowstorm dumps around 9 inches of snow at Ft. Snelling.
8	1933	Arctic air blows across the state with a morning low of -55 at Warroad.
9	1899	The all-time record low is set in Minnesota with -59 at Leech Lake Dam.
10	1857	Extreme cold at Fort Ripley. E.J. Baily, assistant surgeon, notes: "Thermometer -50 at 6 a.m. Mercury frozen in charcoal cup. Thermometer at Little Falls 16 miles from the fort -56 at 6 a.m. The lowest degree of cold on record in the territory."
11	1932	Mizpah picks up 13 inches of snow.
12	1988	Duluth has a temperature of -31, while Rapid City sits comfortably at 59.
13	1872	Snowstorm buries Sibley County with 12-foot drifts.
14	1923	"Black Dust Blizzard" ends after 2 days. Blowing dirt from North Dakota creates "dark drifts."
15	1921	Early blast of spring weather invades state. Winona reaches a high of 67.
16	1903	Pokegama Dam records -59, tying the state record low at the time (Feb. 9, 1899, at Leech Lake Dam). It would not be broken for another 93 years (Feb. 2, 1996).
17	1981	A record high of 55 in the Twin Cities. Crocuses being to bloom.
18	1979	This is one of the rare occasions that Lake Superior has completely frozen over.
19	1928	A dark dust storm moves across Minnesota, causing city lights to be turned on during the daytime in the Twin Cities.
20	1981	Due to the long spell of warm weather, with temperatures in the 60s, a farmer near Le Center begins plowing alfalfa ground.
21	1965	Strong storm winds clocked at 45 mph in the Twin Cities.
22	1922	Blizzards, ice storms, and thunderstorms across Minnesota. Winds hit 50 mph in Duluth, while thunderstorms are reported in the Twin Cities. Heavy ice over southeast Minnesota, with 2 inches of ice on wires near Winona.
23	1981	Warmth returns to state with a high of 55 at Pipestone and a high of 52 at Luverne.

FEBRUARY WEATHER HISTORY

On This Day in February

Day	Year	Weather
24	1835	Temperature at Ft. Snelling falls 26 degrees in only 3 hours.
25	1934	Late-season cold snap with a low of -46 at Big Falls.
26	1896	A balmy high of 60 degrees is reported at Maple Plain. The warm weather hampers the annual ice-cutting on Lake Independence to store for summer use.
27	1948	Severe ice storm over central Minnesota. At the St. Cloud weather office, a half inch of clear ice is measured. Sixty-five telephone poles are down between St. Cloud and Rice.
28	1981	Ice has melted on Lake Minnetonka. Boaters enjoy the early thaw.
29	2000	Early spring with a high of 61 in the Twin Cities.

Source: Minnesota State Climatology Office: DNR Waters

Sir Spamalot

The year 2007 marked seventy years of Spam—not the kind you get in e-mail, but the kind you get at the grocery store.

The "miracle meat" made its debut in 1937 when executives at the Austin, Minnesota, George A. Hormel & Company, the largest independent meat and food processor in the United States, needed to find a way to use surplus pork shoulder. George's son, Jay, developed a chopped ham and pork shoulder product called spiced ham (aka Spam) that needed no refrigeration.

In World War II, U.S. servicemen called Spam the "meat that failed its physical." But Soviet leader Nikita Khrushchev wrote in his biography *Khrushchev Remembers,* "There were many jokes going around in the army, some of them off-color, about American Spam; it tasted good nonetheless. Without Spam, we wouldn't have been able to feed our army."

In 1959, the one-billionth can of Spam was produced; the six-billionth-can mark was reached in 2002. The Spam Museum in Austin claims—with tongue in cheek, of course—that within its walls "lies the sum of all human knowledge" and "all of life's questions will be deliciously answered."

"The February sunshine steeps your boughs and tints the buds and swells the leaves within."

— William Cullen Bryant

February in the Garden

Plants on Vacation • Winter Burn • The Attraction of Shrubbery

Plants on Vacation

A lot of folks plan vacations to warmer destinations in February, hoping that by the time they return to Minnesota spring will have arrived.

But your indoor garden just might miss you while you're away. Here are some suggestions to make sure your houseplants will survive—and thrive—in your absence:

- Fill a sink with about an inch of water. Place your houseplants on empty, upside-down, plastic or glass containers so that they sit above the water. Water the plants thoroughly, and then cover the sink with plastic sheeting or a tarp. This will keep your plants in a moist, humid environment, and reduce the need for water. Your plants should be fine for two weeks.

- If you have too many plants to put in one sink, set them all in the bathtub. Turn on the shower and drench them. Then drape a plastic covering over the plants. If you do not have a window in your bathroom to bring in natural light, set up a fluorescent light on a timer set for twelve hours.

- Mulch very large plants with damp newspaper to prevent a rapid loss of moisture. A dampened towel will also work.

- An alternative to the sink or bathtub method for creating humidity is to double-pot houseplants. First, plant in a clay pot. Set the clay pot inside a larger plastic container. Fill the empty space between the pots with peat moss that you have watered. Moisture will move from the moist peat moss through the clay pot to the soil.

- Remember: In winter, turn down your thermostat to 60 or 65 degrees Fahrenheit. Plants fare better in a cooler climate.

Winter Burn

Winter burn is caused by a sudden drop in temperature. The damage it causes can be seen on evergreens in late winter, when needles turn red and brown. On a bright February day, the sunlight reflected from a white snowy surface could cause the temperature in a tree's leaves or needles to rise as much as fifty or sixty degrees Fahrenheit above the air temperature. This can initiate cellular activity. If clouds or a building then quickly block the sun's light, the temperature drops suddenly and foliage is injured or killed.

By planting trees sensitive to winter burn on sites where they will receive some winter shade, the effects of winter burn can be reduced. Yew, arborvitae, and hemlock are particularly susceptible. These trees should not be planted on the south or southwest sides of buildings or in places highly exposed to wind and sun. Another way to protect against winter burn is to prop pine boughs against or over evergreens to shield them from wind and sun and to catch most of the snow.

The Attraction of Shrubbery

It may still be winter outside, but with seed catalogs starting to arrive in the mailbox, it's not too early to start thinking about spring planting.

Planting shrubs that provide food and shelter for wildlife will bring motion and life into your yard. Consider the following varieties:

Shrubs that provide bird food:

Bayberry	Dogwood	Rose
Chokeberry	Elderberry	Viburnum
Coralberry	Juneberry or Serviceberry	

Shrubs that provide bird shelter:

Arborvitae	Coralberry	Viburnum
Chokeberry	Elderberry	Yew

Shrubs that attract butterflies:

Dogwood	Lilac	Spirea
Elderberry	Rose	Viburnum

Gladys's

February Household Tips

With a plethora of inspiring Minnesota writers out there (see "Minnesota Writes" in this chapter), many Minnesotans have impressive book collections. Knowing how to care for your private library (and knowing how to prevent musty odors!) is a must. Here are a few sure-fire tips:

Caring for Books

• Maintain a moderate humidity level in the room where your books are stored. High humidity, such as in an attic or basement, can attract insects, cause mold growth, and cockle pages. Extremely low humidity, as found above hot radiators, can dry out leather bindings and deteriorate adhesives.

• Keep books away from direct sunlight. It will fade leather and cloth.

• Put similar-sized books next to each other on the shelf vertically. This will help to prevent warping. Lay very large books on their sides if they are too thick or heavy to support their own weight.

• Be sure not to push books together too tightly on the shelf, as this may damage the bindings.

• Dust your books about once a year by gently running a clean, dry, soft brush (such as a shaving brush) along the top edge. You may want to shelve your books in a closed glass case to minimize the amount of dust and grime that will accumulate.

• Remove a book from the shelf by slightly pushing back the adjoining books on each side and grasping the book by its spine.

Removing Musty Odors from Books

• The smell of mildew comes from a biological growth on books that are stored in damp, dark, cool locations.

• To rid your books of a musty smell, move them to a drier (but still cool; about 60 degrees Fahrenheit) environment. Make sure that air can circulate around them. This should render the growth dormant. If the mildewed books are stored for an extended period under such conditions, the smell will eventually disappear on its own. The same technique can be applied to dry books affected by active mold.

• Exposure to circulating air and sunlight outdoors may help; however, be aware that it could also result in some fading of the book's materials.

- If you can see mold, do not attempt to clean it off until the book is thoroughly dry. Premature cleaning attempts will only grind the mold into the book and cause stains that may be impossible to remove.
- An alternative is to put the books in an airtight container with baking soda or charcoal for a week or longer. Keep the baking soda or charcoal from touching the books by placing it in a smaller, lidless container inside the larger one. Monitor the container periodically to see that no mold is growing and to check the status of the odor.

Mars Bars

February 14 is Valentine's Day, a holiday often celebrated by gifting candy. One of the most famous candy companies of all time was started in Minnesota by Frank Mars.

Mars was born in Hancock, Minnesota, in 1882. Because he had a mild case of polio that impaired his ability to walk, his mother kept him entertained by teaching him to hand-dip chocolate. At age nineteen, he began to sell Taylor's Molasses Chips for a living. In 1902, Mars married Ethel Kissack, and two years later their son, Forrest Mars (Sr.), was born in Wadena.

In 1911, Frank and his second wife, Ethel Healy, started making and selling butter cream candies from their kitchen in Tacoma, Washington. Nine years later, they moved to Minneapolis, where Frank founded the Mar-O-Bar Company, which manufactured chocolate candy bars. In 1923, he introduced the Milky Way bar, which soon became the largest selling candy bar on the market. A few years later, he incorporated the company under the name Mars, Inc. In 1929, he moved the business to Chicago. He died in 1934.

Forrest Mars entered the family business in 1929, and took it over after his father's death. During Forrest's tenure, Mars became the world's largest candy company. In 1935, he diversified with a pet-food line for the British market; and in 1941, he created M&Ms candies. In 1942, when a hard-covered rice impervious to insects was developed for U.S. troops in tropical conditions, Forrest opened the first commercial rice parboiling plant in Houston, Texas. That company later became known as Uncle Ben's. Forrest Mars died in 1999.

In 1982, M&Ms became the first candy in space when it was chosen by the first space shuttle astronauts to be included in their food supply. And in 1995, New York's Empire State Building colored its lights blue to announce the launch of the new, blue M&Ms.

MARCH

"The March wind roars

Like a lion in the sky,

And makes us shiver

As he passes by.

When winds are soft,

And the days are warm and clear,

Just like a gentle lamb,

Then spring is here."

— AUTHOR UNKNOWN

Does March really bring spring to Minnesota? There are differing opinions on the topic.

While March 21 can signify gradually warming temperatures and a dramatic growth of plants, it has also been known to snow well into May. Temperatures as high as 112 degrees Fahrenheit—and as low as 4 degrees Fahrenheit—have been recorded around the state during this month. Yet lakes in Minnesota's far north may not be free of ice until mid-May. March can be hail season, and it can also bring the worst tornadoes. According to Minnesota mythology, a snowstorm always occurs during the state high school basketball tournament. In a word, spring in Minnesota is unpredictable.

And "unpredictable" seems just about right for the Land of 10,000 Lakes. After all, the first state forest was treeless. The "Red River Valley"—that iconic song about America's West—was written about the Red River of northern Minnesota. And a famous Scottish author's largest collection of work, featuring a certain fictional detective in London, is preserved here.

So, when the third month of the year rolls around, is it truly spring in Minnesota? Read through this month's chapter for the clues. You don't need to be a Sherlock to figure it out.

Oil Spills — Not Just an Ocean Thing

In January 1963, cold weather in Mankato caused steel tanks containing three million gallons of soybean oil to crack. The oil burst out,

Mark Your Calendar

Mark Your
MARCH
CALENDAR

Minneapolis Home & Garden Show
**www.minneapolishomeand
gardenshow.com**

St. Patrick's Day Parade, St. Paul
www.stpatsassoc.org

St. Urho's Day, Finland
www.finlandmnus.com

flooding into the streets and eventually flowing into the Blue Earth and Minnesota rivers. It then leaked into the Mississippi River, where it combined with more than a million gallons of industrial oil that had bled into the river from an oil company in Savage a month earlier.

It wasn't until March that the Department of Health's Water Pollution Control Commission managed to get both companies to stop the flow of oil. When the ice began to melt on the Mississippi River, oil was even found in the wetlands along the riverbank. Also found were more than ten thousand dead ducks near Hastings and Red Wing.

Minnesota's *Artists*

The arts have always been highly valued in Minnesota (see "An Evening at the Theater," October chapter), and the state has no dearth of famous cartoonists, painters, and illustrators. Below are just a few:

After graduating from West Point, **Seth Eastman** (1808–1875) was transferred to Fort Snelling in 1830. Hoping to preserve the customs of an endangered people, Eastman began to paint watercolor scenes of Dakota Sioux life. He was one of the first American artists to use photography as an aid in his painting.

Philadelphia artist **George Catlin** traveled to North, Central, and South America in the mid 1800s to paint native peoples, whom he recognized as "a vanishing race." On two journeys— in 1835 and in 1836—he spent time in Minnesota studying the Sioux. During his stay, he painted his name in red on some rocks near Richmond, now known as Catlin's Rocks.

Wanda Hazel Gag was born in New Ulm in 1893. She attended the St. Paul School of Art and the Minneapolis School of Art, and received a scholarship to the Art Students League in New York City. Her well-known and prototypical children's book *Millions of Cats* was published in 1928.

Cartoonist **Charles Schulz** was born on November 26, 1922, in Minneapolis, and he grew up in St. Paul. Much like his famous alter ego Charlie Brown, Schulz described himself as the "epitome of unachievement." His first comic strip, "Li'l Folks," began appear-

ing in the *St. Paul Pioneer Press* in 1947. The strip's characters were a group of preschoolers, with Charlie Brown among them. United Feature Syndicate purchased the strip in 1950 and renamed it "Peanuts." It ran for almost fifty years without interruption and appeared in more than 2,600 newspapers in seventy-five countries.

An Objibwa born and raised on the Red Lake Reservation, **Patrick Des Jarlait** became the painter from the "Land of Sky Blue Waters." He created the Hamm's Beer bear in 1952 for TV advertisements. He went on to become a successful watercolor artist.

It is said Hutchinson native **Les Kouba** started the wildlife art boom in America with his 1974 work *Headin' for Shelter*. At age eleven, he sold his first painting for eight dollars to a prosperous German farmer who lived near Hutchinson. It depicted a deer at the water's edge with pine trees in the background.

Mary GrandPré was born in South Dakota in 1954, but spent most of her life in Minnesota. She earned a degree from the Minneapolis College of Art and Design and began her career as a conceptual illustrator for local editorial clients. GrandPré has illustrated all of the American editions of the *Harry Potter* novels.

Sad Days for the Sioux

On December 26, 1862, Minnesota was the site of the largest official execution in American history.

After the "Sioux Uprising," 303 Native Americans were sentenced to death. President Lincoln reviewed each case personally and granted a reprieve to all but thirty-nine men.

In Mankato on a bitterly cold winter day, the warriors—while singing a war song—were led to the twenty-four-foot gallows. Each man placed the rope around his own neck and continued singing while the cap was placed over his head. W. H. Dooley, whose entire family had been killed at Lake Shetek, cut the rope, and all thirty-eight men (one man received a last-minute reprieve) were hung simultaneously in front of four thousand cheering citizens.

On March 3, 1863, Congress passed a law that called for the removal of the Dakota Sioux from Minnesota as punishment for the uprising. It began on May 4, when 770 people, mostly women and children, were forced to board the steamboat Davenport anchored at Fort Snelling. They were taken to reservations in the Dakota Territory.

Reservations Today

Only the Dakota tribes who remained friendly to the whites were allowed to stay in the state, so there are just four Sioux reservations in Minnesota:

Lower Sioux Indian Reservation in Redwood County

Prairie Island Indian Community in Goodhue County

Shakopee-Mdewakanton Sioux Community in Scott County

Upper Sioux Indian Reservation in Yellow Medicine County

The Chippewa (Ojibwa) have seven reservations:

Bois Forte Indian Reservation with three sections:
• Nett Lake in Koochiching and St. Louis counties
• Deer Creek in Itasca County
• Lake Vermilion in St. Louis County

Fond du Lac Indian Reservation in Carlton and St. Louis counties

Grand Portage Indian Reservation in Cook County

Leech Lake Indian Reservation in Beltrami, Cass, Hubbard, and Itasca counties

Mille Lacs Indian Reservation in Mille Lacs, Aitkin, and Pine counties

Red Lake Indian Reservation in Beltrami and Clearwater counties and also scattered throughout Lake of the Woods (including Northwest Angle), Koochiching, Marshall, Pennington, Polk, Red Lake, and Roseau counties

White Earth Indian Reservation in Mahnomen, Becker, and Clearwater counties

Minnesota High School League State Championships
Boys Basketball

Year	School		Year	School
1913	Fosston High School		1948	Bemidji High School
1914	Stillwater High School		1949	Saint Paul Humboldt High School
1915	Red Wing High School		1950	Duluth Central High School
1916	Virginia High School		1951	Gilbert High School
1917	Rochester High School		1952	Hopkins Senior High School
1918	Waseca High School		1953	Hopkins Senior High School
1919	Albert Lea High School		1954	Brainerd High School
1920	Red Wing High School		1955	Minneapolis Washburn High School
1921	Minneapolis Central High School		1956	Minneapolis Roosevelt High School
1922	Red Wing High School		1957	Minneapolis Roosevelt High School
1923	Aurora High School		1958	Austin High School
1924	Two Harbors High School		1959	Wayzata High School
1925	Saint Paul Mechanic Arts High School		1960	Edgerton High School
1926	Gaylord High School		1961	Duluth Central High School
1927	Minneapolis South High School		1962	St. Louis Park High School
1928	Moorhead High School		1963	Marshall High School
1929	Moorhead High School		1964	Luverne High School
1930	Saint Paul Mechanic Arts High School		1965	Minnetonka High School
1931	Glencoe High School		1966	Edina High School
1932	Thief River Falls High School		1967	Edina High School
1933	Red Wing High School		1968	Edina High School
1934	Chisholm High School		1969	Rochester John Marshall High School
1935	Austin High School		1970	Sherburn High School
1936	Bemidji High School		1971	Melrose High School (Class A) Duluth Central High School (Class AA)
1937	Minneapolis Edison High School			
1938	Thief River Falls High School		1972	Saint James High School (A) Mounds View High School (AA)
1939	Mountain Lake High School			
1940	Breckenridge High School		1973	Crisholm High School (A) Anoka High School (AA)
1941	Buhl High School			
1942	Buhl High School		1974	Melrose High School (A) Bemidji High School (AA)
1943	Saint Paul Washington High School			
1944	Minneapolis Patrick Henry High School		1975	Chisholm High School (A) Little Falls High School (AA)
1946	Austin High School		1976	Minneapolis Marshall-University High School (A) Bloomington Jefferson High School (AA)
1947	Duluth Denfeld High School			

continued next page

Minnesota High School League State Championships

Boys Basketball (continued)

Year	School
1977	Winona Cotter High School (A) Prior Lake High School (AA)
1978	Lake City High School (A) Prior Lake High School (AA)
1979	Lake City High School (A) Duluth Central High School (AA)
1980	Bird Island-Lake Lillian High School (A) Minneapolis North High School (AA)
1981	Bird Island-Lake Lillian High School (A) Anoka High School (AA)
1982	Winona Cotter High School (A) Bloomington Jefferson High School (AA)
1983	Barnum High School (A) Woodbury High School (AA)
1984	Pelican Rapids High School (A) White Bear Lake High School (AA)
1985	DeLaSalle High School (A) White Bear Lake High School (AA)
1986	LeSueur High School (A) Bloomington Jefferson High School (AA)
1987	Norman County West High School (A) Bloomington Jefferson High School (AA)
1988	DeLaSalle High School (A) Rocori High School (Cold Spring) (AA)
1989	Rushford High School (A) Owatonna High School (AA)
1990	Lake City High School (A) Owatonna High School (AA)
1991	Crisholm High School (A) Cretin-Derham Hall High School (AA)
1992	Austin Pacelli High School (A) Anoka High School (AA)
1993	Maple River High School (A) Cretin-Derham Hall High School (AA
1994	St. Agnes High School (A) Minneapolis Washburn High School (AA)
1995	Minneapolis North High School
1996	Minneapolis North High School

Year	School
1997	Hancock High School (A) Caledonia High School (AA) Simley High School (AAA) Minneapolis North High School (AAAA)
1998	Norman County East High School (A) DeLaSalle High School (AA) Saint Thomas Academy (AAA) Minnetonka High School (AAAA)
1999	Southwest Minnesota Christian HS (A) DeLaSalle High School (AA) Saint Paul Highland Park HS (AAA) Mounds View High School (AAAA)
2000	Southwest Minnesota Christian HS (A) Litchfield High School (AA) Minneapolis Patrick Henry HS (AAA) Tartan High School (AAAA)
2001	Southwest Minnesota Christian HS (A) Kenyon-Wanamingo Area HS (AA) Minneapolis Patrick Henry HS (AAA) Osseo High School (AAAA)
2002	Southwest Minnesota Christian HS (A) Litchfield High School (AA) Minneapolis Patrick Henry HS (AAA) Hopkins Senior High School (AAAA)
2003	Mankato Loyola High School (A) Litchfield High School (AA) Minneapolis Patrick Henry HS (AAA) Minneapolis N. Community HS (AAAA)
2004	Russell-Tyler-Ruthton Area HS (A) Braham High School (AA) Mankato West High School (AAA) Chaska High School (AAAA)
2005	Russell-Tyler-Ruthton Area HS (A) Braham High School (AA) Shakopee High School (AAA) Hopkins Senior High School (AAAA)
2006	Rushford-Peterson Area HS (A) Braham High School (AA) DeLaSalle High School (AAA) Hopkins Senior High School (AAAA)
2007	Ellsworth (A) Holy Family Catholic (AA) St. Thomas Academy (AAA) Buffalo (AAAA)

Minnesota High School League State Championships

Girls Basketball

Year	School
1974	Glencoe High School
1975	Academy of Holy Angels
1976	Redwood Falls St. Paul Central High School
1977	New York Mills High School Burnsville High School
1978	New York Mills High School (A) Bloomington Jefferson HS (AA)
1979	New York Mills High School (A) St. Paul Central High School (AA)
1980	Albany High School (A) Little Falls High School (AA)
1981	Heron Lake-Okabena Area HS (A) Coon Rapids High School (AA)
1982	Moose Lake High School (A) St. Cloud Apollo High School (AA)
1983	Henderson High School (A) Albany High School (AA)
1984	Crisholm High School (A) Little Falls High School (AA)
1985	Staples High School (A) Little Falls High School (AA)
1986	Midwest Minnesota High School (A) St. Louis Park High School (AA)
1987	Lourdes High School (A) Mankato East High School (AA)
1988	Tracy-Milroy Area High School (A) Edina High School (AA)
1989	Storden-Jeffers Area High School (A) Osseo High School (AA)
1990	Lourdes High School (A) St. Louis Park High School (AA)
1991	Lourdes High School (A) Burnsville High School (AA)
1992	Tracy Area High School (A) Burnsville High School (AA)
1993	Lourdes High School (A) Bloomington Jefferson HS (AA)
1994	The Blake School (A) Bloomington Jefferson HS (AA)

Year	School
1995	Lourdes High School (A) Rochester Mayo High School (AA)
1996	Tracy-Milroy Area High School (A) Hastings High School (AA)
1997	Hancock High School (A) New London-Spicer Area HS (AA) Alexandria High School (A) Rochester Mayo High School (AA)
1998	Christ's Household of Faith (A) The Blake School (AA) Minneapolis N. Community HS (AAA) Bloomington Jefferson HS (AAAA)
1999	Brandon-Evansville Area HS (A) The Blake School (AA) Minneapolis N. Community HS (AAA) Cretin-Derham Hall HS (AAAA)
2000	Fosston High School (A) Lourdes High School (AA) New Prague High School (AAA) Osseo High School (AAAA)
2001	Fosston High School (A) St. Michael-Albertville High School (AA) Marshall High School (AAA) Lakeville High School (AAAA)
2002	Kittson Central High School (A) New London-Spicer Area HS (AA) Marshall High School (AAA) Lakeville High School (AAAA)
2003	Fosston High School (A) Lourdes High School (AA) Minneapolis N. Community HS (AAA) Woodbury High School (AAAA)
2004	Wabasso High School (A) The Breck School (AA) Minneapolis N. Community HS (AAA) Hopkins Senior High School (AAAA)
2005	Elgin-Millville High School (A) Lourdes High School (AA) Minneapolis N. Community HS (AAA) Bloomington Kennedy HS (AAAA)
2006	Fulda High School (A) Cannon Falls Area Schools (AA) Benilde-St. Margaret's School (AAA) Hopkins Senior High School (AAAA)
2007	Fulda High School (A) Pipestone Area High School (AA) Becker High School (AAA)

Minnesota High School League State Championships

Boys Hockey

Year	School
1945	Eveleth High School
1946	Roseau High School
1947	St. Paul Johnson High School
1948	Eveleth High School
1949	Eveleth High School
1950	Eveleth High School
1951	Eveleth High School
1952	Hibbing High School
1953	St. Paul Johnson High School
1954	Thief River Falls High School
1955	St. Paul Johnson High School
1956	Thief River Falls High School
1957	International Falls High School
1958	Roseau High School
1959	Roseau High School
1960	Duluth East High School
1961	Roseau High School
1962	International Falls High School
1963	St. Paul Johnson High School
1964	International Falls High School
1965	International Falls High School
1966	International Falls High School
1967	Greenway High School (Coleraine)
1968	Greenway High School
1969	Edina High School
1970	Minneapolis Southwest High School
1971	Edina High School
1972	International Falls High School
1973	Hibbing High School
1974	Edina East High School
1975	Grand Rapids High School
1976	Grand Rapids High School
1977	Rochester John Marshall High School
1978	Edina East High School
1979	Edina East High School
1980	Grand Rapids High School
1981	Bloomington Jefferson High School
1982	Edina High School
1983	Hill-Murray High School

Year	School
1984	Edina High School
1985	Burnsville High School
1986	Burnsville High School
1987	Bloomington Kennedy High School
1988	Edina High School
1989	Bloomington Jefferson High School
1990	Roseau High School
1991	Hill-Murray High School
1992	Greenway HS (Coleraine)/Nashwauk-Keewatin Area HS (Tier II) Bloomington Jefferson HS (Tier I)
1993	Eveleth-Gilbert High School (Tier II) Bloomington Jefferson HS (Tier I)
1994	Warroad High School (A) Bloomington Jefferson HS (AA)
1995	International Falls High School (A) Duluth East High School (AA)
1996	Warroad High School (A) Apple Valley High School (AA)
1997	Red Wing High School (A) Edina High School (AA)
1998	Eveleth-Gilbert High School (A) Duluth East High School (AA)
1999	Benilde-St. Margaret's School (A) Roseau High School (AA)
2000	The Breck School (A) Blaine High School (AA)
2001	Benilde-St. Margaret's School (A) Elk River Area High School (AA)
2002	Totino Grace High School (A) Academy of Holy Angels (AA)
2003	Warroad High School (A) Anoka High School (AA)
2004	The Breck School (A) Centennial High School (AA)
2005	Warroad High School (A) Academy of Holy Angels (AA)
2006	Saint Thomas Academy (A) Cretin-Derham Hall High School (AA)
2007	Hermantown High School (A) Roseau High School (AA)

Minnesota High School League State Championships
Girls Hockey

Year	School
1995	Apple Valley High School
1996	Roseville Area High School
1997	Hibbing/Chisholm Area High School
1998	Apple Valley High School
1999	Roseville Area High School
2000	Park Center (Brooklyn Park)
2001	Bloomington Jefferson High School
2002	Benilde-St. Margaret's School (A) / South St. Paul High School (AA)

Year	School
2003	The Blake School (A) / South St. Paul High School (AA)
2004	Benilde-St. Margaret's School (A) / Elk River Area High School (AA)
2005	Academy of Holy Angels (A) / South St. Paul High School (AA)
2006	South St. Paul High School (A) / Eden Prairie High School (AA)
2007	The Blake School (A) / Stillwater High School (AA)

March Recipe
Minnesota Wild Rice Creamy Chicken Soup

It turns out that the old folk wisdom was right: Chicken soup is good for you when you have a cold. According to modern researchers, homemade chicken soup inhibits the production of neutrophils, white blood cells that promote cold symptoms such as a runny nose and cough. Sipping warm soup can also clear the sinuses. And, well, heck; chicken soup is just good comfort food. You'll like this Minnesota version of the old standard.

Minnesota Wild Rice Creamy Chicken Soup

2 cups cooked chicken, diced
2 medium onions, diced
2 stalks celery, diced
2 carrots, diced
4 slices bacon, diced
1/4 cup butter, halved

4 cups chicken broth
1/2 cup Minnesota wild rice
1 cup milk
1 tablespoon flour
salt and pepper to taste
1/8 teaspoon nutmeg (optional)

Using the Basic Soak Method below, prepare rice for recipe. In a stockpot, sauté onions, celery, carrots, and bacon in half of the butter until the vegetables are tender. Stir in the broth, wild rice, and milk. Combine flour with remaining butter and whisk into the soup. Cook, stirring constantly, until soup thickens and bubbles. Add diced chicken and season with salt and pepper to taste.

Basic Soak Method:
Rinse a half cup of uncooked rice in a strainer. Soak in three cups of water overnight (twelve hours). Drain rice. Into three cups of fresh water, add rice and half a teaspoon of salt and bring to a boil. Reduce heat and simmer for ten minutes. Drain rice. Rice can now be used in any wild rice recipe.

Printed with permission from Minnesota.gov

The Red River Valley

Admit it: the first thing you thought of when you read the title was the song, right? It probably conjured up visions of the American West. But the "original" Red River Valley song belonged to the Red River of the North, which actually lies closer to Winnipeg, Manitoba, Canada, than it does to the Twin Cities.

This northern valley was once the bed of the glacial Lake Agassiz (see "Slip, Sliding Away," February chapter). When the last glacier melted, the lake drained toward Hudson Bay; today, the Red River Valley region has some of the most fertile farmland and best catfish fishing in Minnesota.

The Red River has a meandering, twisting, and two-sided personality. While its waters remain calm during other seasons, the Red River can turn into raging floodwaters in spring. The Red River flows north, so when the spring-melt begins upstream (south), the lower part of the river remains frozen. The incoming melted water, then, has no place to go but over the banks. When it does, the water can spread out over hundreds of square miles, due to ancient Lake Agassiz's flat bed.

The Red River of the North also has a tie to the West. The valley represents the beginning of the Great Plains and has its own version of the "wagon train." Red River Oxcarts are a colorful part of Minnesota's history. Starting in the 1820s, they were used to transport tons of furs from the Red River country to St. Paul. It took more than a month for the carts to travel the distance. Long trains of fifty to one hundred carts could be heard for miles because of their ungreased, wooden axles that went screeching along the bumpy trail at the slow rate of twenty miles a day. By 1858, almost six hundred Red River Oxcarts were making regular trips along the route.

Some Fun River Facts

- Minnesota is the only state with the source of three major river systems: the Mississippi, the St. Lawrence, and the Red River of the North.

- You can walk across the Mississippi River on stepping-stones at Itasca State Park.

- The Mississippi River travels 2,348 miles from Lake Itasca to the Gulf of Mexico.

- With more than 90,000 miles of shoreline, Minnesota has more shoreline than the states of California, Florida, and Hawaii combined.

- The St. Croix River is approximately 164 miles long. The St. Croix National Scenic Riverway is a 252-mile-long corridor, which consists of the St. Croix and Namekagon Rivers (see "The Wild and Scenic St. Croix River," October chapter).

- It is said the Temperance River got its name in the 1800s because it had no "bar" at its mouth. At one time, its waters flowed so deep and so strong into Lake Superior that there was no build-up of debris—or no sandbar.

"Red River Valley"
Writers of the Words and Music are Unknown

This early Canadian version of "The Red River Valley" is about a young Métis woman whose heart was broken by a white trader or soldier. Using the same tune, the song was later adapted to the other Red River—the one between Texas and Oklahoma—and became much more famous.

From this valley they say you are going,
I shall miss your blue eyes and sweet smile,
And you take with you all of the sunshine,
That has brightened my pathway a while.

As you go to your home by the ocean
May you never forget those sweet hours
That we spent in the Red River Valley
And the love we exchanged 'mid its bowers.

There never could be such a longing
In the heart of a pale maiden's breast
As dwells in the heart you are breaking
With love for the boy who came west.

And the dark maiden's prayer for her lover
To the Spirit that rules all this world
Is that sunshine his pathway may cover
And the grief of the Red River Girl.

CHORUS
So consider a while ere you leave me
Do not hasten to bid me adieu,
But remember the Red River Valley
And the half-breed that loved you so true.

A Treeless Forest

Minnesota's first state forest was established in 1900 when Governor John Pillsbury donated a thousand acres in Cass County to the state to become the Pillsbury State Forest.

The land, however, was all cut-over pineland. It had to be reseeded to actually become a forest.

Mystery at Blue Mounds State Park

Stonehenge. Easter Island Maoi. The Standing Stones of Stenness. To the list of mysterious rocks, add Blue Mounds State Park.

At the south end of this park, located in Rock County, is a line of rocks that runs 1,250 feet from east to west. No one knows who built this construction, but we do know that it marks perfectly where the sun rises and sets on the spring and fall equinoxes.

It's Elementary, My Dear Watson

The Sherlock Holmes Collections at the University of Minnesota Library—over fifteen thousand items—constitutes the largest institutional collection of material related to Sherlock Holmes and his creator, Sir Arthur Conan Doyle, in the world.

March Normals for Duluth

Day	High	Low	Mean	Precip.	Snowfall
1	29	10	20	0.04	0.4
2	29	11	20	0.04	0.4
3	29	11	20	0.04	0.4
4	30	12	21	0.04	0.4
5	30	12	21	0.05	0.4
6	30	12	21	0.05	0.4
7	31	13	22	0.05	0.5
8	31	13	22	0.05	0.5
9	31	14	22	0.05	0.5
10	32	14	23	0.05	0.5
11	32	14	23	0.05	0.5
12	32	15	24	0.05	0.5
13	33	15	24	0.05	0.5
14	33	16	24	0.06	0.5
15	33	16	25	0.06	0.5
16	34	16	25	0.06	0.5
17	34	17	26	0.06	0.5
18	35	17	26	0.06	0.5
19	35	18	26	0.06	0.5
20	36	18	27	0.06	0.4
21	36	19	27	0.06	0.4
22	36	19	28	0.06	0.4
23	37	19	28	0.06	0.4
24	37	20	29	0.06	0.4
25	38	20	29	0.06	0.4
26	38	21	30	0.06	0.4
27	39	21	30	0.06	0.4
28	39	21	30	0.06	0.4
29	40	22	31	0.06	0.4
30	40	22	31	0.06	0.4
31	41	23	32	0.06	0.4

MARCH WEATHER

March Normals for International Falls

Day	High	Low	Mean	Precip.	Snowfall
1	28	5	17	0.02	0.3
2	28	6	17	0.02	0.3
3	29	6	18	0.03	0.3
4	29	7	18	0.03	0.3
5	30	7	18	0.03	0.3
6	30	7	19	0.03	0.3
7	31	8	19	0.03	0.3
8	31	8	20	0.03	0.3
9	31	9	20	0.03	0.3
10	32	9	21	0.03	0.3
11	32	10	21	0.03	0.3
12	33	10	22	0.03	0.3
13	33	11	22	0.03	0.3
14	34	11	23	0.03	0.3
15	34	12	23	0.03	0.3
16	35	12	23	0.03	0.3
17	35	13	24	0.03	0.3
18	36	13	24	0.03	0.3
19	36	14	25	0.03	0.3
20	37	14	25	0.03	0.3
21	37	15	26	0.03	0.3
22	38	15	26	0.03	0.3
23	38	16	27	0.03	0.3
24	39	16	27	0.03	0.3
25	39	17	28	0.03	0.3
26	40	17	28	0.03	0.3
27	40	17	29	0.04	0.3
28	41	18	30	0.04	0.3
29	41	19	30	0.04	0.2
30	42	19	31	0.04	0.2
31	43	20	31	0.04	0.2

Source: National Oceanic and Atmospheric Administration (NOAA)'s National Weather Service

These climate normals are an average of thirty years of data between 1971 and 2000. Every ten years, the National Weather Service recalculates the normals using the next interval of thirty years. In 2010, the new normals will be recalculated using the period of 1981 to 2010.

MARCH WEATHER HISTORY

On This Day in March

Day	Year	Weather
1	1966	"The Blizzard of '66" hits the state and lasts 4 days. Aitken gets 23 inches of snow.
2	1966	By the end of the big blizzard, the snow depth at International Falls reaches a record 37 inches.
3	1977	Snowstorm across the state. More than 400 school closings in Minnesota and Wisconsin.
4	1935	Extremely damaging ice storm in Duluth; at the time, the worst ice storm in Duluth's history. The lights begin to go out in the city by 6:00 p.m. due to power lines breaking. By the next morning, Duluth is virtually isolated from the outside world except for shortwave radio.
5	1966	Blizzard finally ends in the upper Midwest. Some wind gusts from the storm have topped 100 mph.
6	1836	Twelve-day cold spell at Ft. Snelling. Seven nights reach the double-digits below zero.
7	1987	Heat wave across state brings earliest 70s to the Twin Cities. The record high for the day is 73, breaking the old record by 13 degrees. Citizens wear shorts and begin turning over dirt in their gardens for planting.
8	1892	Blizzard hits Minnesota with 70 mph winds at Easton. People are able to walk out of their second-story windows.
9	1999	Light, fluffy snow piles up to 16 inches in the Twin Cities.
10	1948	Late winter cold wave with -44 reported at Itasca.
11	1878	The ice melts off Lake Minnetonka due to one of the warmest winters on record.
12	1954	A "yellow snowstorm" is caused by Texas dust.
13	1851	Before the spring green-up, dry grassy areas are a fire risk. Prairie fires blaze in Minnesota.
14	1870	Severe snow and wind storm across Minnesota and Iowa. First use of the term "blizzard" by the Estherville, Iowa, *Northern Vindicator* newspaper.
15	1941	"Ides of March Blizzard." Winds reach hurricane force at the Twin Cities and 32 people die.
16	1942	Two tornadoes hit Baldwin, Mississippi, only 24 minutes apart.
17	1965	"Great St. Patrick's Day Blizzard." Two feet of snow dumped at Duluth. 19 inches at Mora.
18	1968	The earliest tornado to hit Minnesota.
19	1977	The energy emergency, caused by extended cold, finally ends in Minnesota.
20	1991	Early tornado hits Faribault County from Bricelyn to Wells.
21	1953	Tornado hits the northern St. Cloud area with high winds from Martin to Stearns County.
22	1991	Ice storm begins during the afternoon and ends as heavy, wet snow. Duluth is coated with as much as 6 inches of ice. The 850-foot, WIDO-TV tower topples. Four million pine trees are damaged or destroyed, with the heaviest damage at G. C. Andrews State Forest near Moose Lake in Pine County.

MARCH WEATHER HISTORY

On This Day in March

Day	Year	Weather
23	1966	Snowstorm brings a foot of snow to southern Minnesota.
24	1851	Heat wave across Minnesota with 60s and 70s common.
25	1843	Snowstorm from Mississippi to Maine. Three inches fall on Natchez.
26	1913	"Great Miami River Flood in Ohio." 10 inches of rain falls over a wide area, causing 467 deaths.
27	1956	Winds in Austin hit 70 mph. A 5-ton roof slams into a motel, causing $100,000 in damage.
28	1924	A drought is broken in southern Minnesota when 25 inches of snow falls.
29	1986	Record warmth with July-like temperatures. The Twin Cities hits 83 degrees.
30	1938	Springtime flooding hits Warroad and Grand Marais.
31	1843	The low at Ft. Snelling is -11.

Source: Minnesota State Climatology Office: DNR Waters

The Beginning of Tornado Season

Tornadoes are among the most devastating storms in the world, and the United States has the greatest frequency of them. "Tornado Alley" encompasses parts of Texas, Oklahoma, Kansas, Missouri, East Nebraska, and West Iowa. Minnesota lies along the north edge of this treacherous region.

In Minnesota, tornadoes have occurred in every month from March through November. The earliest verified tornado in Minnesota in any year occurred on March 18, 1968, north of Truman, and the latest on November 16, 1931, east of Maple Plain. Historically and statistically, almost three-quarters of all tornadoes in Minnesota have occurred during the three months of May (16 percent), June (33 percent), and July (27 percent).

In 1931, a tornado hit the Empire Builder train near Moorhead, lifting five seventy-ton cars, tossing one eighty feet away into a ditch. Here are some more notable tornadoes from Minnesota's history:

- The tornado that struck Rochester on August 21, 1883, at 6:36 p.m., killed 37 people and injured many others. This was a large factor in the creation of the Mayo Clinic (see "Rochester's Famed Mayo Clinic," November chapter).

- On April 14, 1886, at 4:00 p.m., the deadliest tornado in Minnesota history razed parts of St. Cloud and Sauk Rapids, leaving 72 dead and 213 injured. 11 members of a wedding party were killed, including the bride and groom.

- On June 22, 1919, at 4:45 p.m., 59 lives were lost when the second deadliest killer tornado in Minnesota history roared through Fergus Falls.

- On August 17, 1946, about an hour apart, tornadoes slashed through the cities of Mankato and North Mankato (5:40 p.m.)—leaving 11 dead and 60 injured—and Wells (6:50 p.m.), where more than 200 people were hurt. continued on page 55

Source: Minnesota State Climatology Office: DNR Waters

*Spring in the Garden • Signs of Spring: Phenology •
Average Frosts and Growing Seasons*

Spring in the Garden

Around mid-March, Minnesota gardeners start looking for budding crocuses and red-winged blackbirds along the roadside. When you notice nature getting ready, it's time to prepare your own garden for summer's bounty.

- When the night temperature begins to stay above freezing, pull the winter mulch up from around your plants to allow the surrounding soil to warm up.

- Pull dead leaves from hostas.

- Remove buckets and other windbreaks from roses.

- Place unplanted spring-flowering bulbs in a plastic bag filled with damp potting soil and store in the refrigerator at 35 degrees. Plant as the ground thaws in early spring. Dig a hole three times deeper than the height of the bulb; add sand, compost, and bulb food; then cover with soil.

- Start flowering annuals and warm-season vegetable seeds inside.

- Check your hand tools. Clean and sharpen blades. Have your mower serviced if you didn't do it in the fall.

- Clean and sterilize terracotta pots, planters, and starter trays by using a bleach and water solution of one part bleach to ten parts water. Rinse thoroughly; then dry. If you haven't broken the chemical habit yet, make sure to dispose of any old products. Before discarding, however, check with your county or city waste management office for guidance on throwing out or recycling hazardous chemicals.

- Clean out birdhouses and set up.

- Continue to feed birds with suet, peanut butter, and sunflower seeds (see "Peanut Butter Suet Cookies," December chapter).

Signs of Spring *Phenology*

"Phenology" is derived from the Greek word *phaino*, meaning "to show" or "appear." It is the study of periodic plant and animal life-cycle events that are influenced by environmental changes—particularly seasonal variations in temperature and precipitation driven by weather and climate.

Below is some recent spring phenology for a site in Maplewood, just north of St. Paul.

Frost Leaves the Ground	
2001	April 4
2002	April 12
2003	April 11
2004	March 28
2005	April 10
2006	April 2

First Red-winged Blackbirds Heard		First Western Chorus Frogs Heard		Crabapples Blooming		Lilacs Blooming	
1999	March 22	1999	April 3	1999	May 2	1999	May 10
2000	March 4	2000	April 13	2000	May 2	2000	May 4
2001	March 28	2001	April 11	2001	May 9	2001	May 13
2002	March 25	2002	April 12	2002	May 17	2002	May 25
2003	March 19	2003	April 10	2003	May 7	2003	May 13
2004	March 8	2004	April 5	2004	May 6	2004	May 9
2005	March 12	2005	April 3	2005	May 3	2005	May 9
2006	March 10	2006	April 10	2006	May 5	2006	May 6
2007	March 13						

Average Frosts and Growing Seasons

Region	Growing Season	Average Last Spring Frost	Average First Autumn Spring
Duluth	144 days	May 10	October 5
Minneapolis	175 days	March 19	October 19
St. Paul	182 days	March 13	October 26

The Beginning of Tornado Season continued from page 53

- The most damaging series of tornadoes in Minnesota whipped across the west and north sections of the Twin Cities metro area between 6:00 p.m. and 9:00 p.m. on May 6, 1965. 14 people were killed and 685 injured, with damages in excess of $50 million.

- The greatest March tornado outbreak in Minnesota history occurred March 29, 1998. Two people died in a series of 13 tornadoes that struck St. Peter and Comfrey especially hard.

- The most recent killer tornado in Minnesota (through 2007) occurred on September 16, 2006. A ten-year-old girl died in Rogers.

Some Minnesota Tornado Statistics

1950–2007	Totals	Annual Averages
Tornadoes	1,482	25.60
Tornado Deaths	94	1.62
Tornado Injuries	1,862	32.10

Gladys's

March Household Tips

March means "spring," and "spring" often brings to mind "spring cleaning." Having sparkling windows to throw open when the weather warms and carpets free of stains will help shake off the winter and sharpen your outlook on life—or at least your view on it.

Treating Carpet Stains

Mud, Coffee, Alcoholic Beverages, and Soft Drinks: If the spot is mud, let it dry completely; then brush or vacuum off as much as possible. If the spot is a beverage, dilute with cold water and blot up the excess. Then treat any of the residual stain with a solution of one teaspoon of liquid dish detergent, one teaspoon of white vinegar, and one quart of warm water. Let the carpet dry and vacuum gently.

Tar: Scrape off as much as you can. Then dab with paint thinner on a cotton ball. Blot dry.

Red Wine: Dilute the stain with white wine, then clean the spot with cold water and cover with table salt. Wait ten minutes, then vacuum up the salt.

Candle Wax: Use the "cold" or "hot" method. Press an ice cube against the wax stain. When the wax hardens, pull it off. Or, cover the wax with paper towels or brown paper. Iron with a warm iron so the wax melts and is absorbed. Use clean paper until all the wax is removed. If colored candle wax leaves a stain, treat it with a little paint thinner on a white cotton ball. Vacuum when dry.

Vomit: Treat quickly. Blot up as much as possible, then dilute immediately with baking soda and water or club soda. Apply a solution of one part ammonia and ten parts water. Rinse with cold water, let dry, and vacuum.

Urine: Treat with a solution of one teaspoon of liquid dish detergent, one teaspoon of white vinegar, and one quart of warm water. Let the carpet dry and vacuum gently.

How to Clean Windows

Windows should be cleaned on the outside and inside at least twice a year to keep them looking clear and grime-free:

- Choose a cloudy day for your window-washing task. Direct sunlight dries cleaning solutions before you can polish the glass properly.
- Use a sponge or squeegee to wash windows, along with a commercial or homemade cleaner (see below). Use a long-handled sponge/squeegee combination for large windows.
- Wash one side of a window with vertical strokes and the opposite side with horizontal stokes. If a streak appears, you'll know which side of the window it is on.
- Wash windows from the top down. Do not let window cleaners drip on the windowsill. They can harm paint and varnish.
- You can eliminate tiny scratches on glass by polishing them with toothpaste.
- Use a damp cotton swab or soft toothbrush to clean corners.
- Polish windows to a sparkling shine with crumpled newspaper. The paper will also leave a film that resists dirt.

Homemade Glass Cleaner

You can make glass cleaner using two tablespoons of ammonia (or three tablespoons of vinegar or lemon juice), one-half cup rubbing alcohol, and one-fourth teaspoon dishwashing detergent. Pour all ingredients into a spray bottle, fill the bottle to the top with water, and shake well.

Dancin' the Night Away

World Champion Marathon Dancer, 3,780 Continuous Hours" is written on Minnesota-born Callum de Villier's tombstone in Minneapolis's Lakewood Cemetery.

De Villier (1907–1973) made the *Guinness Book of World Records* by dancing 1,448 hours in the Kenwood Armory in Minneapolis in 1928. He topped that total a few years later in Massachusetts when he and a partner danced for five months—from December 28, 1932, to June 3, 1933; 3,780 hours or 157 days—taking only brief medical and restroom breaks.

The marathon dancing craze lasted about ten years, from 1925 to 1935. In the 1969 film *They Shoot Horses, Don't They?* the record was erroneously attributed to others, but Callum set it right and won the title from *Guinness*.

"Up from the sea,
the wild north wind is blowing
Under the sky's gray arch;
Smiling I watch
the shaken elm boughs, knowing
It is the wind of March."
— WILLIAM WORDSWORTH

APRIL

"*Winter's done,*

and April's in the skies,

Earth,

look up with laughter in your eyes!"

— CHARLES G.D. ROBERTS

The old saying goes: "April showers bring May flowers," and the expression seems to suggest that this month will usher in the changing of the Earth's palette from winter's whites, grays, and browns, to spring's more colorful, floral hues. But more than flowers make Minnesota colorful at this time of year.

April is the month that rainbow smelt, blue, green, and black-crowned herons, and bluebirds return to the state. Even the reds of the pipestone in Minnesota rocks become uncovered in the warming temperatures. Color is unleashed everywhere.

True to the saying, about two-thirds of Minnesota's annual precipitation is received during the growing season, which begins in April. So, pull out the umbrellas, rush outside, and get ready to delight in the coming colors.

Rain, Rain, Come Our Way

You may notice that birds fly less and perch more in trees or on the ground just before a storm. It is thought that the lighter, low-pressure air that brings weather changes makes it harder for birds to fly.

Average Precipitation and High and Low Temperatures in April

Place	Avg. Precip. (Inches)	Avg. High Temp.	Avg. Low Temp.
Bemidji	1.7	49	28
Duluth	0.8	39	29
Int'l Falls	1.5	50	27
Minneapolis	2.2	56	36
Moorhead	1.7	51	30
Rochester	2.6	55	34
St. Cloud	1.9	53	32
Windom	2.2	55	34

Source: Minnesota State Climatology Office: DNR Waters

Play Ball!

The opening day for the Minnesota Twins was Friday, April 21, 1961. They played in the Metropolitan Stadium and lost to the Washington Senators, 5-3.

The Twins' first World Series appearance occurred in 1965, and their first player to step to the plate during the series was Zoilo Versalles, "the Cuban Comet." He socked a three-run homer to win Game One against the Los Angeles Dodgers. Although the Twins lost the series at three games to four, that year Versalles won the American League Most Valuable Player award. Vice President Hubert Humphrey (who previously served as mayor of Minneapolis and two terms as a U.S. Senator from Minnesota) threw the first ball of the 1965 World Series.

In 2006, Zoilo Versalles became the sixteenth member of the Minnesota Twins Hall of Fame.

Retiring the Greats

The Minnesota Twins have retired five numbers in honor of the players who wore them:

No. 3 Harmon Killebrew: number retired August 11, 1974. He was one of the best home-run hitters in baseball history, with 573 career home runs. During his fourteen seasons with the Twins, he hit 475 homers. In 1969, he was named the American League's Most Valuable Player. Nicknamed "Killer," Killebrew was the first Minnesota Twins player to be elected to the Baseball Hall of Fame (on January 10, 1984).

No. 29 Rod Carew: number retired July 19, 1987. Rod Carew won seven American League batting titles during his twelve years with the Twins. He finished his career with 3,053 hits, placing him sixteenth on the all-time hit list. He is one of only twenty-one players to collect three thousand or more career hits. He was elected to the Baseball Hall of Fame on January 8, 1991.

No. 6 Tony Oliva: number retired July 14, 1991. Nicknamed "Tony-O," Tony Oliva was the only player to win batting titles in his first two seasons and was the winner of three in his fifteen-year career with the Twins, which still stands as the club's longevity mark. When knee injuries cut his career short, he became a batting coach.

No. 14 Kent Hrbek: number retired on August 13, 1995. Ken Hrbek played for the Twins for thirteen years and is best remembered for his Game Six grand slam in the 1987 World Series and for his tag of Ron Gant in Game Two of the 1991 World Series.

No. 34 Kirby Puckett: number retired on May 25, 1997. Considered by some to be the greatest Twin ever, "Puck" played for the Twins for twelve seasons. His shining moment came on October 26, 1991, during Game Six of the World Series versus Atlanta. He went 3-for-4, made a leaping catch off the Plexiglas, and robbed Ron Gant of a sure extra-base hit. He became the ninth player to end a World Series game with a home run on the final pitch when he homered off Charlie Leibrandt in the eleventh inning to force a seventh game. He was inducted into the Baseball Hall of Fame in 2001 and into the World Sports Humanitarian Hall of Fame in 2000.

Pipestone and Portage

Minnesota has two federal monuments: Grand Portage National Monument and Pipestone National Monument.

Established in 1937, Pipestone National Monument in southwest Minnesota is the site of a type of red-colored stone found nowhere else but here. For centuries, Native Americans of the Great Plains used the soft pipestone to make ceremonial pipes for use in councils and healing practices. The sacred pipes were sometimes even buried with the dead.

Pipestone was widely traded throughout North America. When European artist and explorer George Catlin came to the quarries in the 1830s, he made sketches and sent pieces of the rock out for chemical analysis. Because of this, some mineralogists called the stone "catlinite."

Since the founding of the national monument in 1937, quarry excavation has been limited to Native Americans of all tribes. Demonstrations of pipe-making are held throughout the summer months in the Upper Midwest Indian Cultural Center, located inside the site's visitor center.

Grand Portage National Monument is located on the North Shore, within the boreal forest of Lake Superior in northeastern Minnesota. As part of the Grand Portage Indian Reservation, it preserves a four hundred-year-old center of fur trading activity and Ojibwa heritage. From 1778 until 1802, Kitchi Onigaming, "the Great Carrying Place" or Grand Portage, connected the summer headquarters of the North West Company and other French and English fur trading businesses on Lake Superior to smaller posts located on the Pigeon River, just over eight miles away. Summer rendezvous were held here, involving indigenous families, French voyageurs, Scottish clerks, and Montreal and London agents.

Later, Grand Portage became a major gateway into the interior of the continent for exploration, trade, and commerce. It was the link that connected Lake Superior and Montreal with the system of lakes, rivers, and trading posts farther west, which eventually reached the Pacific Ocean and the Beaufort Sea.

Pipestone Legend

"At an ancient time, the Great Spirit, in the form of a large bird, stood upon the wall of rock and called all the tribes around him, and breaking out a piece of the red stone formed it into a pipe and smoked it, the smoke rolling over the whole multitude. He then told his red children that this red stone was their flesh, that they were made from it, that they must all smoke to him through it, that they must use it for nothing but pipes: and as it belonged alike to all the tribes, the ground was sacred, and no weapons must be used or brought upon it."

— Dakota account of the origin of pipestone, recorded by George Catlin, 1835

Smelting Party

The rainbow smelt runs in April on the North Shore of Lake Superior used to be legendary, a spring ritual as much as deer hunting was to the fall. But that was in the 1960s and 1970s, when anyone with a big net, plastic bag, or garbage can could count on taking home a huge catch of the silver-colored, six- to nine-inch fish. The run would last a week and a half, beginning at Minnesota Point and swinging around to Duluth, and then up the North Shore to the Canadian border. Commercial fisheries harvested as much as four million pounds in 1976, and crowds of amateur anglers would gather on the beach to cook their smelt over open fires and have all-night parties.

The smelt abundance actually had its birth much earlier, in 1912. That year, smelt, a native of the Atlantic and Pacific oceans, entered the Great Lakes accidentally when they escaped from Crystal Lake in Michigan where they had been stocked as forage fish. The smelt entered Lake Michigan through connected waters and quickly spread to other Great Lakes. They were first found in Lake Huron in 1925, in Lake Ontario in 1929, in Lake Superior in 1930, and in Lake Erie in 1932. In 1946, they were found in the Minnesota waters of Lake Superior.

During the 1950s, sea lampreys from the Atlantic Ocean began to decimate the natural populations of native trout in Lake Superior. With far fewer predators, the smelt population flourished, growing into the huge numbers that peaked in the 1970s.

Then, they began to disappear. Reaching a critical mass, their numbers naturally tapered off. But other, not-so-natural factors were also at work: predation by stocked trout, chinook salmon, coho salmon, and other species began to affect smelt numbers. And with sea lampreys under control by trapping and poisons, the stocked fish had little to fear while enjoying their smelt snacks.

As Lake Superior is restored to a more natural state, it is unlikely that smelt will ever return to the boom days of the '60s and '70s. There is still a smelt run most years, but it is minor compared to that of forty years ago. Today, the run usually starts about April 21 and continues off-and-on until May 7.

It Was That Big …
As of 2008, the state muskellunge record is 54 pounds. The muskie was caught in Lake Winnibigoshish in 1957.

Source: Minnesota Department of Natural Resources

Duluth

One of the World's Fastest and Freshest

The world's largest freshwater inland port, Duluth is the third largest of Minnesota's cities in terms of population but one of its most handsome. With its Wisconsin counterpart, Superior, Duluth is one-half of Lake Superior's "Twin Ports." The two cities sit where the Saint Louis River winds its way into the great lake; and while Superior is on the flat river delta, Duluth rests on the dramatic, six hundred- to eight hundred-foot granite bluffs of the rocky North Shore.

Duluth extends for 26 miles along the west end of Lake Superior, ranging in width from less than a mile to never more than four miles. The narrow city is named after the French trader Daniel Greysolon, also known as Sieur Du Luth, who landed here around 1679. In a meeting with the Dakota Sioux that year, he claimed all of the area for France by nailing the royal emblem to a tree. For the next ten years, Du Luth tried to enforce French authority in the area and dealt with the factions of Native Americans who used the site for transportation to what is now northern Minnesota and Canada.

In 1692, Hudson's Bay Company set up a small post at Fond du Lac, located a few miles upstream from the mouth of the Saint Louis River on the grounds of a former Indian village. When the settlement began to grow, it was renamed in honor of Du Luth.

It was not until 1792 that Jean Baptiste Cadotte of the North West Company opened the next trading post, on the Wisconsin side of the St. Louis River. A fire destroyed the post in 1800, but German émigré John Jacob Astor soon built a new post on the Minnesota side of the river. The Indians, however, continued to trade with their familiar English and French partners, and Astor's store struggled. But when Astor convinced the United States Congress to ban foreigners from trading in American territory in 1816, his American Fur Company took off.

In 1855, the construction of locks at Sault Sainte Marie on the east end of Lake Superior allowed ships to pass from Duluth to the large cities on the lower Great Lakes. Duluth grew as a shipping port for grain, coal, and lumber. In the late 1860s, the city became the northern terminus of financier Jay Cooke's Lake Superior & Mississippi Railroad, which connected Saint Paul with the Great Lakes. Duluth grew dramatically.

By 1873, Duluth rivaled Chicago as a grain-shipping port. The opening of the Mesabi Range, the largest iron-mining district in the world, in 1891 secured the city's role as a major shipper of iron ore. The city was swarmed with thousands of immigrants who came to work in the mines.

Today Duluth is an international port, shipping iron ore to steel plants on the lower lakes, and grains and wood products to the eastern United States and Europe.

Duluth Facts

In 1933 a black bear broke into the coffee shop of Duluth's largest hotel, the Hotel Duluth (afterward renamed the "Black Bear Lounge").

The official opening of the **St. Lawrence Seaway** in 1959 brought ocean traffic to the port of Duluth.

Bob Dylan was born Robert Zimmerman in Duluth in 1941. His first band as a teenager in Hibbing was "The Golden Chords." Dylan ran away from home many times before leaving permanently, traveling across the country by hopping freight trains.

In the 1940s, Duluth was nicknamed Minnesota's **"air-conditioned city."**

The **Duluth-Superior Harbor** has more than 110 docks on the 49-mile harbor frontage. It has 17 miles of dredged channels, varying from 23 to 27 feet in depth. It has two entrances: the natural Superior Entry and the manmade Duluth Ship Canal (see "A State of Contention," August chapter).

The 510-foot-long **Aerial Lift Bridge,** which connects Minnesota Point with the mainland in Duluth, takes 55 seconds to rise to its complete height of 138 feet. Two 450-ton concrete blocks counterbalance the 900-ton lift. It is one of the fastest of its kind in the world.

Brainerd's Pitted Outwash Plain

With their warm, clear, shallow waters and sandy shores, the lakes around Brainerd in north-central Minnesota are a natural choice for those looking for some water-based recreation. You can thank the glaciers for providing your pleasure.

Geologists term this area a "pitted outwash plain." This kind of feature occurs when the front of a glacier is stalled and streams of melting glacial water flow down a slope. As the glacier then recedes, large ice blocks at the front of the glacier fall off, making depressions in the land. The wet sand and gravel then bury the ice blocks. When the blocks themselves eventually melt, the dents become lakes and marshes. The hundreds of depressions and pits in the soil surrounding Brainerd, ranging from a few feet to several miles across, are the result of this kind of glacier action.

It is estimated that 80 to 85 percent of Minnesota's lakes formed in ice-block depressions.

"The first of April, some do say,

Is set apart for All Fools' Day.

But why the people call it so,

Nor I, nor they themselves do know.

But on this day are people sent

On purpose for pure merriment."

— POOR ROBIN'S ALMANAC, 1790

The First Buying and Selling Co-Operative
The Grange

The Patrons of Husbandry, popularly known as "The Grange," was founded in St. Paul in 1867 by government clerk Oliver Hudson Kelley and six associates to help farmers protect their interests.

The expansion of the railroads brought an increasing amount of settlers into Minnesota's open prairies, and railroad officials often selected the sites for towns. First would come the boxcar station, quickly followed by a store, church, schoolhouse, and homes. Without the benefit of a railway, some older settlements were abandoned or forgotten. Many farmers in the older villages were unhappy with their bare subsistence living: the growing markets were located far from their homes, railroads discriminated against them through excessive rates, and agents falsely graded their grain. It was no wonder that Kelley's Grange movement spread more rapidly in Minnesota than in any other part of the country. By the close of 1869, forty of the forty-nine local Granges in the United States were located in Minnesota. By 1875, the national Grange had 850,000 members.

Through his Grange organization, a farmer could air grievances and give them voice in the legislature by endorsing Granger candidates. The first of the "Granger Acts" was passed in 1871, which led to laws limiting the rates railroads could charge. Three years later, the Grangers had gained control of the state legislature.

By the 1880s, however, Granger influence waned. But it could be said that the Grange Movement was the first time in Minnesota history that the voices of farmers had truly been heard.

Herons Herald Spring

Six species of herons come to live in Minnesota during the spring and summer: great blue herons, black-crowned night herons, green herons, great egrets, American bitterns, and least bitterns. More than eight thousand great blue herons alone migrate from the South to Minnesota every spring to nest and raise their young.

Spring is the best time to spot heron nests high in the trees before they leaf out. In the Twin Cities, the largest heron colony is on Pig's Eye Island, only five miles from the St. Paul city center. The Pig's Eye Island Heron Rookery Scientific and Natural Area, created in 1986, is the seasonal home to more than two thousand great blue herons.

Northwest Sportshow, Minneapolis
www.northwestsportshow.com

Last Chance Bonspiel, Hibbing
www.hibbingcurling.com

Minneapolis-St. Paul International
Film Festival
www.mnfilmarts.org

April Recipe
Grandma's Scalloped Asparagus

One of the earliest spring vegetables to be harvested, asparagus comes in around mid-April and grows for about two months. Asparagus tolerates a great range of temperatures: it grows in the Imperial Valley of Southern California in 115-degree heat and in Minnesota where temperatures can plunge to 40 degrees below zero.

According to the University of Minnesota Extension, the state has great potential for becoming a large asparagus-producing region. Here it grows on many different soils, ranging from sandy and coarse-textured to fine-textured clay. Enjoy this gourmet vegetable in a scalloped version.

Grandma's Scalloped Asparagus
From Carter's Red Wagon Farm

2 lbs. asparagus, trimmed and cut into one-inch pieces
2 cups milk
1/3 cup butter or margarine
1/4 cup flour
1/4 teaspoon salt
1/4 teaspoon pepper

4 hard-cooked eggs, sliced
1 cup cooked ham, chicken or cubed beef
1/2 cup shredded cheddar cheese
1/2 cup bread crumbs
2 teaspoons butter, melted

Cook the asparagus in 1/2 cup boiling water for three minutes (asparagus will still be crisp). Drain, reserving liquid. Add milk to the reserved liquid. In a medium saucepan, melt 1/3 cup butter and stir in the flour, salt, and pepper. Stir into the milk mixture all at once. Cook and stir until thickened and bubbly. Remove from heat. Cover the bottom of a greased two-quart casserole dish with half of the asparagus. Arrange half of the eggs over the asparagus. Put in half of the meat. Spoon in half of the sauce; sprinkle with half of the cheese. Repeat layers. Sprinkle with bread crumbs and drizzle with melted butter. Bake in 425°F oven for twenty minutes or until bubbly. Serve over rice, pasta, toast, or biscuits. Serves four.

APRIL WEATHER

April Normals for Duluth

Day	High	Low	Mean	Precip.	Snowfall
1	41	23	32	0.06	0.3
2	42	23	33	0.06	0.3
3	42	24	33	0.06	0.3
4	43	24	34	0.06	0.3
5	43	25	34	0.07	0.3
6	44	25	35	0.07	0.3
7	45	25	35	0.07	0.3
8	45	26	36	0.07	0.3
9	46	26	36	0.07	0.3
10	46	27	36	0.07	0.2
11	47	27	37	0.07	0.2
12	47	28	37	0.07	0.2
13	48	28	38	0.07	0.2
14	48	28	38	0.07	0.2
15	49	29	39	0.07	0.2
16	49	29	39	0.07	0.2
17	50	30	40	0.07	0.2
18	50	30	40	0.07	0.2
19	51	30	41	0.07	0.2
20	51	31	41	0.07	0.2
21	52	31	42	0.07	0.2
22	52	32	42	0.07	0.2
23	53	32	42	0.07	0.2
24	53	32	43	0.07	0.2
25	54	33	43	0.07	0.1
26	55	33	44	0.07	0.1
27	55	33	44	0.07	0.1
28	56	34	45	0.08	0.1
29	56	34	45	0.08	0.1
30	57	35	46	0.08	0.1

"The first day of spring is one thing, and the first spring day is another.
The difference between them is sometimes as great as a month."

— HENRY VAN DYKE, *FISHERMAN'S LUCK*, 1899

APRIL WEATHER

April Normals for International Falls

Day	High	Low	Mean	Precip.	Snowfall
1	43	20	32	0.04	0.2
2	44	21	32	0.04	0.2
3	44	21	33	0.04	0.2
4	45	22	33	0.04	0.2
5	46	22	34	0.04	0.2
6	46	23	34	0.04	0.2
7	47	23	35	0.04	0.2
8	47	24	35	0.04	0.2
9	48	24	36	0.04	0.2
10	48	25	36	0.04	0.2
11	49	25	37	0.04	0.2
12	50	25	37	0.04	0.2
13	50	26	38	0.04	0.2
14	51	26	39	0.04	0.2
15	51	27	39	0.04	0.2
16	52	27	40	0.05	0.2
17	52	28	40	0.05	0.2
18	53	28	41	0.05	0.2
19	53	29	41	0.05	0.2
20	54	29	42	0.05	0.2
21	55	30	42	0.05	0.2
22	55	30	43	0.05	0.2
23	56	31	43	0.05	0.2
24	56	31	44	0.05	0.2
25	57	32	44	0.05	0.1
26	57	32	45	0.05	0.1
27	58	32	45	0.05	0.1
28	59	33	46	0.06	0.1
29	59	33	46	0.06	0.1
30	60	34	47	0.06	0.1

Source: National Oceanic and Atmospheric Administration (NOAA)'s National Weather Service

These climate normals are an average of thirty years of data between 1971 and 2000. Every ten years, the National Weather Service recalculates the normals using the next interval of thirty years. In 2010, the new normals will be recalculated using the period of 1981 to 2010.

APRIL WEATHER HISTORY

On This Day in April

Day	Year	Weather
1	1960	The satellite "Trios 1" is launched from Cape Canaveral. Even though it only lasted two-and-a-half months, it took over nineteen thousand pictures of clouds.
2	1920	The temperature falls to 8 degrees in Pipestone. The high the day before was 74.
3	1982	A sharp cold front causes the temperature at Lamberton in Redwood County to drop from 78 to 7 degrees. This 71-degree change in 24 hours is the maximum 24-hour temperature change in Minnesota history.
4	1928	Severe thunderstorms rumble through east-central Minnesota. Anoka suffers $100,000 in damages.
5	1929	Tornado cuts a path from Lake Minnetonka through north Minneapolis and leaves six dead.
6	1964	Snowstorm hits Minnesota with 9 inches at Fosston and 8.7 at Park Rapids.
7	1857	Cold snap hits United States. Snow falls in every state.
8	1805	John Sayer at the Snake River Fur Trading Post (near present-day Pine City) writes: "The most tempestuous day of the year. Pines and other trees fell near the fort."
9	1931	Severe dust storms reported in St. Paul.
10	1877	Topography is altered by two great storms on the Virginia and Carolina coast. The Oregon Inlet is widened by almost a mile.
11	1929	Downpour in Lynd (near Marshall) dumps 5.27 inches of rain in 24 hours.
12	1931	July-like temperatures across state with 90 degrees at Beardsley in west-central Minnesota.
13	1949	Snowstorm dumps more than 9 inches at the Twin Cities.
14	1886	St. Cloud/Sauk Rapids tornado leaves 72 dead. 80 percent of all buildings in Sauk Rapids leveled as the tornado expanded to 800 yards across. When it crosses the Mississippi, it knocks down two iron spans of a wagon bridge, and local witnesses say the river was "swept dry" during the tornado crossing. The forecast for that day called for local rains and slightly warmer with highs in the 50s.
15	2002	Early heat wave over Minnesota. Faribault hits 93 degrees while the Twin Cities see their earliest 90-degree temperature with a high of 91.
16	1939	Rain, snow, sleet, and ice storms begin across southern Minnesota. Despite the fact that there are many phone and power outages, farmers are jubilant about the much-needed moisture.
17	1965	The Mississippi River crests at St. Paul 4 feet above the previous record. High water records are set all the way down to Missouri in later days.
18	2004	A strong cold front whips up winds of 55 mph over southern Minnesota. The wind causes black clouds of soil to lift into the air, reducing visibility. Some old-timers remarked that it reminded them of the storms from the 1930s Dust Bowl Era.
19	1820	A tornado hits the camp that would soon become Ft. Snelling. This is the first tornado ever reported in Minnesota. It damages the roof of a barracks, but no one is injured.
20	1970	Snow falls across much of Minnesota.

APRIL WEATHER HISTORY

On This Day in April

Day	Year	Weather
21	1910	Snowstorm hits northeastern Minnesota. Duluth picks up 6.5 inches.
22	1874	Cold outbreak across Minnesota. The low at the Twin Cites is 23 degrees.
23	1885	Denver picks up 23 inches of snow in 24 hours.
24	1854	Summertime at Ft. Snelling, with temperatures in the 80s.
25	1996	Heavy snow over northern Minnesota. 10 inches of snow at Baudette. The International Falls airport closes for only the second time in history.
26	1954	Downpour in Mora. Nearly 7 inches of rain fall in 10 hours.
27	1921	Late-season blizzard at Hibbing. The temperature was 75 degrees 3 days before.
28	1966	Snowstorm leaves 10 inches of snow on the ground across a wide chunk of northern Minnesota.
29	1984	Late-season snow blankets the Twin Cities with 6.6 inches.
30	2004	After a high temperature of 91 the day before in the Twin Cities, the mercury tumbles to 47 degrees by morning. St. Cloud sheds 50 degrees over 12 hours.

Source: Minnesota State Climatology Office: DNR Waters

The Bluebirds Return

Bluebirds return to the Upper Midwest in April, so have your birdhouses out by the first of the month.

Some Fun Bluebird Facts

- Bluebirds are thought to be a symbol of happiness.

- Although seeing a bluebird is considered a sign of spring, some return as early as February and linger until late December.

- Bluebirds eat a wide range of insects and wild fruit but like to eat mealworms at bird feeders.

- Bluebirds live in open woodlands, roadsides, farmlands, orchards, and occasionally suburbs and city parks.

- They are found in every county in Minnesota.

- They are considered Minnesota's most popular songbird.

April in the Garden

Pruning Deciduous Trees • How to Keep Garden Pests Away • Average Frosts and Growing Seasons

Pruning Deciduous Trees

Light pruning of deciduous trees—removing just the small, damaged, or diseased branches—can be done at almost any time of year, but late winter to early spring (March or April), once the threat of severe cold has passed, is the best time for more extensive pruning. This is the time before new growth begins, when pruning wounds heal quickly, and when there are very few active insects and disease spores to infest pruning cuts. And particularly in early spring, trees produce a hormone that stimulates the growth of a special protective layer of bark (callus tissue) that is similar to scar tissue. Some trees, however, "bleed" or exude sap from cuts if pruned in early spring. It is better to prune elms, maples, birches, and black walnuts after they leaf out in the spring and their sap flow has slowed down.

There are only a few valid reasons to ever prune a tree: Prune young trees to establish a strong framework; prune established trees to maintain a strong structure, promote healthy growth, and to improve flowering and fruiting. Strive to retain the particular tree species' natural shape and eliminate only diseased or broken branches, double leaders (two top stems splitting from the main trunk), weak crotches (two mature-top stems that have a "Y" formation), or branches that cross and rub against each other. Prune off healthy, lower branches only for safety and clearance reasons. Lower limbs are the tree's best defense against disease and old age.

- Wait two to four years after planting before pruning a tree for structure. The more top growth (branches and leaves), the faster trees recover from transplanting.

- Sterilize pruning tools (a pruning saw, pruning loppers, and hand pruning shears) with a ten-percent bleach solution to prevent the spread of disease.

- Remove dead and damaged branches first. Always make a pruning cut at a bud or an adjoining side branch so that no branch stubs remain to cause rotting and disease.

- If the branches to be cut away are large, make an initial undercut to prevent the bark from tearing with the weight of the branch as it falls from the tree.

- Prune water sprouts (upright shoots on branches) and suckers (upright shoots at the base of the trunk) as close to their bases as possible.

- Let tree cuts heal on their own rather than treat them with wound dressing. Since they keep wood damp, wound dressings encourage decay.

- For safety, consult a competent arborist for very large jobs.

How to Keep Garden Pests Away

Chewing insects, such as worms, caterpillars, beetles, and grasshoppers, as well as sucking insects, such as aphids and leafhoppers, can cause serious damage to gardens and the vegetables they produce. When trying to solve a garden-pest problem, always start with the simplest solution and then move up the ladder of complication until something works.

There are two simple practices that can greatly reduce insect problems: rotating crops and regular sanitation habits. Keep plants washed with a spray of soapy water. If washing doesn't get rid of insects, add garlic, salad oil, and cayenne pepper to the soapy spray.

Till your soil over each fall and rotate the position of vegetables each year. Interplant marigolds, garlic, and chives in vegetable rows to discourage pests. And try to enlist the aid of your pests' natural enemies: birds feed on insects, and predatory insects such as lady beetles and praying mantises may also help.

Average Frosts and Growing Seasons

These chart averages are based on 44 years of data (1948–1992) and show the medium frost dates (32 degrees Fahrenheit) for various regions.

Region	Growing Season	Average Last Spring Frost	Average First Autumn Spring
Minneapolis/ St. Paul	160 days	April 2	October 6
Morris	143 days	May 8	September 27
St. Cloud	138 days	May 12	September 24

Gladys's

April Household Tips

April means the smelt are running and the muskie fishing is good. But just as you start dreaming of that fresh fish dinner and cast your rod, the hook sinks into your skin and snaps you back to reality. Here's how to get that hook removed while you're out in the wilds and what to watch for in the days following.

Removing a Fishhook from Your Skin

Do not act hastily; take the time to assess your wound. Panic can do more harm than good. Fishhooks have a barb, a backward facing point that is meant to prevent the hook from being pulled free. If a fishhook is implanted but the barb is still showing, you can simply pull it out the way it went in.

If the hook is embedded past the barb, **do not** pull on the line. Instead:

• If you have ice, rub it over the spot where the hook is caught until sensation dulls. Then push the hook forward in the direction of the hook's curve until the barb pokes out of the skin through the shortest possible distance.

• Cut the barb with wire cutters and pull the shank out in the opposite direction.

• Wash the wound carefully with soap and water and hold it under cool, running water for five to ten minutes.

• Apply an antiseptic, such as hydrogen peroxide.

• If the wound is still bleeding, apply pressure with a clean cloth and elevate it.

• When the bleeding stops, bandage the wound.

Of course, if a fishhook is embedded in the skin and you are able to get to a doctor, do so. If the fishhook is embedded in the eye or face or near an artery, seek a doctor immediately. As soon as possible after the injury, check to see if the victim has had a tetanus shot in the past ten years and watch for signs of infection.

Signs of Infection

Injuries that break the skin, such as punctures, lacerations, bites, stings, or burns, can provide an opening through which infection-causing bacteria, viruses, and fungi can enter. In the hours that follow an injury, watch carefully for the following signs, and contact a physician immediately if any of them should develop:

- Swelling of the affected part
- Throbbing pain
- Tenderness
- A sensation of heat
- Joint aches
- A green, yellow, or white discharge (pus) from the wound
- Red streaks radiating from the wound
- Inflammation—more than a red rim just around the wound
- Fever that has no other known cause, such as the flu
- Shaking chills
- Overall weakness
- Swollen, tender lymph glands in the groin, armpit, or neck

Some Fun City Facts

Blue Earth is the birthplace of the ice cream sandwich and home of the world's largest statue of the Jolly Green Giant.

Cloquet has the only Frank Lloyd Wright-designed gas station; is the home of the World's Largest Voyageur, erected on an island in the St. Louis River; and is the birthplace of actress Jessica Lange.

Grand Rapids is the birthplace of Frances Gumm (aka Judy Garland) and is the home of the Judy Garland Museum.

Hastings has a total of sixty-three buildings on the National Register, including thirty-three commercial buildings, twenty-eight private homes, and two churches. Wildlife artist Terry Redlin is from Hastings.

Mabel is "Rural America's Steam Engine Capital."

Mendota was the site of the first permanent white settlement in Minnesota (founded around the same time as Fort Snelling); has the oldest church in continuous use in Minnesota (St. Peter's Catholic Church, est. 1842); and was the site of John Jacob Astor's American Fur Company's chief trading center with the Dakota Sioux in the Minnesota Territory.

Minneapolis is the birthplace of retired professional wrestler and former Minnesota governor Jessie ("The Body") Ventura.

Kansas is the only other state that has both a **Minneapolis** and a **St. Paul.**

Pine City has what is perhaps the world's largest chainsaw sculpture, an enormous voyageur carved from a huge, thirty-five-foot redwood log, which came from an old-growth California forest. It was placed in Riverside Park to commemorate the first European explorers in the area.

Rochester had a three-day gold rush in the 1860s; the first fully accredited school of nursing; caves at Quarry Hill Park dug in the 1880s to refrigerate food and preserve cadavers for the state hospital; and a corncob-shaped water tower built by Libby's in 1931.

Virginia (city) was destroyed by fires twice, in 1893 and 1900.

MAY

"*The fair maid who, the first of May*

Goes to the fields at break of day

And washes in dew from the hawthorn tree

Will ever after handsome be."

— MOTHER GOOSE NURSERY RHYME

Dating back to the time of the Druids, May Day traditionally celebrated the end of winter weather in the Northern Hemisphere. Maypoles, a custom rooted in Germanic paganism, were often set up. Long, colorful ribbons were draped from the top, and children would dance with them, weaving the streamers in and out and around the pole.

If you were an elementary schoolchild in the United States anytime during the latter half of the twentieth century, you probably remember making May Day baskets out of a milk carton or other small container. You'd fill it with flowers or treats and were told to leave it on someone's doorstep, ring the bell, and run away.

Today still, communities with a large Swedish population often have May Day celebrations. Minneapolis holds an annual May Day Parade and Festival in conjunction with the In the Heart of the Beast Puppet and Mask Theatre.

But there's another Minnesota May tradition that's even more widespread: the annual fishing opener, usually on the second weekend of the month. Since it coincides with Mother's Day, it's a wonder how many Minnesotans have honored their mothers by bringing home a big fish on her special day. With Minnesota ranking first in the number of fishing licenses issued per capita, however, it's more likely that mom was right on the lake beside them!

Gustavus Adolphus College

Gustavus Adolphus College, a private liberal arts college located in St. Peter, was founded in 1862. Approaching its 150th anniversary, it is one of the oldest educational institutions in the state.

In 1963, the college became the site of the first American memorial to Swedish philanthropist Alfred Nobel when it dedicated the Alfred Nobel Hall of Science. Twenty-six Nobel laureates attended the dedication ceremony—the largest single gathering of Nobel Prize-winners outside of Sweden to that date.

The college boasts another important first: The earliest recorded women's football game occurred at the college in 1923. The "Heavies" team played the "Leans."

"The Lone Eagle"
and Other Famous Minnesotans

Charles Lindbergh, Jr.

One of Minnesota's most famous residents was aviator Charles Lindbergh, Jr., called "the lone eagle." On May 20, 1927, he became the first to fly solo nonstop across the Atlantic—from New York to Paris. The trip in his single-engine plane took 33.5 hours. Lindbergh's 1953 book, *The Spirit of St. Louis,* won a Pulitzer Prize for biography.

Lindbergh's father was a lawyer and a U.S. congressman from Minnesota from 1907 to 1917, and his grandfather had been a prominent member of the Swedish Parliament before immigrating to Minnesota's frontier in 1859.

Boogie Woogie Bugle Girls

Born in Minnesota to a Greek immigrant father and a Norwegian-American mother, the three Andrews Sisters—Patty, LaVerne, and Maxene—achieved world fame with their 1937 recording of a translated Yiddish tune, "Bei Mir Bist Du Schön." The record sold 350,000 copies and held the *Billboard* No. 1 slot for five weeks. During the 1940s, their popularity soared, especially as they traveled abroad to entertain troops during World War II.

On August 5, 2006, the Andrews Sisters Trail in Mound, Minnesota, was officially named and presented to the public. When told of the winding, half-mile path on Lake Minnetonka, Patty Andrews said, "No one knows how many, many, wonderful memories we have from Mound and what Mound meant to us." The trail is the only physical recognition for the singing trio anywhere in the world.

Other Famous Minnesotans

Loni Anderson, Louie Anderson, Richard Dean Anderson (aka "MacGyver"), James and Peter Aurness (aka James Arness and Peter Graves), Jim Brandenburg, Warren Burger, Ethan and Joel Coen, William Demarest, William O. Douglas, Bob Dylan, Mike Farrell, F. Scott Fitzgerald, Judy Garland, Jean Paul Getty, Terry Gilliam, Tippi Hedren, George Roy Hill, Hubert Humphrey, Garrison Keillor, Jessica Lange, Tom Laughlin (aka T. C. Frank or "Billy Jack"), Sinclair Lewis, Walter Mondale, LeRoy Neiman, Prince Rogers Nelson (aka Prince), Marion Ross, Jane Russell, Winona Ryder, Charles Schulz, Lea Thompson, Cheryl Tiegs, Vince Vaughn, Jesse Ventura (born James Janos), Gig Young, Steve Zahn.

K Rations and the Wars

Although no one claimed they were a taste sensation, K rations got a lot of World War II soldiers through some hungry times.

The non-perishable, pocket-sized meals were developed by Dr. Ancel Keys, director of the University of Minnesota's Laboratory of Physiological Hygiene, in 1941. The U.S. War Department had asked Keys to design a ready-to-eat meal that combat soldiers could easily carry with them. Keys went to a local grocery store and selected some inexpensive foods that would provide energy: hard biscuits, dry sausages, hard candy, and chocolate bars.

At an army base, Keys tested the twenty-eight-ounce, 3,200-calorie meals on six soldiers. While the best the soldiers could say about the taste was that they were "better than nothing," the foods successfully relieved hunger. The United States Army added a few extra items and had the Cracker Jack Company produce a waxed paper ration box for the food that was about the same size as a Cracker Jack box. The packs were named "K rations," possibly in honor of their creator.

Memorial Day
In Service to the Country

During World War I, Minnesotans in uniform totaled 123,325. During World War II, that number jumped to more than 300,000.

- 1,432 Minnesotans died in World War I
- 6,255 Minnesotans died in World War II
- 700 Minnesotans died in Korea
- 1,072 Minnesotans died in Vietnam
- 72 Minnesotans died in Afghanistan and Iraq (as of March 2008)

It's Outta Here!

On May 4, 1984, baseball player Dave Kingman did something no one else had ever done in the city's Metrodome.

In the fourth inning of a game between Kingman's Oakland Athletics and the Minnesota Twins, the six-foot, six-inch first baseman hit a baseball 180 feet straight up in the air. And it never came down.

The ball had found its way through an eleven-inch drainage hole in the Metrodome's roof. The umpires called the play a ground rule double.

About a week later, the ball was poked down to the field by John Beane of the maintenance crew, who stood on the outside roof and used a long stick to nudge it loose. The ball, which brought a new ruling into the books, now resides at the Baseball Hall of Fame in Cooperstown, New York.

Know Your State Symbols

"Minnesota" comes from the Dakota Sioux word meaning "cloudy water" or "sky-tinted water" (sometimes interpreted as "Land of Sky-Blue Waters"), which refers to the Minnesota River. The first time the prospect of statehood arose in congress, the state's name was spelled "Minasota."

On May 11, 1858, Minnesota became the thirty-second state in the union, with Henry Sibley serving as the first governor. And although Minnesota is called the "Land of 10,000 Lakes," some statisticians say there are actually 11,842 lakes of more than ten acres, and one counter claims there are actually 15,291 lakes in total.

Test your knowledge by seeing if you know the following state facts (before reading the correct answers, that is!):

Animal: white-tailed deer
Bird: common loon
Butterfly: monarch
Capital: St. Paul, est. 1849
Drink: milk
Fish: walleye
Flower: showy lady's slipper (pink and white)
Fruit: Honeycrisp apple
Gemstone: Lake Superior agate
Grain: wild rice
Mammal: gopher
Motto: L'Etoile du Nord (The Star of the North)
Muffin: blueberry

Mushroom: morel
Nicknames: North Star State; Gopher State; Land of 10,000 Lakes
Photograph: "Grace," depicting an elderly man bowing his head and giving thanks, taken in Bovey, Minnesota, in 1918 by Eric Enstrom
Quarter: The design features a tree-lined lake with two people fishing, a loon on the water, and a textured outline of the state surrounding the words, "Land of 10,000 Lakes"
Seal: a waterfall and a forest represent the state's natural features; a Native American and a farmer symbolize the state's people
Song: "Hail! Minnesota"
Tree: red (Norway) pine

State Geography

Total area: 84,068 square miles (twelfth largest state)
Total land area: 79,610 square miles
Total water area: 4,458 square miles
Highest point: Eagle Mountain in Cook County, 2,301 feet
Lowest point: Lake Superior shore, 602 feet
Longest distance from north to south: 411 miles
Widest distance from east to west: 357 miles
Average width: 240 miles
Northernmost point in the contiguous forty-eight states: Northwest Angle
Geographic center: Crow Wing, southwest of Brainerd

From Fires Come Flour Inventions

On May 2, 1878, at 7:00 a.m., the largest flour mill in the United States at the time blew up. The roof of the Washburn A Mill in Minneapolis was sent sailing five hundred feet into the air by the force of the explosion, and the seven-story building was demolished. The resulting fire spread to the Minneapolis business district, and eighteen people were killed.

The reason for the explosion remains a mystery. Dr. R. J. Taylor of Galesburg, Illinois, however, came up with a plausible theory. He proposed that the flour drifting in the mill's air had formed "nitroglycerin," and could easily have been ignited by the slightest spark. He estimated the force of the explosion to have been the equivalent of 30,323 twenty-five-pound kegs of gunpowder going off.

Researchers in dust explosions later learned that mill dust suspended in the air would explode like gunpowder when ignited. Cadwallader Washburn rebuilt the mill and installed dust catchers. He also began to use corrugated rollers made of porcelain or steel—as opposed to the millstone methodology—which in addition to lessening the chance of fire, revolutionized the industry by increasing the amount of flour produced from the grains of wheat.

Since Minnesota's wheat was spring wheat, the flour made from it was of a darker color and tended to be speckled as compared with that of the winter wheat flour of other states. Yet spring wheat was the only variety ideally suited to Minnesota's weather.

When French-Canadian Edmund La Croix perfected a "middlings purifier" to remove the speckles, or chaff, from the wheat, his new milling process was quickly adopted in all the Minneapolis mills. The purifier, combined with the rollers, increased the efficiency of mills from 25 to 90 percent. By 1885, Minnesota's flour had become the most popular in the world.

Minnesota, (Not Quite the) Land of the Free
The Dred Scott Decision

Dr. John Emerson, a military surgeon from Missouri, took his slave Dred Scott with him when he was transferred to a post in Illinois and later, in 1836, to Fort Snelling. There, Scott met and married Harriet Robinson, another slave, and had two children. In 1842, Dr. Emerson and his wife moved back to Missouri, taking the Scott family with them.

In 1843, however, Dr. Emerson died, and Mrs. Emerson hired out the Scotts for service to other families. In 1846, Dred Scott decided to sue for his family's freedom, arguing that under the terms of the Missouri Compromise, the fact that he and Dr. Emerson had lived in a free state (Illinois) and a free territory (the Fort Snelling site) made him a free man.

For the next ten years, the case moved from court to court, finally winding up at the U.S. Supreme Court. In a majority decision, the court held that as a slave, Scott was not a U.S. citizen and thus was not entitled to sue for freedom in federal court; he had never been free and would have to remain a slave.

However, in 1850, Mrs. Emerson remarried. Her new husband was a U.S. congressman from Springfield, Massachusetts, and an avowed abolitionist. To avoid embarrassment, she arranged to transfer the Scott family to Dred's original owner, the Peter Blow family in the state of Virginia. On May 26, 1857, Peter's son, Taylor Blow, granted the Scotts their freedom. On September 17, 1858, fifteen months after he was freed, Dred Scott died. Harriet died shortly thereafter.

Once, Mounds Abounded

At one time, there were ten to twenty-five thousand Indian mounds in Minnesota. Built by native peoples of the Woodland Period (800 B.C. to the time of historic contact with European-Americans), the mounds are mostly gone today. Erosion, agriculture, and road building have contributed to the loss of almost eighty percent of these earthworks.

What remains are located near deciduous forests and along rivers, streams, and lakes. They stand as low as one foot to as tall as forty feet high, and from five feet to more than 150 feet wide. The mounds are found in groups of two to more than two hundred. Some were built as fortifications; some for burials.

The 2,200-year-old Grand Mound near International Falls is believed to be the largest surviving prehistoric structure in the Upper Midwest. It is about forty feet high and 325 feet around. Built by a group of people called the Laurel Indians, the mound was closed permanently to visitors in 2007 because of its sacred nature.

Walleye Season

May marks the opening of wall-eye fishing season, and Minnesotans do love to catch what many consider to be the best-tasting freshwater fish. Each year, anglers in Minnesota keep 3.5 million walleyes, for a total of four million pounds. The average walleye caught and kept is about fourteen inches long and weighs slightly more than one pound.

Named for its pearlescent eye that reflects light, the walleye is the state fish of Minnesota. But there could be some bad news on the horizon. Scientists say that within a few decades some Minnesota lakes will probably be too warm for walleye to thrive.

For now, the Minnesota Department of Natural Resources is working to ensure the continuance of the walleye population by protecting its habitat, enforcing catch-limit regulations, and stocking fish where natural reproduction is limited and other fish species will not be harmed.

The Minnesota record walleye was caught in Seagull River (Cook County) on May 13, 1979, and weighed seventeen pounds, eight ounces. It was 35.8 inches long.

State Record Fish

Species	Weight (lbs-ozs)	Length/girth (inches)	Where caught	County	Date
Bass, Largemouth	8–15	23.5/18	Auburn Lake	Carver	10/05/2005
Bass, Rock (tie)	2–0	13.5/12.5	Osakis Lake	Todd	05/10/1998
	2–0	12.6/12.4	Lake Winnibigoshish	Cass	08/30/2004
Bass, Smallmouth	8–0	n/a	West Battle Lake	Otter Tail	1948
Bass, White	4–2.4	18.5/15.1	Mississippi River Pool 5	Wabasha	05/04/2004
Bluegill	2–13	n/a	Alice Lake	Hubbard	1948
Bowfin (tie)	10–15	32/15	Mary Lake	Douglas	07/15/1983
	10–15	31/14.8	French Lake	Rice	08/26/1992
Buffalo, Bigmouth	41–11	38.5/29.5	Mississippi River	Goodhue	05/07/1991
Buffalo, Black	20–.5	34.2/20	Minnesota River	Nicollet	06/26/1997
Buffalo, Smallmouth	20–0	32/23.75	Big Sandy	Aitkin	09/20/2003
Bullhead, Black	3–13.12	17.17/14.96	Reno Lake	Pope	06/08/1997
Bullhead, Brown	7–1	24.4/n/a	Shallow Lake	Itasca	05/21/1974
Bullhead, Yellow	3–10.5	17.87/11.75	Osakis Lake	Todd	08/05/2002
Burbot	19–3	36.25/22.75	Woods	Lake of the Woods	02/17/2001
Carp	55–5	42/31	Clearwater Lake	Wright	07/10/1952
Carpsucker, River	3–15	19.5/14	Mississippi River	Ramsey	03/09/1991
Catfish, Channel	38–0	44/n/a	Mississippi River	Hennepin	1975
Catfish, Flathead	70–0	n/a	St. Croix River	Washington	1970
Crappie, Black	5–0	21/n/a	Vermillion River	Dakota	1940
Crappie, White	3–15	18/16	Lake Constance	Wright	07/28/2002
Drum, Freshwater (Sheepshead)	35–3.2	36/31	Mississippi River	Winona	10/05/1999

Species	Weight (lbs-ozs)	Length/girth (inches)	Where caught	County	Date
Eel, American	6–9	36/14	St. Croix River	Washington	08/08/1997
Gar, Longnose	16–12	53/16.5	St. Croix River	Washington	05/04/1982
Gar, Shortnose	4–9.6	34.6/10	Mississippi River	Hennepin	07/22/1984
Goldeye	2–13.1	20.1/11.5	Root River	Houston	06/10/2001
Hogsucker, Northern	1–15	14.25/7.12	Sunrise River	Chisago	08/16/1982
Mooneye	1–15	16.5/9.75	Minnesota River	Redwood	06/18/1980
Muskellunge	54–0	56/27.8	Lake Winnibigoshish	Itasca	1957
Muskellunge, Tiger	34–12	51/22.5	Lake Elmo	Washington	07/07/1999
Perch, Yellow	3–4	n/a	Lake Plantaganette	Hubbard	1945
Pike, Northern	45–12	n/a	Basswood Lake	Lake	05/16/1929
Pumpkinseed	1–5.6	10.1/12.12	Leech Lake	Cass	06/06/1999
Quillback	6–14.4	23/18	Mississippi River	Ramsey	04/06/1991
Redhorse, Golden	3–15.5	20.12/12.37	Root River	Fillmore	04/30/2007
Redhorse, Greater	12–11.5	28.5/18.5	Sauk River	Stearns	05/20/2005
Redhorse, River	12–10	28.38/20	Kettle River	Pine	05/20/2005
Redhorse, Shorthead	7–15	27/15	Rum River	Anoka	08/05/1983
Redhorse, Silver	9–15	26.6/16.87	Big Fork River	Koochiching	04/16/2004
Salmon, Atlantic	12–13	35.5/16.5	Baptism River	Lake	10/12/1991
Salmon, Chinook (King)	33–4	44.75/25.75	Poplar River	Cook	09/23/1989
(tie)	33–4	42.25/26.13	Lake Superior	St. Louis	10/12/1989
Salmon, Coho	10–6.5	27.3/n/a	Lake Superior	Lake	11/07/1970
Salmon, Kokanee	2–15	20/11.5	Caribou Lake	Itasca	08/06/1971
Salmon, Pink	4–8	23.5/13.2	Cascade River	Cook	09/09/1989
Sauger	6–2.75	23.87/15	Mississippi River	Goodhue	05/23/1988
Splake	13–5.44	33.5/19	Larson Lake	Itasca	02/11/2001
Sturgeon, Lake	94–4	70/26.5	Kettle River	Pine	09/05/1994
Sturgeon, Shovelnose	5–9	36/11.87	Mississippi River (near Red Wing)	Goodhue	06/04/2007
Sucker, Blue	14–3	30.4/20.2	Mississippi River	Wabasha	02/28/1987
Sucker, Longnose	3–10.6	21/10.25	Brule River	Cook	05/19/2005
Sucker, White	9–1	24.25/16.25	Big Fish Lake	Stearns	05/01/1983
Sunfish, Green	1–4.8	10.25/10.62	North Arbor Lake	Hennepin	06/14/2005
Sunfish, Hybrid	1–12	11.5/12	Zumbro River	Olmsted	07/09/1994
Trout, Brook	6–5.6	24/14.5	Pigeon River	Cook	09/02/2000
Trout, Brown	16–12	31.4/20.6	Lake Superior	St. Louis	06/23/1989
Trout, Lake	43–8	n/a	Lake Superior	Cook	05/30/1955
Trout, Rainbow (Steelhead)	16–6	33/19.5	Devil Track River	Cook	04/27/1980
Trout, Tiger	2–9.12	20/9.62	Mill Creek	Olmsted	08/07/1999
Tullibee (Cisco)	5–11.8	20.45/16.40	Little Long Lake	St. Louis	04/16/2002
Walleye	17–8	35.8/21.3	Seagull River	Cook	05/13/1979
Walleye-Sauger Hybrid	9–13.4	27/17.75	Mississippi River	Goodhue	03/20/1999
Warmouth	0–6.2	7.3/7	Airport Lake	Winona	03/06/2007
Whitefish, Lake	12–4.5	28.5/20	Leech Lake	Cass	03/21/1999
Whitefish, Menominee (Round)	2–7.5	21/9.1	Lake Superior	Cook	04/27/1987

Source: Minnesota Department of Natural Resources

The First Wilderness
Boundary Waters Canoe Area Wilderness

The glaciers did it again: They carved one of the most beautiful areas in Minnesota and on the continent. The Boundary Waters Canoe Area Wilderness (BWCAW) is filled with rugged cliffs, deep canyons, gentle hills, towering rocks, sandy beaches, and several thousand lakes and streams. It is the largest federal wilderness east of the Rocky Mountains, as well as the first one anywhere, and the only lakeland wilderness in the United States.

The 1.3-million-acre wilderness extends for 150 miles along the Minnesota-Canada border and is adjacent to Canada's million-acre Quetico Provincial Park. It is bordered on the west by Voyageurs National Park and on the south by two million more acres within the Superior National Forest. It contains over twelve hundred miles of canoe routes, some twenty-five thousand lakes, fifteen hiking trails, and approximately two thousand campsites.

Here, where the rocks are three billion years old and the wolves and loons call, you can experience solitude, nature, and a Minnesota that looks like it must have looked when the French-Canadian voyageurs arrived two hundred years ago. With few exceptions, motors are not allowed, and planes have to fly at a designated altitude.

The best time for a Boundary Waters canoe trip is late May to mid-September. Permits are required for all overnight visits to the wilderness area.

Five Fun Facts About Faribault

Alexander Faribault was the son of a French-Canadian fur trader and a Dakota Sioux woman. In 1826, he established a fur trading post on the Cannon River. In 1834, the post was relocated to the Straight River, one mile upstream of its junction with the Cannon River; the site is now the city of Faribault.

Faribault has a claim to something no other place in the United States can claim: it is the producer of **cave-aged blue cheese**. In fact, Faribault was home to the first blue cheese plant in the nation. In 1936, cheesemaker Felix Frederiksen purchased several caves in the bluffs along the Straight River to cure his cheese. The caves had formerly been used to brew beer.

Actor **Marlon Brando** attended boarding school at Faribault's Shattuck Military School. In 1943, during his final year, he was expelled. He was invited back the next year, but Brando decided not to finish school.

Around 1859, there was a **"ginseng rush"** in Minnesota. In one week of that year alone, six tons of ginseng were brought to Faribault for export.

In the 1920s especially, Faribault was known for its **peony farms.** In the mid- and late twenties, Brand Peony Farms developed an active breeding program and developed a national peony reputation.

A Hole in One

Born in 1918 in Minneapolis, Patty Berg took up golf at the age of thirteen. By 1934, she had won the city championship. Four years later, she won the national Woman's Amateur title and was well on her way to becoming the first of the great women golfers.

When America entered World War II, Berg joined the armed forces and served as a lieutenant in the Marines until 1945. The next year, she became the first winner of the inaugural U.S. Women's Open.

Her hole-in-one during the 1959 open at Churchill Valley Country Club in Pittsburgh made her the first woman to record an ace in a United States Golf Association competition. She won eighty-three golf tournaments between 1935 and 1964.

All her life, Berg remained an ambassador for the game she loved. She helped found the Ladies Professional Golf Association and served as its first president, starting in 1948. She once said, "Always keep learning. It keeps you young."

Berg became one of the original members of the Hall of Fame of Women's Golf in 1951, and was also in the first class inducted into the World Golf Hall of Fame in 1974.

May Recipe
Pecan Crusted Minnesota Walleye

Minnesotans love walleye—even made it their state fish—and it is estimated that on opening day in May, 25 percent of the 1.2 million anglers who fish Minnesota each year will be sitting in a boat or standing on shore in an attempt to catch the green and gold goodie. Here's a great recipe for yours.

Pecan Crusted Minnesota Walleye

2 Minnesota walleye fillets
   (½ lb. each)
3 cups all-purpose flour
   seasoned with salt and pepper
1 large egg, slightly beaten
¾ cup finely chopped pecans
2 tablespoons butter

2 tablespoons minced scallions
1 ripe pear, peeled and cut into slices
¼ cup white wine
Juice of ½ lemon
¼ cup heavy cream
2 tablespoons blue cheese

Dredge walleye in flour, shake off excess, dip in egg, and coat in pecans. Melt butter in a pan and sauté walleye for six minutes on each side. Transfer the fillets to a plate and cover to keep warm. Drain excess grease.

Cook the scallions and the pear slices in the pan for one to two minutes. Add wine and cook a few more minutes. Add cream, and season with salt and pepper. Add lemon juice. At the last minute, add the blue cheese and spoon over the fish.

Printed with permission from Minnesota.gov

MAY WEATHER

May Normals for Duluth

Day	High	Low	Mean	Precip.	Snowfall
1	57	35	46	0.08	0.1
2	58	35	47	0.08	0.1
3	58	36	47	0.08	0.1
4	59	36	48	0.08	Trace Amt.
5	59	37	48	0.08	Trace Amt.
6	60	37	48	0.08	Trace Amt.
7	60	37	49	0.08	Trace Amt.
8	61	38	49	0.08	Trace Amt.
9	61	38	50	0.08	0
10	61	38	50	0.09	0
11	62	39	50	0.09	0
12	62	39	51	0.09	0
13	63	39	51	0.09	0
14	63	40	51	0.09	0
15	63	40	52	0.09	0
16	64	40	52	0.09	0
17	64	41	52	0.09	0
18	65	41	53	0.10	0
19	65	41	53	0.10	0
20	65	42	53	0.10	0
21	65	42	54	0.10	0
22	66	42	54	0.10	0
23	66	43	54	0.10	0
24	66	43	55	0.11	0
25	67	43	55	0.11	0
26	67	43	55	0.11	0
27	67	44	55	0.11	0
28	67	44	56	0.11	0
29	68	44	56	0.12	0
30	68	44	56	0.12	0
31	68	45	56	0.12	0

MAY WEATHER

May Normals for International Falls

Day	High	Low	Mean	Precip.	Snowfall
1	60	34	47	0.06	0.1
2	61	35	48	0.06	0.1
3	61	35	48	0.06	0.1
4	62	35	49	0.06	0
5	62	36	49	0.06	0
6	63	36	50	0.06	0
7	63	37	50	0.07	0
8	64	37	50	0.07	0
9	64	37	51	0.07	0
10	65	38	51	0.07	0
11	65	38	52	0.07	0
12	66	39	52	0.07	0
13	66	39	52	0.08	0
14	66	39	53	0.08	0
15	67	40	53	0.08	0
16	67	40	54	0.08	0
17	67	41	54	0.08	0
18	68	41	54	0.08	0
19	68	41	55	0.09	0
20	69	42	55	0.09	0
21	69	42	55	0.09	0
22	69	42	56	0.09	0
23	69	43	56	0.09	0
24	70	43	56	0.1	0
25	70	43	57	0.1	0
26	70	44	57	0.1	0
27	70	44	57	0.1	0
28	71	44	57	0.11	0
29	71	45	58	0.11	0
30	71	45	58	0.11	0
31	71	45	58	0.11	0

Source: National Oceanic and Atmospheric Administration (NOAA)'s National Weather Service

These climate normals are an average of thirty years of data between 1971 and 2000. Every ten years, the National Weather Service recalculates the normals using the next interval of thirty years. In 2010, the new normals will be recalculated using the period of 1981 to 2010.

MAY WEATHER HISTORY

On This Day in May

Day	Year	Weather
1	1966	Winter takes a last stab at Minnesota with a low of 5 degrees at Cook. Hard freeze over rest of the state.
2	1954	Late season snowstorm dumps over half a foot of snow at International Falls.
3	1905	Western Minnesota is pelted with hail.
4	1926	From winter to summer in one day. Morris temperature rises from 32 to 89.
5	1965	At least seven tornadoes hit southern Minnesota, just a preview of what would happen the following day.
6	1965	Six tornadoes hit an eleven-county area, including the western Twin Cities. Fourteen people are killed; 683 injured. Three of the tornadoes hit Fridley.
7	1916	Strong winds sweep across the state and cause sandstorms over southern Minnesota. Great damage done to standing timber in the northern part of the state. In Duluth, a boy trying to cross St. Louis Bay drowns in the waves that capsize his boat. Many fires are started, one of which destroys 30 million feet of lumber.
8	1924	Snowstorm brings 4 inches to parts of the state. Minneapolis sees a half-inch of snow, with St. Paul picking up an inch. Winds of 50 mph accompany the snow, and heavy coats are brought back out of the closet.
9	1966	Hard freeze over the state with temperatures in the teens as far south as Caledonia.
10	1934	"The Classic Dust Bowl." Near daytime blackout in the Twin Cities and west central Minnesota. Automobiles have their headlights on due to the dust. Drifts of dust and soil 6 inches deep cover the roads in Fairmont.
11	1915	A waterspout is seen at Lake Mills.
12	1922	From shorts to sweaters at Morris. The temperature drops from 91 to 26.
13	1872	Hail reported the size of pigeon eggs in Sibley County. Lightning burns down a barn near Sibley and kills a horse tied up inside.
14	1896	Coldest-ever May reading in lower 48 states with a -10 at Climax, Colorado.
15	1969	Storm in Synnes township dumps 8 inches of rain in three hours.
16	1934	Hot spell, with temperatures over 100 across much of Minnesota.
17	1915	Old Man Winter's last hurrah with 5 inches of snow along Lake Superior.
18	1980	Mt. St. Helens erupts. The smoke plume rises to eighty thousand feet, and the cloud circles the earth in nineteen days. Brilliant sunsets are seen across Minnesota for days afterward.
19	1975	Strong winds cause more than $2 million in damages across Fridley, Mounds View, and New Brighton.
20	1892	Very late-season snowfall over central Minnesota. Maple Plain receives 4 inches of snow, with 3 inches falling in Minneapolis. This is the latest significant snow on record for the Twin Cities and one of the latest widespread snowfalls in Minnesota.
21	1960	Downpour at New Prague dumps 10 inches of rain in a 48-hour period.

MAY WEATHER HISTORY

On This Day in May

Day	Year	Weather
22	1925	Temperature takes a nosedive from 100 to freezing in 36 hours at New Ulm and Tracy.
23	1914	Early heat wave across the state with 103 at Tracy.
24	1925	After seeing a high of 99 degrees two days earlier, the Twin Cities pick up a tenth of an inch of snow.
25	1862	Hail the size of hickory nuts falls on the Dakota Mission in Renville County.
26	1929	Tornado rakes Freeborn County and causes $10,000 in damages to farms.
27	1930	"Great Empire Builder Tornado." A direct hit derails the famous train in Norman County.
28	1965	Late-season snow falls across all of Minnesota, with Duluth and Caribou reporting an inch.
29	1947	Freak snowstorm over far southern Minnesota, northern Iowa, and southern Wisconsin. Worthington, Minnesota, picks up an inch.
30	1985	Tornado hits Lakefield. The Twin Cities report winds of 67 mph.
31	1934	Extreme heat in Minnesota with 107 in St. Paul and 106 in Minneapolis. Rush City reaches 110. There are numerous cases of heat ailments among people and livestock.

Source: Minnesota State Climatology Office: DNR Waters

The Ten Largest Cities (By Population) in Minnesota

Minneapolis	382,618	Rochester	85,806	Eagan	63,557
St. Paul	287,151	Bloomington	85,172	Coon Rapids	61,607
Duluth	86,918	Brooklyn Park	67,338	Burnsville	60,220
		Plymouth	65,894		

The total population of Minnesota on April 1, 2000, was 4,919,479.

Source: United States Census, April 2000

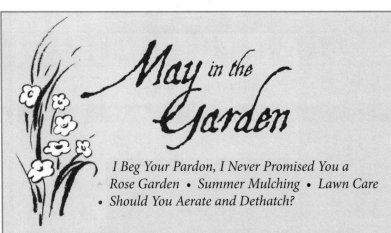

May in the Garden

I Beg Your Pardon, I Never Promised You a Rose Garden • Summer Mulching • Lawn Care • Should You Aerate and Dethatch?

I Beg Your Pardon, I Never Promised You a Rose Garden

The Minnesota Rose Society was organized in 1939 to foster the hobby of growing roses in Minnesota and surrounding areas. Here are the society's tips:

Ten Commandments of Growing Roses
(Adapted by Jim Beardsley from *Anyone Can Grow Roses,* Fourth Edition by Dr. Cynthia Westcott; printed with permission from the Minnesota Rose Society, www.minnesotarosesociety.org)

- **I. Locate Beds Properly** Thou shalt plant away from competition with trees and shrubs in an area of at least six hours of sun; in good, well-drained, previously prepared soil.
- **II. Prepare Soil Thoroughly** Thou shalt prepare the soil to a depth of eighteen to twenty-four inches, incorporating organic matter and other amendments generously to create a sandy loam with a pH of 6.5–6.8.
- **III. Plant Carefully** Thou shalt plant good-quality, disease-resistant varieties, suitable for your area and only as many as you can successfully manage. Thou shalt typically space your roses, thirty-six to forty-two inches on center, in a well-prepared hole, eighteen inches deep by twenty-four inches wide.
- **IV. Prune with Common Sense** Thou shalt commence spring pruning once growth has started and thou shalt remove all dead, diseased, three-eighths-inch-or-less-in-diameter stems and crossing growth.
- **V. Feed Judiciously** Thou shalt fertilize your roses on a regular basis beginning right after pruning, using a complete fertilizer at least monthly. Thou shalt not apply nitrogen-containing fertilizer after August 15.
- **VI. Water Prudently** Thou shalt water, water, water, carefully making certain that the foliage has time to dry before evening. Thou shalt make sure that your roses receive at least one inch of water each week. Thou shalt also water well before applying fertilizer or spraying and after applying fertilizer.
- **VII. Mulch and Relax** Thou shalt mulch your roses after the soil warms to reduce and conserve water, decrease diseases, and rebuild soil structure. Thou shalt take time to enjoy your roses.

- **VIII. Treat for Diseases and Pests Regularly** Thou shalt develop and implement a regular fungicide spray program to prevent diseases. Thou shalt only use chemicals according to directions and thou shalt protect thyself when mixing, applying, and during cleanup.
- **IX. Winter Protection** Thou shalt employ winter protection on the roses that require such and shalt do so around October 15.
- **X. Love Your Roses** Thou shalt love your roses enough to know when they are healthy and not disturb them with unnecessary attention, application of chemicals, or fuss over every little thing.

Extra commandment: XI. Join a Rose Society

- Thou shalt join a rose society to learn more, experience the fun, and meet new friends.

Summer Mulching

A summer mulch can be a great aid in growing roses and some varieties of vegetables, such as vine crops, unstaked tomatoes, and potatoes. Under plants and between rows, mulches help control weeds, provide a more uniform soil temperature, reduce sunburn, and allow you to water your garden less.

Mulches, however, can also cause problems. They provide a beneficial habitat for slugs, which can proliferate in a wet year. Wait to apply a mulch until the soil has warmed up in the spring. If put on too soon, the soil remains cool and will slow the growth of warm-season vegetables.

Organic mulches. Because they are often agricultural by-products, many organic mulches are inexpensive. Ground corncobs, cocoa-bean hulls, buckwheat, grass clippings, old hay, pine needles, shredded leaves and bark, and chipped bark are examples of organic mulches. They add humus and nutrients to the soil as they decompose. Apply a two- to four-inch layer in mid-spring. In late fall, turn over with a spading fork to evict overwintering rodents and insects.

Inert mulches. Although inert mulches last longer than organic ones, they lack the soil-building qualities that decomposition provides. Black plastic film, plastic fabric such as spun-bonded polypropylene, asphalt paper, crushed stones, pebbles, gravel chips, and fiberglass insulation are some common inert mulches. Very effective at curbing weed growth, plastic mulches are also good soil-warmers and speed the growth of heat-loving crops such as tomatoes, peppers, and eggplants. Before winter, roll up and store plastic mulches.

Lawn Care

With a few simple practices, you can enjoy a healthy lawn throughout the spring, summer, and fall: just water, fertilize, and mow. Properly doing these three things is your best defense against weeds, disease, and insects:

- Established lawns need about one inch of water per week from either rain or irrigation. If your soil is composed of clay, apply the water once a week. Sandy soils should receive one-half inch of water twice a week. (See "Watering Tips" below.) *continued next page*

continued from previous page

- Having your soil tested will tell you what type of fertilizer to use and the amount to apply for every thousand square feet.

- Keeping the grass longer and mowing more frequently will keep your lawn healthier and better able to fight off weeds. Cut so that the grass is three to three-and-one-half inches high. Mow often enough so that you remove no more than one-third (about one inch) of the total height. Leave short clippings on the lawn. Rake and compost longer clippings, or use a mulching mower to cut them down in size.

Watering Tips

- Your lawn is too dry if your footprints persist, the leaves start to roll, or the color turns bluish-gray.

- Before watering the lawn, set several straight-sided cans under the sprinkler to measure the water applied. Once filled with the required amount of water, turn off the sprinkler and move it to the next location. Take note of the pressure used and the time it took to apply the needed water for an idea of how long you need to water next week.

- Water early in the day to reduce the amount lost to evaporation.

Should You Aerate and Dethatch?

A "thatch" is a layer of partially decomposed grass plants. While a thin layer—one-half inch or less—benefits your lawn by conserving moisture and reducing wear, anything greater than one-half inch should be removed. Thatch is not caused by short grass clippings left on the lawn to decompose.

"Vertical mowers," or dethatching machines, can be used to remove the layer of thatch. These machines cut through the thatch and pull it to the surface. Since this is stressful on lawns, it should only be done in May or in early September when the lawn is actively growing. Once the thatch is cut, rake and compost it. If your lawn is thin, now is the time to overseed it; the disturbed lawn provides a perfect surface for the seed to contact the soil and germinate.

Aeration also reduces soil compaction and allows thatch to decompose. Compacted lawns—usually those growing in clay soils or in high traffic areas—are poorly drained, limit root growth, and result in thin, unhealthy lawns. By removing plugs of soil from the lawn, aerators allow air, water, and nutrients to reach the plant roots. Aeration is also most effective when done in May or in early September.

Of course, the best cure is prevention. To keep thatch from becoming a problem, do not overwater or overfertilize your lawn. And avoid excessive use of insecticides that may harm earthworms. They are nature's aerating machines (see "Be a Friend of the Earth … worms!," June chapter).

Gladys's

May Household Tips

For warm-weather aficionados, May marks the beginning of can't-wait-to-get-outside-and-have-some-fun season. That also means bumps-bruises-and-cuts season. Here are some tips for what to keep in your medicine cabinet—and what to keep locked away.

What to Keep in a Medicine Cabinet
- Two mercury thermometers; one oral, one rectal
- Medicine dropper and calibrated measuring spoon
- Petroleum jelly
- Tweezers
- Adhesive tape
- Gauze pads
- Adhesive bandages

What to Keep in a Locked Cupboard or Closet
Medicines (prescription or over-the-counter) should be stored outside the bathroom to protect them from dampness, light, and heat, which can cause drugs to deteriorate. A dry, dark, and cool place, such as the top of a linen closet, is better, preferably in a locked container and out of a child's reach. Of course, if the label says to, keep those medicines refrigerated.
- Analgesics (relieves pain)
- Antibiotic ointments (reduces risk of infection; such as Bacitracin or Neosporin)
- Antacids (relieves heartburn and upset stomach)
- Antihistamines (relieves allergy symptoms; such as Benadryl or Sudafed)
- Syrup of ipecac (induces vomiting)
- Decongestants (relieves stuffy nose and other cold symptoms)
- Aspirin and aspirin substitutes; adult and child (reduces fever; such as acetaminophen [Tylenol] and ibuprofen [Advil])
- Hydrocortisone and calamine lotion (relieves itching and inflammation)
- Antiseptics (helps stop infection; such as rubbing alcohol, alcohol wipes, and disinfectants)
- Athlete's foot spray or cream
- Laxatives (relieves constipation)

JUNE

"There are three good reasons

to be a teacher—

June, July, and August."

— AUTHOR UNKNOWN

Summer is here, and to paraphrase Oscar Hammerstein's lyrics, "June is bustin' out all over" Minnesota. Temperatures have been known to jump up to the nineties or higher, skies sometimes do burst open with thunderstorms, and agricultural soils split apart as crops begin to bloom and push up from below.

June is the perfect time to open one's mind as well. Minnesotans seem to never tire of stretching their imaginations—from creating popular fictitious towns to finding historic rocks that may or may not be fakes;

from fabricating a make-believe woman who can cook up a storm to manufacturing a fantastic male superhero capable of marvelous feats.

And if mental gymnastics are not your thing, there are other Minnesotans who used the summer to make tracks in the more physical fields. Croquet clubs, rollerblades, and tennis racquets have been their instruments of choice.

So why not go wild when summer starts? It only comes once a year, and some claim it is the state's shortest season.

A Flour That Wins the Gold

On June 8, 1880, the Washburn Crosby Company of Minneapolis was awarded the three top prizes for its flour at the first Miller's International Exhibition in Cincinnati: the Bronze Medal for "Parisian Flour," the Silver Medal for "Extra Flour," and the Gold Medal for "Superlative Flour." "Gold Medal" became the brand name on the firm's best grade of flour.

In 1931, the company, which by then had become General Mills, introduced one of the first packaged mixes, called "Bisquick." Consisting of flour, shortening, salt, and baking powder, Bisquick was developed by a sales executive named Carl Smith.

Today, Bisquick remains the country's top convenience baking mix, with a leading share of the market.

We're Having a Heat Wave:
Record High Temperatures and Average Annual Rainfall

Place	Recored High Temp.	Ave. Annual Rainfall (in inches)
Bemidji	107	23
Duluth	106	30
Int'l Falls	103	24
Minneapolis	108	27
Moorhead	114	19
Rochester	108	29
St. Cloud	107	26
Windom	106	28

Source: Minnesota State Climatology Office: DNR Waters

A Snapshot of Minnesota Agriculture

Minnesota is a leading producer and a major exporter of agricultural products. In 2006, the state's farm cash receipts totaled $9.7 billion. Agricultural exports were estimated at $2.9 billion.

Minnesota's Top Five Agricultural Commodities, 2006

	Value of Receipts (in thousand dollars)	Percent of State Total Farm Receipts	Percent of U.S. Value
1. Corn	2,029,081	20.8	9.3
2. Hogs	1,751,000	17.9	12.4
3. Soybeans	1,676,210	17.0	9.9
4. Dairy products	1,073,670	11.0	4.6
5. Cattle and calves	925,531	9.5	1.9
All commodities	**9,769,512**		**4.1**

Source: United States Department of Agriculture

Minnesota's Top Five Agricultural Exports, 2006

Exports are increasingly important to Minnesota's economy. Measured as exports divided by farm cash receipts, the state's reliance on agricultural exports was 30 percent in 2006.

Soybeans and products — $830 million   **Wheat and products** — $241 million
Feed grains and products — $827 million   **Vegetables** — $138 million
Live animals and red meat — $336 million

Source: United States Department of Agriculture

Minnesota Farming Facts

According to Minnesota House of Representatives research, the state is ranked highly among all the states in several areas of production:

- **First** in sugar beets, turkeys, sweet corn, and green peas for processing.
- **Second** in canola and cultivated wild rice.
- **Third** in soybeans, spring wheat, hogs and pigs, and American cheese.
- **Fourth** in corn, oats, edible beans, flaxseed, and mink pelts.
- **Fifth** in total cheese, ice cream, honey, total cash receipts, and total agricultural exports.

In 2005, the state was home to approximately 79,600 farms totaling 27.5 million acres, for an average acreage of 345.

Stories in Stone

The Kensington Runestone

The drawings of Cro-Magnons on cave walls in Europe and the pictographs and petroglyphs of Native Americans in America have shown us that stones can tell stories of the people who came before us. Minnesota has its own famous stories in stone, one of which still ignites controversy and imaginations more than one hundred years after being unearthed.

In 1898, a Swedish immigrant farmer, Olof Öhman, and his son were clearing a field near Kensington, fifteen miles west of Alexandria, when they came upon a large stone wrapped in the roots of an old, aspen tree. The stone—thirty-six inches long, five-and-a-half inches thick, fifteen to sixteen inches wide, and weighing 230 pounds—had strange, runic symbols etched on it, followed by what appeared to be the date 1362. The inscriptions were then sent to Scandinavian languages professors at the University of Minnesota, and while the academics recognized some of the runic markings, they declared the stone a forgery since some of the symbols, they said, were too modern and unknown in the fourteenth century.

Interest in the "Kensington Runestone" soon lapsed, and Öhman put it to use as a stepping-stone to one of his farm's outbuildings. But in 1907, Hjalmar Holand, a Viking studies enthusiast who likely heard about the stone as a student at the University of Wisconsin, showed up on Öhman's doorstep and asked to purchase the stone. Luckily, Öhman had placed the stone with the incised side down. Holand deciphered the runic script to read:

> *"8 Goths and 22 Norwegians on an exploration journey from Vinland westward. We had camp by 2 skerries [rocky inlets] one day's journey north from this stone. We were out to fish one day. After we came home, we found 10 men red with blood and dead. AVM [Ave Maria] save us from evil. We have 10 of our party by the sea to look after our ships 14 days' journey from this island. Year 1362."*

Holand was convinced the stone was authentic, believing it to be proof that the Vikings had beat Columbus to the New World by at least one hundred years. Until he died in 1963, Holand defended his stance through speeches, articles, and books—such as his *The Kensington Stone: A Study in Pre-Columbian American History* (1932). To back up his case for the authenticity of the stone, Holand called upon yet more stones: three huge granite boulders located on the shore of Big Cormorant Lake. These "anchor stones," as he called them, each had a triangular hole an inch wide and nine inches deep cut into it, which Holand said once held rings to moor Viking ships.

After a 1948 exhibition at the Smithsonian Institution, promoters brought the stone back to Minnesota for a showing at the 1949 Territorial Centennial festivities. Alexandria then started billing itself as the "Birthplace of America," and local Kiwanis club members financed the construction of a granite replica of the stone at five times its original size. The replica was placed at the eastern edge of the city in 1951. In 1958, the Alexandria chamber of commerce built a museum to house the original stone.

Even today, the Kensington Runestone still stirs up controversy. There are rumors that one of Öhman's neighbors, Sven Fogelblad, once studied runes and that Öhman himself was a trained stonemason. They could have collaborated on a fraud. The

fact that the late nineteenth century was the time of P.T. Barnum's famous hoaxes adds to the suspicion that the two could have been trying to amuse themselves and their neighbors. On the other hand, there are a few pieces of evidence that fight for the credibility of the stone's story. The first were the discoveries of the Vinland Map in 1957 and the ruins of a Viking camp at L'Anse-aux-Meadows in Newfoundland in 1960. The second is Cornell University Italian language and literature Professor Robert Hall's 1982 and 1994 books, which claim that the stone is authentic. Finally, the publication of Houston, Texas, amateur language researcher Richard Nielsen's 1982 book disputes several earlier claims of forgery. And, as if that wasn't enough, the name of the National Football League's Minnesota Vikings was inspired by the notoriety of the Kensington Runestone.

Perhaps, given the state's penchant for bigger-than-life stories, there's even room for a third explanation. The truth, for now, remains etched in stone.

A Passion for Peat

A rarity in the world, peatlands cover a large portion of northwestern Minnesota. In fact, Minnesota has more than six million acres of peatland, more than any other state except for Alaska.

When the last glacier that scraped across Minnesota retreated at the end of the Ice Age, it left lakebeds and depressions in which decaying mosses and grasses collected. With poor drainage and a cool climate, conditions were ideal for the formation of the dark brown or black peat, which is comprised of dead and decayed plant matter that has accumulated in a wet environment. Stagnant waters inhibited the circulation of oxygen, causing a dearth of bacteria, worms, and other decomposing agents; Minnesota's cool temperatures further slowed the decomposition process. As subsequent peat accumulated and drainage was further hampered, it created its own spongy, organic growing topography.

Peat up to ten feet thick discourages humans, but encourages adaptable, hardy plant and animal species. Black spruce and tamaracks survive by sending out new roots from their trunks into the uppermost and best oxygenated layers of the peat bog. Several colorful orchids thrive, as well as mosses and sedges that grow nowhere else. Pitcher plants, bladderworts, and sundews find unique ways to adapt to this nutrient-poor but water-rich place, such as devouring insects. Bog lemmings, great gray owls, and several warblers and sparrows even prefer peat lands to other environments.

Minnesota's peatlands are particularly significant to researchers because they are among the few in the world that are free of permafrost, making it easier to investigate their formation and development. And because the state's peat lands occur at the edges of three biomes, they are home to a unique gathering of life.

The rate of accumulation in Minnesota peatland is between two and five inches per one hundred years.

MARK YOUR CALENDAR

Mark Your
JUNE
C A L E N D A R

Grand Old Day, St. Paul
www.grandaye.com/grandoldday

Minnesota Inventors Congress, Redwood Falls **www.invent1.org**

Corn & Clover Carnival, Hinckley
www.hinckleychamber.com

Grandma's Marathon, Duluth
www.grandmasmarathon.com

Locusts Among Us

In the late 1870s, locusts took a liking to southwestern Minnesota. In June 1873, Rocky Mountain locusts devoured almost everything in sight. And they kept coming for the next four years.

The grasshoppers ate—and ate—barley, buckwheat, spruce, and tobacco, not to mention fence posts, leather, dead animals, and sheep's wool. They ate the blankets that were placed over the crops to protect them. One common comment at the time was that "grasshoppers ate everything but the mortgage."

By 1877, a plague of billions were eating Minnesota and driving farmers off their land. Some wondered if settlement of the prairie had been a mistake. One farmer said, "wheat and grasshoppers could not grow on the same land, and the grasshoppers already had the first claim."

On April 26, 1877, Governor Pillsbury declared a state day of prayer, asking residents to plead for deliverance from the pests. Over the following two days, an April snowstorm with hard frost set in, freezing some of the locusts and causing a hasty departure in others. Whether dead or fled, they left, never to return.

Scientists still debate the causes of the 1870s infestation and the reasons for its end. Following that plague, the Rocky Mountain locust became extinct. We may never know why.

"The whole prairie was bare and brown. Millions of brown grasshoppers whirred low over it. Not a green thing was in sight anywhere. All the way [to church], Laura and Mary brushed off grasshoppers. When they came to the church, brown grasshoppers were thick on their petticoats. They lifted their skirts and brushed them off before they went in. But careful as they were, the grasshoppers had spit tobacco-juice on their best Sunday dresses."

— Laura Ingalls Wilder,
On the Banks of Plum Creek
(1937)

Rollin' Along in Summer

Rollerblades may have first caught your attention in the 1980s, but as the saying goes, "Everything old is new again."

The very first in-line skates were invented in Holland in the early 1700s. An unknown Dutchman attached wooden spools to strips of wood and nailed them to his shoes so he could skate in the summer. His new, dry-land skates were called "skeelers."

But in 1863, an American developed the conventional rollerskate model, with the wheels positioned at the four corners of a rectangle, making it the more popular design for over a century.

Then in 1980, two Minnesota brothers, Scott and Brennan Olsen, discovered the old in-line skate inside a sporting goods store and got an idea. Looking for a way to train for winter hockey all summer long, they made some improvements to the older skate model and began manufacturing the first Rollerblade in-line skates in their parents' basement.

Three years later the Olsens founded Rollerblade, Inc., and the term "rollerblading" came to mean the sport of in-line skating. Hockey players and both alpine and Nordic skiers were soon seen cruising the streets of Minnesota during the summer on their Rollerblade skates.

Winning Wimbledon

St. Paul-born Jeanne Arth was the first Minnesota tennis player to compete overseas and the first Minnesotan to win Wimbledon.

By the time Arth entered the College of St. Catherine in St. Paul in 1952, she was already a polished tennis player who was ranked fourth in the nation. While in college, she won three straight doubles titles at the National College Girls Championships.

After graduating in 1956 with her teaching degree, Arth joined the international tennis circuit. Two years later, she and partner Darlene Hard captured the U.S. Doubles Championship as an unseeded team, winning a three-set match against the top seed. They defended their title the following year. In 1959, they won Wimbledon.

Arth was inducted into the Minnesota Tennis Hall of Fame in 1979, the Minnesota Sports Hall of Fame in 1986, and was named one of *Sports Illustrated's* Top 50 Minnesota Athletes of the 20th Century.

Being Young Like Betty Crocker

People may accuse her of being a "fake," but Betty Crocker has stood the test of time.

In the late 1910s and early 1920s, the Washburn Crosby Company of Minneapolis—one of the six million companies that merged into General Mills in 1928—was inundated with thousands of baking questions. In 1921, company executives decided that cooking advice would seem more authentic and intimate if it came from one person, so they created a fictional woman who was an expert in the kitchen. They used the last name of a retired company executive, William Crocker, and combined it with the first name "Betty," a warm, friendly, all-American name. "Betty's" written signature came from a secretary, who won a contest among the female employees of the mill.

By 1940, a survey revealed that 90 percent of the country's women knew who Betty Crocker was and that they rated her as the second most famous woman in America, after Eleanor Roosevelt.

Betty's look has undergone many changes since 1936 when she was given a face. In fact, she's had seven "face-lifts." In 1955, she became younger; in 1965, she resembled Jackie Kennedy; the 1969 version looked like Mary Tyler Moore; the 1972 version donned a businesslike appearance; and the 1980 version got more casual. The 1986 Betty weathered a debate regarding a change in her racial background. Company officials decided "consumers see Betty Crocker as white." But in 1996 she finally became multicultural, with slightly darker skin, giving her a more "ethnic" look. In all of her reincarnations, however, Betty was true to her style: she always wore a red dress, jacket or sweater, with white at her neck.

Although she's now eighty-eight years old, she doesn't look a day over thirty-five. No wonder she's received numerous marriage proposals. As far as we know she hasn't accepted any—yet.

Croquet, Everyone?

In the late nineteenth century, croquet became one of the earliest outdoor games to become popular in Minnesota. In the early 1940s, the town of Lyle claimed to be the "Croquet Capitol of Minnesota" and boasted what it called "the finest croquet court in the state." Almost every Lyle resident was an avid croquet player.

The Cows Were Looking Grimm

In the mid-1800s, farmers in Minnesota typically fed their cows corn during the winter. But German immigrant Wendelin Grimm had another idea. Grimm arrived in Carver County in 1859 with a small wooden box of seed called "everlasting clover." For the next fifteen years, Grimm planted and collected seeds from the plants that survived the harsh Minnesota winters. And strangely enough, Grimm's cows were starting to look better than all his neighbors' cows—even after winter had dished out its best.

The result of Grimm's selective seeding process was the first winter-hardy alfalfa in North America. It is the source of all modern varieties of alfalfa now grown on more than twenty-five million acres in the United States. Grimm alfalfa became one of Minnesota's prime contributions to agriculture and rivals hybrid corn as the single most important agricultural crop development in North America.

The Most Famous Minnesota Town That Wasn't

One of the most famous towns in Minnesota is the fictional Lake Wobegon, the creation of writer **Garrison Keillor.** Through his popular live radio show broadcast from the Twin Cities called *A Prairie Home Companion,* Keillor painted a portrait of a place where "all the women are strong, the men good-looking, and the children above average."

Born in Anoka in 1942 and named "Gary" at birth, Keillor began the public radio weekly program in 1974. The show's format began as a collection of stories, songs, and ads reminiscent of radio programming in the 1930s. Spoof commercial spots were from fictitious sponsors, such as Rent-A-Raptor and Powdermilk Biscuits, "the biscuits that give shy persons the strength to get up and do what needs to be done." Lake Wobegon was "the little town that time forgot and the decades cannot improve."

On June 13, 1987, Keillor decided to take the variety show off the air so he could work on other projects. In 1993 he began producing *A Prairie Home Companion* again, with an almost identical format. In 2006, Keillor wrote the screenplay for the movie version of *A Prairie Home Companion,* directed by Robert Altman.

Garrison Keillor is a proud advocate for Shy Persons' Rights.

XXXX Marks Pillsbury Quality

On June 4, 1869, after working in his uncle's Minneapolis hardware supply company, twenty-seven-year-old Charles Pillsbury managed to buy a one-third share of the local Frazee and Murphy Flour Mill for $10,000.

Pillsbury set out to make improvements to his newly acquired mill, and purchased more modern equipment that could handle milling Minnesota's very hard wheat. By 1872, he had acquired two more mills and was producing two thousand barrels of flour a day. He reorganized his mills as C. A. Pillsbury and Company and registered the trademark "Pillsbury's Best XXXX." Three "Xs" had been used by bakers to denote quality, so Pillsbury added the extra "X" and the word "Best" to assure his customers that his flour was on a superior plane.

In 1883, the largest flour mill in the world at the time—the Pillsbury A Mill—opened, using all-new roller technology. Built of limestone from the river bluffs, the mill was the first along St. Anthony Falls to have electric lights. It more than tripled the company's output. A few years later, in 1889, Pillsbury sold the mills to an English financial syndicate. He remained managing director, however, and in 1896 the Pillsbury-Washburn Flour Mills Company Ltd. was putting out ten thousand barrels of flour per day.

June Recipe
Minnesota Blueberry Muffins

What makes the recipe below purely "Minnesota" is its blueberries, which are native to the northeastern part of the state—and perhaps some Pillsbury's Best XXXX flour.

Minnesota Blueberry Muffins

½ cup butter (softened)
1¼ cups sugar
2 eggs
2 cups flour
½ teaspoon salt

2 teaspoons baking powder
½ cup milk
2 cups fresh, Minnesota blueberries
1 teaspoon freshly grated orange peel
3 teaspoons sugar

Preheat oven to 375°F. Cream butter and sugar until light. Add the eggs one at a time, beating well after each one is added.

Sift together the flour, salt, and baking powder. Add the dry mixture to the creamed mixture, alternately with the milk. Crush ½ cup blueberries with a fork and mix into batter. Fold in the remaining whole berries and add the orange peel.

Fill large muffin cups (grease the cups or use paper liners). Sprinkle the tops with three teaspoons of sugar. Bake for twenty to thirty minutes. Cool for thirty minutes before removing.

Printed with permission from Minnesota.gov

JUNE WEATHER

June Normals for Duluth

Day	High	Low	Mean	Precip.	Snowfall
1	68	45	57	0.12	0
2	68	45	57	0.13	0
3	69	45	57	0.13	0
4	69	46	57	0.13	0
5	69	46	57	0.13	0
6	69	46	58	0.13	0
7	69	46	58	0.13	0
8	70	47	58	0.14	0
9	70	47	58	0.14	0
10	70	47	59	0.14	0
11	70	47	59	0.14	0
12	70	48	59	0.14	0
13	71	48	59	0.14	0
14	71	48	60	0.14	0
15	71	48	60	0.14	0
16	71	49	60	0.15	0
17	72	49	60	0.15	0
18	72	49	60	0.15	0
19	72	49	61	0.15	0
20	72	50	61	0.15	0
21	72	50	61	0.15	0
22	73	50	61	0.15	0
23	73	50	62	0.15	0
24	73	51	62	0.15	0
25	73	51	62	0.15	0
26	73	51	62	0.15	0
27	74	51	63	0.15	0
28	74	52	63	0.15	0
29	74	52	63	0.14	0
30	74	52	63	0.14	0

"No price is set on the lavish summer;
June may be had by the poorest comer."
— JAMES RUSSELL LOWELL

JUNE WEATHER

June Normals for International Falls

Day	High	Low	Mean	Precip.	Snowfall
1	72	45	58	0.12	0
2	72	46	59	0.12	0
3	72	46	59	0.12	0
4	72	46	59	0.12	0
5	72	47	59	0.12	0
6	72	47	60	0.13	0
7	73	47	60	0.13	0
8	73	47	60	0.13	0
9	73	48	60	0.13	0
10	73	48	61	0.13	0
11	73	48	61	0.13	0
12	74	48	61	0.14	0
13	74	49	61	0.14	0
14	74	49	61	0.14	0
15	74	49	62	0.14	0
16	74	49	62	0.14	0
17	74	50	62	0.14	0
18	75	50	62	0.14	0
19	75	50	62	0.14	0
20	75	50	63	0.14	0
21	75	50	63	0.14	0
22	75	51	63	0.14	0
23	76	51	63	0.14	0
24	76	51	63	0.14	0
25	76	51	64	0.13	0
26	76	51	64	0.13	0
27	76	52	64	0.13	0
28	76	52	64	0.13	0
29	77	52	64	0.13	0
30	77	52	64	0.13	0

Source: National Oceanic and Atmospheric Administration (NOAA)'s National Weather Service

These climate normals are an average of thirty years of data between 1971 and 2000. Every ten years, the National Weather Service recalculates the normals using the next interval of thirty years. In 2010, the new normals will be recalculated using the period of 1981 to 2010.

On This Day in June

Day	Year	Weather
1	1993	St. Cloud reports its latest-ever freezing temperature.
2	1945	Snow and sleet pile up to 4.5 inches at Tower.
3	1955	Seven people die on Lake Traverse when their boat is overturned by strong winds from a thunderstorm.
4	1935	The latest official measurable snowfall in Minnesota occurs at Mizpah on this date, with 1.5 inches.
5	1915	This day marks the first of a long stretch of days of measurable rain at Winton near Ely. Some measurable rain fell every day until June 19. The total amount of rain for the fifteen-day period was over 6 inches.
6	1864	Light frost reported in St. Paul as a chilly air mass moves over the state.
7	1939	Grapefruit-sized hail falls in Rock County killing hundreds of farm animals near Hill.
8	1893	Violent windstorm at Maple Plain. A large-frame house is moved 8 feet from its foundation. Many barns and hay sheds are blown over by the wind. One barn is blown across Dutch Lake.
9	1913	Strange mirage in Duluth. Ships appear to be floating in the air over Lake Superior.
10	1926	Downpour at Mahoning. In forty-five minutes, 3.05 inches fall.
11	2001	Severe weather over central Minnesota. An unofficial wind gust of 119 mph is reported at a seed farm one mile northwest of Atwater. A storm chaser's car was battered when he got too close to the storm.
12	1917	The ice pack finally breaks up in Duluth, one of the latest ever.
13	1991	One dead, five injured when a lightning bolt strikes a tree at Hazeltine Golf Course during the U.S. Open.
14	1956	Eight inches of rain fall in the Ivanhoe area in three and a half hours. Damage to crops totals $100,000.
15	1989	Scattered frost across the state, with the cold spot at Isabella at 29 degrees.
16	1992	A total of twenty-seven tornadoes are reported across Minnesota, the most the state has ever seen in a single day.
17	1954	Hailstorm at St. Cloud injures many people.
18	1850	Territorial Governor Ramsey reports that about halfway between Ft. Ripley and Ft. Snelling on the Mississippi, a severe hailstorm occurred in the evening. One or two hailstones picked up were as large as hen's eggs, and he thought he saw one about the size of a musket ball.
19	1955	Hailstones the size of eggs fall in Roseau County.
20	1861	Rain at Forest City measures 1.17 inches; one observer notes that the rain was "strongly impregnated with sulfur."
21	1989	Fairmont has a wind gust of 76 mph during a severe thunderstorm.
22	1919	Second most deadly tornado in Minnesota history hits Fergus Falls. It destroys half of the town—killing 59 people and destroying 228 houses—and left the other half untouched. Like the No. 1 killer tornado for Minnesota (St. Cloud), it struck on a weekend.

JUNE WEATHER HISTORY

On This Day in June

Day	Year	Weather
23	2002	Just a few weeks after torrential rains hit the area, another round of heavy rain hits northern Minnesota. This time, up to 8 inches fall in a two-day period in small parts of Mahnomen and St. Louis counties.
24	1972	Frost across eastern Minnesota. Duluth sees a low of 35, and Tower bottoms out at 32.
25	2003	Heavy rains across central Minnesota. Elk River picks up 8.19 inches. Maplewood has 4.36 inches in 4 hours, with reports of street flooding in St. Paul. Strong winds topple trees in Richfield.
26	1982	Kulger Township dips to 31 degrees. Duluth registers 36.
27	1908	Tornado hits Clinton in Big Stone County.
28	1876	The latest ice breakup in Duluth.
29	1930	Heat wave across state. Canby gets up to a sizzling 110 degrees.
30	1863	Note written on a June 1863 meteorological form at Ft. Ripley: "Drought is very severe. The grass upon the prairie is nearly or quite dried up. The Mississippi River at this point is lower than was ever known before. The amount of moisture which fell during the last six months ending June 30, 1863, was 4.27 inches."

Source: Minnesota State Climatology Office: DNR Waters

Bats About You This Summer

Minnesota's most common bat, the little brown myotis, is found throughout the state.

Put up a bat house and welcome this little mammal to your yard for a mosquito-light summer; the little brown bat can eat five to six hundred mosquitoes per hour.

"It is the month of June,

The month of leaves and roses,

When pleasant sights

salute the eyes,

And pleasant scents the noses."

— NATHANIEL PARKER WILLIS

June in the Garden

A Checklist for Your Summer Garden • Be a Friend of the Earth ... worms! • You Can Be a Butterfly Gardener

A Checklist for Your Summer Garden

- If you haven't put down your summer mulch yet, do so now as the soil warms up (see "Summer Mulching," May chapter).
- Finish pruning spring-flowering shrubs in early June. This will give them time to develop flower buds for next spring.
- Remove flowers (called "deadheading") on annuals and most perennials as they fade to encourage continual bloom. Cut the flowering stem with a knife or garden shears back to the first set of leaves or flower buds. Not all annuals need deadheading, however: ageratums, cleomes, gomphrenas, impatiens, narrowleaf zinnias, wax begonias, and pentas drop their dead blooms.
- Plant summer-bedding marigolds to attract birds.
- Perform the last pinching of chrysanthemums to promote full, bushy plants.
- Keep newly planted trees, shrubs, and hedges well watered and make sure your garden has one inch of water per week.
- Tie climbing roses to trellises.
- Feed roses. Do not, however, use overhead sprinklers to water them, especially late in the day. Roses are especially prone to disease if their leaves stay wet at night.
- Watch for aphids and fungus on roses. Aphids should be washed off and left on the ground. Leaves with fungus should be cut off and burned.
- Stake young tomato plants; late-staking may cause rot.
- Harvest vegetables and herbs. Do the last picking of rhubarb at the end of June. This allows the roots to start storing energy for next season.
- Weed often.
- Watch your garden. At night, look for the glow of fireflies. In the early morning, try to spot night predators, such as owls, bats, foxes, opossums, and raccoons.
- Plan a trip to see Minnesota's native lady slippers in bloom. The yellow varieties start flowering about June 10; the showy lady slipper usually begins to bloom around the Fourth of July.

Be a Friend of the Earth … worms!

You've heard it said over and over again: Earthworms are nature's tillers (see "Should You Aerate and Dethatch?", May chapter). They eat their weight in soil every day, mixing layers of soil and compost while digging tunnels. The thin tunnels provide passageways in the soil through which air and water can circulate, and they bring surface plant material down into soil, enriching it.

When it rains and the soil floods, worms come to the surface to avoid drowning. But when the sun comes out, earthworms can get disoriented and die. Be a friend to one of your garden's best friends and caretakers by finding new homes for the surfaced worms you notice in your garden.

There is one area in Minnesota, however, that is not a welcome home for earthworms. Since all earthworms in Minnesota are invasive, nonnative species probably introduced from Europe, Minnesota's hardwood forests developed before the arrival of earthworms. Without worms, fallen leaves decompose slowly, creating a spongy, organic, "duff" layer. This nutrient-rich leaf litter is the natural growing environment for native woodland wildflowers, hardwood forest tree seedlings, and ferns. The duff also provides habitat for ground-dwelling animals and helps prevent soil erosion.

When earthworms invade the forest, they eat the leaves that create the duff layer. Big trees may survive, but many seedlings, flowers, and ferns die.

So keep earthworms in your garden, and do not dump them in the woods. After fishing, always dispose of unwanted bait in the trash.

You Can Be a Butterfly Gardener

You've planted all the right flowers to attract, retain, and encourage butterfly populations. Yet you're still not seeing as many of the graceful, brightly colored insects that you'd like. Here are some tips to further draw them to your garden:

- Butterflies are sensitive to insecticides, herbicides, and pesticides, so do not use them in your butterfly area.
  - Mud provides a source of amino acids and salt for male butterflies. Put a small bucket of wet sand or mud in the corner of your garden.
  - Butterflies appreciate dark stones that offer a great spot to warm their bodies in the sun.
  - Overripe fruit, such as a smashed banana, makes a great butterfly lure. Any fermented fruit combined with beer or wine, or honey and sugar, poured over a sandy surface will also attract butterflies.

Gladys's

June Household Tips

Our household animal companions—and our feathered friends in the backyard—sometimes need a helping hand when injured. While out and about this summer, you may come across a dog, cat, or bird that requires medical attention. Use the guidelines below to safely assist them.

How to Handle Injured Animals

Dogs

- Approach an injured dog cautiously and quietly. Use his name a lot if you know it and speak gently to him. Let the dog sniff the back of your closed fist—not your open hand, which may make the dog think you are going to hit him.
- Many dogs won't need a muzzle, but if you are worried about being bitten or the dog is not known to you, make an improvised muzzle from a tie or a bandage. If the dog has a chest injury or trouble breathing, DO NOT use a muzzle.
- To move a dog, pull him onto a blanket or slide a blanket under him. If possible, enlist the help of two other people to support his head, back, and pelvis as you lift him together.

Cats

- Cats in pain may bite or lash out with their claws. Approach softly, keep your face well away, and wear heavy gloves if possible.
- Reach down from above and hold the cat firmly but gently by the scruff (back) of her neck. Most cats will go limp, since this mimics the way their mothers carried them as kittens. Then place your other hand under her hindquarters for support.
- DO NOT raise or prop up a cat's head because her airway may become blocked. Wrap her in a blanket or towel to prevent any struggling as you transport her to the veterinarian.
- To move a frightened cat, cover her with a towel for a minute or two. After she becomes calmer, slide the rest of the towel underneath and lift her up as a bundle.

Birds

- Make sure a bird is really injured BEFORE you try to help it. Young birds on the ground are not necessarily abandoned. If you see no visible signs such as limping, dragging a wing, or falling over, leave the bird alone.

- To pick up an injured bird, gently scoop it up with both hands, with your index and middle fingers on either side of its head.
- If you find a baby bird, try to find the nest and replace the baby bird inside it. Birds do not have a true sense of smell, so the myth that parent birds will reject their baby if touched by a human is not true.
- The most important thing is to keep an injured bird warm. Birds chill quickly and are susceptible to pneumonia. You can warm up a small songbird simply holding it in your hands.
- Place the injured bird in a dark, quiet place, preferably in a small box for about ten minutes. If the bird does not wake up or fly away within that time frame, call a bird rehabilitator.

Native Americans AIM to End Racism

In 1968 in Minneapolis, Ojibwas Dennis Banks, George Mitchell, and Clyde Bellecourt joined together to form the American Indian Movement (AIM) in response to the discrimination they saw in the Twin Cities. Through the organization, the AIM leaders spoke out against high unemployment and slum housing, and fought for treaty rights and reclamation of tribal land.

AIM leaders drew the attention of the FBI and the CIA, who were watching for revolutionary fervor during the 1970s. It seemed confrontation was inevitable. In February 1973, AIM leader Russell Means (Oglala Lakota) and his followers took over the small Indian community of Wounded Knee, South Dakota, on the Pine Ridge Reservation, in protest of the reservation's president and his allegedly corrupt governing practices.

FBI agents were dispatched to remove the AIM occupiers, and a standoff ensued. Over a period of seventy-one days, two people were killed and twelve hundred were arrested. The AIM leaders were tried in a Minnesota court and, after an eight-month trial, were acquitted of any wrongdoing. The Wounded Knee incident succeeded in drawing worldwide attention to the plight of American Indians.

It's a Marvel
Born in Zumbrota, Minnesota, in 1910, C. C. Beck was the original artist for the comic book superhero series *Captain Marvel*.

Short Geography Lesson
The closest body of saltwater to Minnesota is Hudson Bay.

JULY

"Those who desire

to give up freedom

in order to gain security

will not have,

nor do they deserve,

either one."

— BENJAMIN FRANKLIN

Although it technically isn't the case, The Fourth of July remains our mental-marker for the middle of summer. School lets out in early June and starts in late August, so at the beginning of July, we're pretty much into picnics and boating, parks and burgers. You'll find Minnesota-style inspiration for all of these things in this chapter.

July also brings to mind two of Minnesota's most iconic resources: lakes and lumbering. Has anyone ever actually counted every lake in the state? Although there's an "official" number, tally-takers disagree but have generally reached the consensus that there are more than ten thousand, for sure. But with at least one in six Minnesotans out on the lake in the summer (and that's just the boat owners, and not counting the ones who join in for the ride), most would rather just enjoy their lakes than count the ones others may be enjoying.

Like the lakes, the number of trees in Minnesota has confounded people since white settlers first arrived and tried to take stock. Nineteenth-century loggers thought we'd never run out. We now know we can, but sustainable forestry practices enacted in the twentieth century are making sure that trees will count in the future.

If the Fourth is the mental midpoint, then we're halfway through the summer and halfway to fall—appropriate for a state sitting on the forty-fifth line of latitude, halfway between the North Pole and the equator.

"If the first of July be rainy weather,

It will rain, more or less, for four

weeks together."

— JOHN RAY,
COLLECTION OF ENGLISH
PROVERBS (1670)

Hottest Day
Beardsley reached 114°F on July 29, 1917. It was the hottest day in Minnesota history, and was matched in Moorhead on July 6, 1936.

Average Precipitation and High and Low Temperatures in July

Place	Avg. Precip. (Inches)	Avg. High Temp.	Avg. Low Temp.
Bemidji	3.3	80	56
Duluth	3.9	78	55
Int'l Falls	3.9	79	54
Minneapolis	3.8	84	62
Moorhead	3.1	83	59
Rochester	4.1	81	60
St. Cloud	3.6	82	58
Windom	3.6	84	61

Source: Minnesota State Climatology Office: DNR Waters

Minnesota's Oldest Industry

When the first white settlers arrived in Minnesota, there were 31,500,000 acres of virgin forest (about 60 percent of the state). Approximately 40 percent of the land was covered with pine, spruce, and fir forests, while aspens and birches covered nearly 20 percent.

Minnesota's oldest manufacturing industry is lumbering. The first sawmill was built at St. Anthony Falls in 1822, construction for the buildings of the new Fort Snelling. Just seventeen years later, in 1839, the first commercial sawmill was erected at Marine on the St. Croix River. Before the St. Croix timber was exhausted, 133 mills were operating in the area. Loggers thought the vast stands of red and white pines in Minnesota would last at least a thousand years.

With the coming of the railroads in the 1870s, the lumbering industry became "Big Business." The growth was due not only to the settlement of the newly accessible prairie, but also by the railroads themselves, which required huge supplies of lumber for their own building needs.

A decade later, lumbering operations began to move into the more northern sections of the state. Larger and more efficient mills took the place of the simpler plants. By the end of the nineteenth century, forty thousand men were working in timber. By 1905, the peak year for lumbering,

more than two billion board-feet of lumber were cut in Minnesota.

However, in the mid-1930s, less than one hundred years since the first commercial sawmill was built, Minnesota's gigantic lumbering era was over. The best forestland had been devastated, and the lumber companies moved on to the Pacific Northwest. They left behind thousands of unemployed loggers, hundreds of marginal farms, and dozens of nearly-deserted towns.

In 1993, Minnesota completed a comprehensive study of the state's timber harvest and wrote an impact statement. It resulted in the passing of the 1995 Sustainable Forest Resources Act and created the Minnesota Forest Resources Council taskforce, charged with recommending policies and practices to protect and provide sustainable management for the state's forests.

10,000 Lakes and More

Although Minnesota boasts ten thousand lakes, it turns out the statement is quite modest. Officially, there are 15,291 lakes in the state. And it seems that names for them ran out before the number of bodies of water did. At last count, there are 201 "Mud Lakes," 154 "Long Lakes," and 123 "Rice Lakes."

Here are some facts on some of those many sparkling lakes:

- **Lake Vermilion** in St. Louis County has 290 miles of shoreline, more shoreline than any other lake in Minnesota.

- **Lake Saganaga** in Cook County is the deepest natural lake in Minnesota (240 feet).

- The largest inland lake is **Red Lake** at 288,800 acres or 451 square miles.

Minnesota's largest border lakes are Lake Superior at 20,364,800 acres total, with 962,700 acres in Minnesota; and Lake of the Woods at 950,400 acres total, with 307,010 acres in Minnesota.

The ten largest lakes with their borders entirely inside Minnesota include:

- **Red Lake** (both "Upper" and "Lower")—288,800 acres
- **Mille Lacs Lake**—132,516 acres
- **Leech Lake**—111,527 acres
- **Lake Winnibigoshish**—58,544 acres
- **Lake Vermilion**—40,557 acres
- **Lake Kabetogama**—25,760 acres
- **Mud Lake** (Marshall County)—23,700 acres
- **Cass Lake**—15,596 acres
- **Lake Minnetonka**—14,004 acres
- **Otter Tail Lake**—13,725 acres

According to a popular local legend, Lake Minnewaska, the thirteenth largest lake in Minnesota, is named for a Native American woman believed to be buried in one of the mounds bordering the lake's northern shore.

Four counties have no natural lakes: Mower, Olmsted, Pipestone, and Rock.

If it Looks Like a Duck ...

... it probably is one. Ducks make up the largest group of waterfowl in Minnesota, with twenty-two species that either nest in or visit the state in various seasons.

In 2005, a breeding duck survey estimated there were 632,000 ducks in Minnesota. Although duck numbers decreased 34 percent from 2004, the statewide duck harvest ranks among the Top Ten nationally.

Father of Water Skiing

Eighteen-year-old **Ralph Samuelson** of Lake City, Minnesota, had been thinking during the summer of 1922. If it was possible to ski on snow, then why couldn't you ski on snow in a different form—water?

Samuelson was adept at aquaplaning—standing on a single board tied tightly behind a powerboat—but he wanted water skis that were more like snow skis. After purchasing two pine boards for one dollar each, he boiled the tips in his mother's copper kettle to make them pliable and shaped the ends upwards. He then let them set for two days while making bindings from leather scraps he found at a local harness shop. He bought one hundred feet of sash cord at the hardware store and asked a blacksmith to make an iron ring for a handle to attach to the cord.

Samuelson went to Lake Pepin for a trial run. On July 2, 1922, he discovered that leaning backwards with the ski tips up greatly increased his ability to stay upright. By 1925, he was zipping around Lake Pepin at 80 mph, with folks on shore taking notice. On July 8, 1925, during an exhibition on the lake, Ralph Samuelson made the first water ski jump using a greased four-foot-by-sixteen-foot ramp.

Although a back injury later led him to take up turkey farming, he became known as "the Father of Water Skiing." He was inducted into the Water Ski Hall of Fame in 1982.

Starting the NAACP

Born in slave quarters in Mississippi in 1861, Fredrick McGhee became not only the first black criminal lawyer in Minnesota, but the first black criminal lawyer west of the Mississippi. He opened a practice in St. Paul in 1889.

McGhee lived through a historic episode in U.S. history: the Civil War. The war, Reconstruction, and the racial Jim Crow laws that followed it greatly influenced his life's course. In 1904, along with W. E. B. Du Bois and others, McGhee formed the Niagara Movement, the forerunner of the National Association for the Advancement of Colored People (NAACP). The NAACP, in turn, provided the seeds for the Civil Rights Movement six decades later.

McGhee died in 1912 shortly before his fifty-first birthday. Many years later, NAACP chairman Roy Wilkins said, "It was through [McGhee] that the National Association for the Advancement of Colored People reached St. Paul and [our house at] 906 Galtier Street."

A Prince of a Musician

Prince Rogers Nelson (known as "Prince") was born in Minneapolis in 1958. His father was a jazz pianist and songwriter, and his mother was a singer. When naming his son, Prince's father took his inspiration from the name of his jazz band, the "Prince Rogers Trio."

When his parents separated, Prince moved back and forth between them. During one stint with his father, Prince was given his first guitar. He finally moved into the basement of a neighbor's home and befriended the family's son, with whom he formed a band called "Grand Central," which was later changed to "Champagne."

Champagne dissolved before any recordings were made, but at age eighteen, Prince put together a collection of demo tracks. Three different recording companies offered him contracts. The bidding war was won by Warner Brothers, who offered him not only money but creative control over his songs. His first major-label album release was the 1978 *For You*. As on most of Prince's subsequent albums, he played all the instruments—twenty-seven of them—and wrote most of the music.

Prince's 1984 semi-autobiographical film *Purple Rain* was shot in Minneapolis, mostly on First Avenue. After the movie, Prince developed his own record label, Paisley Park, and in 1987 built Paisley Park Studios in Chanhassen. It was the home for all of his later recording and film work.

Among Prince's No. 1 hits are "When Doves Cry" (1984), "Let's Go Crazy" (1984), "Kiss" (1986), and "Batdance" (1989). In 2008, Prince won a Grammy Award for Best Song Written for Motion Picture, Television, or Other Visual Media: "Song of the Heart" from the film *Happy Feet*.

MARK YOUR CALENDAR

Mark Your JULY CALENDAR

Taste of Minnesota, St. Paul
www.tasteofmn.org

Fourth of July Water Carnival, Bemidji

Wilder Pageant, Walnut Grove
www.walnutgrove.org

Minneapolis Aquatennial, Minneapolis
www.aquatennial.org

Minnesota

First and Last in the Civil War

- During the Civil War, Minnesota was the first state to offer troops to Abraham Lincoln.

- Josias King (Pioneer Guards), a St. Paul surveyor, claimed to be the first Union volunteer in the Civil War.

- The 1st Minnesota Regiment had more losses than any other Northern regiment in the First Battle of Bull Run.

- The 262 men of the 1st Minnesota Regiment are most remembered for their role in the Battle of Gettysburg. On July 2, 1863, Major General Winfield Hancock, commander of the II Corps of the Army of the Potomac, ordered the men to charge a much larger approaching confederate force. Although outnumbered, they attacked with ferocity. Only forty-seven of the 262 men escaped injury or death, but they continued the fight into the next day. Union reinforcements arrived, held the position, and eventually won the Battle of Gettysburg.

- The 82 percent casualty rate of the 1st Minnesota Regiment at Gettysburg stands to this day as the largest loss by any surviving military unit in American history during any single engagement.

- Albert Woolson, who died August 2, 1965, in Duluth at the age of 109, claimed he was the last survivor of the Union army.

Close Encounters of the Loony Kind

Every year in early July, the Minnesota Department of Natural Resources' Nongame Wildlife Program coordinates the state's Loon Monitoring Program. Over a ten-day period, volunteers, called "Loon Rangers," count the official Minnesota state bird (otherwise known as the "great northern diver")on each of the six hundred lakes surveyed for loons. At last tally, Minnesota had almost twelve thousand loons, more than half of the common loons in the lower forty-eight states and three-quarters of the common loons in the Midwest.

Perhaps only the howl of a wolf can equal the call of a loon as the epitome of the North Woods. A loon has four different vocalizations: a wail, a tremolo, a yodel, and a hoot. A salt gland under each eye allows the common loon to adapt to fresh- or saltwater-living.

Islands or secluded bays are preferred places for nests, and the birds usually return to the same site each year. Although loons often mate for life, the female remains attached to her home lake. If another male forces her mate from the lake, she will usually prefer to stay with the lake and mate with the new male.

Loon nests are built right on the water's edge. Typically, the female loon will lay two eggs in mid-May, one day apart. For about a month, the parents share incubating duties and keep an eye out for egg stealers, including ravens, crows, gulls, eagles, and raccoons.

As for humans, if you're a boater, observe no-wake zones on lakes with incubating loons. Waves could wash eggs or chicks out of the close-to-shore nests. If you should find a loon nest or chick, stay as far way as possible to avoid disturbing the loon family.

And, if like me, you'd like to be a loon counter (and have a loon encounter), call the Minnesota Department of Natural Resources.

Spam of Another Kind

During the Great Depression, President Roosevelt devised a plan to stimulate the economy and feed the unemployed. The government would buy livestock from farmers and have packing companies (such as the George A. Hormel & Company of Austin, Minnesota) produce a canned roast beef with gravy for the nation's poor.

Unfortunately, in 1935, only nine months after the program began, it ended, leaving Hormel with five hundred thousand extra cans. To get rid of them, Jay Hormel and company filled the tins with a stew that they called "Dinty Moore." It became a staple in many people's diets and was very popular with campers and hikers, who liked its convenience.

Alien Invasion   *Zebra Mussels*

First found in 1988 in the Great Lakes, zebra mussels have made their way into the Duluth-Superior Harbor and the Mississippi River.

From one-quarter to one-and-a-half inches long, barnacle-like zebra mussels have alternating black- to brownish-colored stripes. They are the only freshwater mussel that can attach to objects, such as boat hulls, nets, boat lifts, submerged rocks, dock pilings, water intake pipes, and aquatic plants. Microscopic larvae may be carried in water.

Introduction of zebra mussels into the Great Lakes is likely to have occurred in 1985 or 1986, when one or more oceangoing ships discharged ballast water into Lake St. Clair. The freshwater ballast, picked up in a European port, contained zebra mussel larvae and possibly juveniles. The mussels found the plankton-rich St. Clair Lake and Lake Erie to their liking and multiplied rapidly. Zebra mussels have severely reduced populations of Minnesota's native mussels and clogged municipal water intake lines; and because they are filter-feeders, taking plankton for food that young native fish rely upon, they are linked to fish and wildlife die-offs that damage whole-lake ecosystems.

What You Can Do

- Learn to identify zebra mussels.

- Remove plants and animals from your boat, trailer, and accessory equipment (anchors, cables, centerboards, trailer hitches, and wheels) before leaving the water access area.

- Drain lake or river water from the livewell and bilge before leaving the water access area.

- Dispose of unwanted live bait in the trash, never into the water. Never dip your bait or minnow bucket into one lake if it has water in it from another. Also, never dump live fish from one body of water into another body of water.

- Wash your boat, downriggers, tackle, and trailer with hot water when you get home. Flush water through your motor's cooling system and other boat parts that normally get wet. It's best to let everything dry for three days before transporting your boat to another body of water.

- If you suspect a new infestation of an exotic plant or animal, report it to the Minnesota Department of Natural Resources or the Minnesota Sea Grant. Record the exact location and store specimens in rubbing alcohol.

The Style of a State *The CCC and the State Parks*

More than eighty-six thousand men served in the Civilian Conservation Corps (CCC) in Minnesota during the 1930s. Along with Works Progress Administration (WPA) crews, CCC workers gave Minnesota twenty-two state parks containing "Rustic Style" constructions that have today put them on the National Register of Historic Places.

The Rustic Style design philosophy emphasized natural features and resulted in edifices that blended in with their environments. They were made with whatever materials were locally available. Throughout Minnesota, Rustic Style buildings reflect the land upon which they reside: in the northern part of the state where timber was plentiful, log construction is prevalent. Stone buildings were more typical in the south and northwest, and a combination of log and stone is common in the central section of the state.

The stonework in these state parks include basalt and sandstone in the east, limestone in the south, quartzite in the southwest, granite and gabbro near Lake Superior, and fieldstone in the north, west, and northwest.

You will find a list of Minnesota Parks placed on the National Register of Historic Places on the following page.

July Recipe Gourmet Burgers

According to Ojibwa legend, Indian people live in Minnesota because of wild rice. It wasn't until the 1950s and early 1960s that farmers in Minnesota started producing cultivated wild rice from seeds gathered in natural wild rice stands.

Wild rice thrives only in flooded soils that have never or seldom been farmed. Minnesota's cultivated wild rice is produced primarily in the north-central peatlands. For your July picnics, make your burgers the Minnesota way—with wild rice.

Gourmet Burgers

1 pound lean ground beef
1 cup cooked wild rice
$1/4$ teaspoon salt

In a large bowl, combine the ingredients well. Shape into five patties; broil, grill, or panfry.

Variations: Add chopped onion, shredded cheese, parsley, basil, garlic, or seasoned salt. Can also be used for meatballs or meatloaf. For convenience, double or triple the recipe and freeze extra patties.

Printed with permission from the Minnesota Cultivated Wild Rice Council

The Minnesota Parks on the National Register of Historic Places:		
Blue Mounds State Park	Interstate State Park	Minneopa State Park
Buffalo River State Park	Itasca State Park	Monson Lake State Park
Camden State Park	Jay Cooke State Park	Old Mill State Park
Charles Lindbergh State Park	Lac Qui Parle State Park	St. Croix State Park
	Lake Bemidji State Park	Scenic State Park
Flandrau State Park	Lake Bronson State Park	Sibley State Park
Fort Ridgely State Park	Lake Carlos State Park	Whitewater State Park
Gooseberry Falls State Park	Lake Shetek State Park	

Dan Patch, a Record-Holding Horse

Dan Patch has been called the "World's Champion Harness Horse" and the "greatest harness horse in the history of the two-wheel sulky," titles he earned when he paced a 1.55-minute mile on September 8, 1906, at the Minnesota State Fairgrounds. It broke the world record.

Patch was born on April 29, 1896. The record he set that day in September would not be topped by pacers and trotters for fifty-four years. (It was broken in 1960 when Adios Butler clocked in at 1:54:3.) It was met only once during that time by Billy Direct, also a pacer, in 1938.

Dan Patch was acquired by Marion Savage of Minneapolis in 1902. Savage guided Patch to the pinnacle of his career. He was kept at the famous Savage Racing Stables, located twenty miles from Minneapolis. The horse's earnings from races and exhibitions totaled more than a million dollars. Each time he raced, his purse ranged from $10,000 to $20,000.

The affection between Patch and Savage was legendary. When Dan Patch died on July 11, 1916, Savage passed away just twenty-four hours later—some say of a broken heart. Savage was in a Minneapolis hospital recovering from a minor operation when Patch died of a heart ailment following an attack of pneumonia. Informed of his horse's passing, Savage did the same the next day. Attending physicians reported that Savage's death was caused by shock resulting from the loss of the horse he worshipped.

During his career, Dan Patch broke world speed records at least fourteen times. Other owners sometimes refused to race their horses against him, leaving Patch to run against the clock.

Dan Patch Days are held annually in Savage, Minnesota, usually attended by descendants of Dan Patch and Marion Savage. The Dan Patch Historical Society was established to collect, preserve, and disseminate historical knowledge and artifacts about the famous horse and Marion Savage.

JULY WEATHER

July Normals for Duluth

Day	High	Low	Mean	Precip.	Snowfall
1	74	52	63	0.15	0
2	75	52	64	0.14	0
3	75	52	64	0.14	0
4	75	53	64	0.14	0
5	75	53	64	0.14	0
6	75	54	65	0.14	0
7	76	54	65	0.14	0
8	76	54	65	0.14	0
9	76	54	65	0.14	0
10	76	54	65	0.14	0
11	76	54	65	0.14	0
12	76	55	66	0.14	0
13	76	55	66	0.14	0
14	76	55	66	0.14	0
15	76	55	66	0.14	0
16	77	55	66	0.14	0
17	77	55	66	0.13	0
18	77	55	66	0.13	0
19	77	55	66	0.13	0
20	77	55	66	0.13	0
21	77	55	66	0.13	0
22	77	55	66	0.13	0
23	77	55	66	0.13	0
24	77	55	66	0.13	0
25	77	56	66	0.13	0
26	77	56	66	0.13	0
27	77	56	66	0.13	0
28	77	56	66	0.13	0
29	77	56	66	0.13	0
30	77	56	66	0.13	0
31	77	56	66	0.13	0

JULY WEATHER

July Normals for International Falls

Day	High	Low	Mean	Precip.	Snowfall
1	77	52	65	0.13	0
2	77	52	65	0.13	0
3	78	53	65	0.12	0
4	78	53	65	0.12	0
5	78	53	65	0.12	0
6	78	53	65	0.12	0
7	78	53	65	0.12	0
8	78	53	66	0.12	0
9	78	53	66	0.11	0
10	78	53	66	0.11	0
11	79	54	66	0.11	0
12	79	54	66	0.11	0
13	79	54	66	0.11	0
14	79	54	66	0.11	0
15	79	54	66	0.11	0
16	79	54	66	0.11	0
17	79	54	66	0.11	0
18	79	54	66	0.1	0
19	79	54	66	0.1	0
20	79	54	66	0.1	0
21	79	54	67	0.1	0
22	79	54	67	0.1	0
23	79	54	67	0.1	0
24	79	54	67	0.1	0
25	79	54	67	0.1	0
26	79	54	67	0.1	0
27	79	54	67	0.1	0
28	79	54	67	0.1	0
29	79	54	67	0.1	0
30	79	54	67	0.1	0
31	79	54	66	0.1	0

Source: National Oceanic and Atmospheric Administration (NOAA)'s National Weather Service

These climate normals are an average of thirty years of data between 1971 and 2000. Every ten years, the National Weather Service recalculates the normals using the next interval of thirty years. In 2010, the new normals will be recalculated using the period of 1981 to 2010.

JULY WEATHER HISTORY

On This Day in July

Day	Year	Weather
1	1964	Tyler picks up more than 6 inches of rain in twenty-four hours.
2	1972	Freezing temperatures at Big Falls in Koochiching County.
3	1947	Tornadoes hit Marshall and Polk counties.
4	1962	Downpour at Jackson: 7.5 inches of rain in two hours.
5	1966	Jumbo hailstones fall at Detroit Lakes. One measures a foot in diameter.
6	1936	Moorhead registers 114 degrees, tying with Beardsley's record high temperature reached on July 29, 1917.
7	2000	Torrential rains douse the Twin Cities with 8 inches in a three-to-five-hour span. Eagan is also hit hard.
8	1974	The Twin Cities reach 101 degrees, the warmest in twenty-six years.
9	1932	Tornado hits near Springfield, causing $500,000 in damage.
10	1899	Twenty-five thousand acres of wheat are damaged or destroyed in Clay, Norman, and Polk counties.
11	1903	Just a reminder that this is still Minnesota: It gets down to 26 at Leech Lake Dam.
12	1863	Cool wave across the state. Frost in Twin Cities area.
13	1933	Odd heat wave affects Grand Marais with a high of 90. Most of Minnesota in the 100s.
14	1936	The hottest day ever in the Twin Cities, with 108 degrees at the downtown Minneapolis office. Seventy-one people die due to the extreme heat.
15	1980	Straight-line winds of nearly 100 mph cause enormous damage, mainly in Dakota County. 100,000 people are without power.
16	2006	"Heat burst" occurs over west-central and central Minnesota. The temperature at Canby jumps from 91 degrees to 100 degrees in forty minutes. At the same time, the dew point temperature drops from 63 to 32 degrees. A heat burst is caused by a dying thunderstorm, with very warm air aloft.
17	1934	Frost damages crops across the north with 34 degrees in Baudette and Roseau.
18	1867	Possibly the greatest "unofficial" rainstorm in Minnesota history. Thirty-six inches are recorded in thirty-six hours near Sauk Center. Disastrous flooding in central Minnesota. The Pomme De Terre River is impassable. A courier attempts to cross on horseback and drowns. Millions of logs are lost on the Mississippi River.
19	1987	The town of Floodwood lives up to its name with nearly 6 inches of rain in two days.
20	1909	Beaulieu in Mahnomen County gets 10.75 inches of rain in twenty-four hours. This record will stand for more than fifty years. Bagley receives an estimated 10 inches.
21	1934	Temperature tops out at 113 at Milan.
22	1972	"The Granddaddy" of flash floods. The greatest downpour ever in Minnesota comes when Ft. Ripley gets 10.84 inches in twenty-four hours. Fourteen inches of rain falls at the Jaschiki farm in Morrison County.

JULY WEATHER HISTORY

On This Day in July

Day	Year	Weather
23	1987	Greatest deluge ever in Twin Cities begins with 10 inches in six hours at the airport.
24	1987	Deluge ends in the Twin Cities. Two-day totals include over a foot of rain at Bloomington. Nearly 10 inches in downtown Minneapolis and nearly 9 inches in St. Paul. At one time, the water is as deep as 13.5 feet on I-494 near East Bush Lake Road. Bloomington's I-494 is closed for nearly five days.
25	1915	Frost hits northeastern Minnesota.
26	1981	Chilly morning, with 33 degrees at Roseau and Wannaska.
27	1910	Giant hailstones in Todd and Wadena counties. One stone weighs 5 pounds.
28	1987	Heavy rain in La Crosse, Wisconsin (near the state line). Their rain bucket picks up 5 inches.
29	1917	Hottest temperature ever recorded in Minnesota, with 114 degrees at Beardsley.
30	1971	Cool spell across state with frost in the north and freezing temperatures reported as far south as Pipestone.
31	1858	Hail the size of fruit cups falls one mile east of Forest City. The hailstones weigh 2.75 ounces.

Source: Minnesota State Climatology Office: DNR Waters

Keep Your Straw Sun Hat Looking Its Best

To reshape a straw hat, use a little steam. Hold the hat over a large pot of boiling water and move it around. Then let it air dry.

Prevention is the key to keeping your summer hat looking great:

- Do not get a straw hat too damp; it could shrink.
- Protect it from water and other stains with a light spray of stain repellent.
- When storing your hat, use a plastic-shaped head or a coffee can.

"In winter I get up at night

And dress by yellow candlelight.

In summer quite the other way

I have to go to bed by day."

— ROBERT LOUIS STEVENSON

July in the Garden

Mid-Summer Planting for Fall Harvest • How to Stake Tomato Plants • Killing Grass Weeds, Keeping the Grass

Mid-Summer Planting for Fall Harvest

In July, once the early maturing vegetables have come in and been harvested, gardeners can plant again for fall crops. You may want to check for your area's average first-frost date, however, so you'll get to them before the winter does!

Crop	Days to Mature	Crop	Days to Mature	Crop	Days to Mature
Basil	30–60	Green onions	60–70	Peas	70–80
Beets	50–60	Kale	40–65	Radishes	30–60
Bush beans	45–65	Kohlrabi	50–60	Spinach	35–45
Cilantro	60–70	Leaf lettuce	40–60	Swiss chard	40–60
Collard greens	40–65	Mustard greens	30–40	Turnips	50–60

How to Stake Tomato Plants

Nothing comes close to the taste of a fresh, ripe tomato straight off the vine. Some gardeners use staking to help them grow healthy plants. Use the tips below in your tomato garden.

Things You'll Need:
- Wooden stakes, six feet long by one-inch square
- Wood preservative
- Strips of cotton cloth for ties

1. **Paint the stakes** with the wood preservative to prevent them from rotting.
2. **Pound the stakes** ten inches into the ground about three inches away from the plant, on its north side. Be careful not to damage buried stems and developing roots.
3. **Loosely tie the vines** to the stake with strips of cotton cloth. Wrap the cotton ties around the tomato stake first, then catch the stem with a loop and tie it with a knot or bow behind the stake. Old nylon stockings will also work as ties.
4. **Prune the plant** to one stem as it grows. If you want two stems, allow a side shoot to grow, but continue to prune the other shoots. When the plant reaches the top of the stake, pinch out the growing part of the shoot. This will allow the plant to focus its energy on the tomatoes.

Killing Grass Weeds, Keeping the Grass

Unfortunately, weeds in your lawn such as ground ivy and quack grass cannot be destroyed by hand-pulling and usually require a total vegetation killer to keep them from taking over your yard. Unfortunately, these products will kill the weeds and any growing plant they touch.

To apply the herbicide safely, paint, sponge, or wipe it on the weed leaves while wearing protective gloves. The herbicide will move through the leaves, down the stems, and into the roots.

To isolate the weeds and make the job easier:
- Remove the top and bottom of a plastic milk jug.
- Position the milk jug over a weed area in your lawn.
- Spray the vegetation killer on the weeds inside the milk jug. The jug will protect the surrounding plants from the harmful herbicide. Remove the jug after the herbicide dries.

Gladys's

July Household Tips

While Minnesotans may long look forward to the warmth of July, the outdoor sun and fun can be hazardous from time to time. In addition to keeping your head covered (see page 131), here are a few tips for keeping your summer safe.

What to Keep in a First Aid Kit

Box of individually wrapped, adhesive bandages (such as Band-Aids)
Absorbent, open-weave bandages (gauze dressings), three medium-size, one large, and one extra large
Sterile gauze (four-inch squares)
Medical adhesive tape
A large, triangular bandage for a sling
Elastic Ace bandages for strains and sprains
Antiseptic solution (such as hydrogen peroxide)

Alcohol wipes
Antiseptic hand cleaner
Triple-antibiotic ointment
Calamine lotion
Selection of safety pins
Small pair of scissors
Round-ended tweezers
Instant cold packs
Acetaminophen and/or ibuprofen
Plastic gloves (at least two pairs)
Thermometer

And don't forget: always wear sunscreen and drink plenty of water.

AUGUST

"Ancient of days!

August Athena!

Where, Where are thy men of might?

Thy grand in soul?

Gone —glimmering through

the dream of things that were."

— GEORGE GORDON NOEL [LORD] BYRON

Augustus, at least the way Lord Byron uses it, means "marked by a majestic dignity or grandeur." The name of the eighth month of the year comes from such a personage, Augustus Caesar.

Minnesota has never been short of "men of might," "those grand in soul," or for that matter, dreamers. Early miners—along with loggers and farmers—used their strength to forge a state, even if they had to dig through rock to make living here possible. Some other Minnesotans have beautified urban settings with works of art; and more than a few have brought joy to their neighborhoods on a summer day with a friendly, community game of softball. These people certainly have a grandness of soul.

The state has its share of dreamers, too, such as a man who imagined skyscrapers and another who envisioned the biggest ball of twine in the world, sitting right in his backyard. Such an unusual thought must have been born in a dream. Good or bad, you can decide.

Read about these august people and mighty men here, in this month—before the dream of summer ends, and fall becomes reality once again.

Minnesota Man Is a Woman

In 1931 on U.S. Highway 59, a crew of road builders dug up a prehistoric skeleton that is estimated by some anthropologists to be at least ten thousand years old. Measurements indicate that she is of ancient *Homo sapiens* species, predating Indians or Eskimos, perhaps making her the oldest known female of America.

Called "Minnesota Man," she lived at the end of the last Ice Age, in the shadow of the glaciers, and was only about fifteen years old at the time of her death. Found twenty feet below the surface in an ancient lake bed, it's likely that she drowned. A conch shell pendant and a small dagger made from an elk's horn were discovered beside her.

In Browns Valley two years later, another ancient skeleton was found.

Amateur archeologist William Jensen discovered the "Browns Valley Man," who lived approximately nine thousand years ago. Tested at the University of Minnesota, the man was between twenty-five and forty years of age, and his features resembled those of a Greenland Eskimo. The skeleton mysteriously disappeared after it was returned to Jensen, and he failed to reveal its location before his death in 1960; however, his family rediscovered it in 1987.

In 1938 in Sauk Valley near West Union, another ancient skeleton was unearthed. The discovery of three ancient skeletons in widely separated locations and from different periods makes Minnesota an unusual—and fortunate—state.

Darwin's Theory *A Big Ball of Twine Evolves!*

What put tiny Darwin (population 276) on the map wasn't its natural beauty or historic buildings. It was The World's Largest Ball of Twine.

It started simply enough. A man named Francis Johnson started the ball from pieces of baler twine he found around his home. But once the cold Minnesota winters hit, he began to devote four hours a day to growing his twine ball. When the ball got too big to stay inside the house, he moved it to the barn and hoisted it with a railroad winch to help wrap it as more twine was added.

Eventually, Johnson rolled the ball into his yard. It was so unusual that people started to stop by for a look and to snap photos. At eleven feet high, thirteen feet in diameter, and weighing 17,400 pounds, the ball was listed in the *Guinness Book of World Records*. Johnson passed away in 1989; and in 1991, the Darwin Community Club transferred the ball to its new home in a Plexiglas gazebo in the center of town.

It took Johnson thirty-nine years to create the "largest sisal twine ball built by one person." Today, like any other town resident, the ball has its own mailbox.

My Son, the Skyscraper

Minneapolis native and architect Leroy Buffington was granted a patent in 1888 for "iron-building construction." His method used a braced, steel skeleton, with the weight of the building distributed on shelves fastened to the frame at each floor. Because of the patent, Buffington called himself "the father of the skyscraper."

One year later, the thirteen-story Tacoma building in Chicago was constructed using a similar technique. But Buffington never saw any patent rights money in that case, or in any other.

A favorite of the Pillsbury family, however, Buffington designed the Pillsbury A Mill, Charles Pillsbury's house, and Pillsbury Hall at the University of Minnesota's Twin Cities East Bank Campus.

Minnesota's first skyscraper wasn't completed until 1929. For many years, the Foshay Tower was the tallest building in Minneapolis, at 447 feet and thirty-two floors. It housed the Foshay public utility empire. Modeled after the Washington Monument, the building was dedicated in extravagant ceremonies on August 30, 31, and September 1, 1929. John Philip Sousa wrote "The Foshay Tower-Washington Memorial March" to commemorate the dedication.

Minneapolis's
First Steps Were Falls

At the same time that St. Paul was growing as a river port on the Mississippi, St. Anthony Falls was roaring upstream. The power of those waters alone meant that a city was sure to arrive on the site.

Soldiers from Fort Snelling, which was initially called Fort St. Anthony, built a sawmill on the west bank of the falls in 1821 and a flour mill in 1823. An entrepreneur from Pennsylvania, Franklin Steele built a cabin on the east bank in 1838, fol-

lowed by another sawmill. Soon Steele owned five sawmills, and his settlement came to be called St. Anthony.

In 1849, an Illinois businessman named Robert Smith, who was a member of Congress, used his political influence to persuade the army to lease him its gristmill and sawmill on the west bank. Although Smith promised the army he had plans to become a resident of Minnesota, he never did. Instead, he subleased the mills to local operators. His "Minneapolis" Mill

Minneapolis Facts

- The doctor at Fort St. Anthony began taking weather observations in January 1820. They have been recorded continuously ever since, giving the Twin Cities one of the most complete weather records in the United States.

- A suspension bridge connected Minneapolis to St. Anthony in 1855, seventeen years before the towns became one city. Something new in bridge engineering, the span was suspended from steel cables that ran across the river from a west bank tower to a tower on Nicollet Island just above the falls. The roadway across the bridge was seventeen feet wide. A toll of twenty-five cents was charged for horse-drawn wagons, five cents for pedestrians, and two cents for swine and sheep.

- There are more than 150 parks in the city.

- The name "Minneapolis" comes from the Dakota word for falls, *Minne ha-ha,* or "laughing water," and the Greek word for city, *polis.* The resulting "Minnehapolis" meant "Laughing Water City." The *h* was silent and was later dropped.

- After World War II, Minneapolis became a leader in the manufacture of computers, electronic equipment, and farm machinery.

- Besides the waters of the great Mississippi River, Minneapolis has twenty-two lakes lying within its borders.

- Minnehaha Park includes the fifty-three-foot-high Minnehaha Falls, made famous in Henry Wadsworth Longfellow's poem "The Song of Hiawatha."

- Half of the state's population lives in the Minneapolis-St. Paul metropolitan area.

Company received a charter from the legislature in 1856.

At the same time across the river, Franklin Steele and his partners obtained a charter from the St. Anthony Falls Water Power Company. The two companies then cooperated to build a dam at the head of the falls to divide the water evenly between them. The dam was completed in 1858. V-shaped, it angled out from each shore and met upstream in the middle of the river. Twenty feet high at the banks and just four feet high at the center, the dam allowed excess water to flow through and channeled the current —full of logs—into log-retention reservoirs on either side.

For their first twenty years, both Minneapolis and St. Anthony were sawmill towns. During the 1850s, six mills sat on the east side of the river and seven on the west. By 1856, the two settlements were turning out twelve million board feet of lumber annually, and the place had become a boomtown. The census of 1860 recorded St. Paul with a population of 10,400; St. Anthony had 3,200, and Minneapolis 2,564.

In 1869, however, water broke through the falls' thinning limestone cap rock. Townspeople feared the whole falls would collapse in a pile of stones and rubble. It wasn't until 1880 that the Army Corps of Engineers was able to build a system of aprons and dams to stabilize the falls.

Minneapolis absorbed St. Anthony in 1872. During the 1880s until the Depression, the city entered a new phase of flour-milling expansion. When a flour-sifting device called "the purifier" was perfected, it enabled millers to produce high-quality flour from inexpensive spring wheat grown in the Upper Midwest. Soon Minneapolis became the biggest milling center in the country.

Today, some of the oldest buildings in Minneapolis sit on the east bank, the site of the old St. Anthony. Upton Block, the oldest brick building in the city, dates from 1855. Minneapolis is the state's most populous city; the 2007 census estimate was 372,811.

Big on the Minneapolis Sculpture Garden

The Minneapolis Sculpture Garden was expanded in 1992 from seven-and-a-half to eleven acres, making it the largest urban sculpture garden in the country at the time.

Claes Oldenburg and Coosje van Bruggen's *Spoonbridge and Cherry* (1985–1988) sculpture located in the garden has become an iconic symbol for the city of Minneapolis. The 5,800-pound spoon and 1,200-pound cherry were built at two shipbuilding yards in New England.

The Iron Ranges of Minnesota

Minnesota has many "riches," and among them are its minerals. After farming and lumbering, iron mining became the state's third important frontier industry.

All three of the state's iron ranges are found in coniferous forests. The Vermilion, the Mesabi, and the Cuyuna ranges were formed about two billion years ago, when life was just beginning to create an oxygen-rich environment on earth. This oxygen dissolved in the seas and combined with iron minerals. When the sea floor eventually turned to sedimentary rocks, it contained rich concentrations of iron; some of the ore was 66 percent pure.

The **Vermilion Range** is located between the present towns of Tower and Ely. George Stuntz, a government surveyor in Duluth and an amateur archeologist, is credited with the discovery of iron ore here while searching for gold in 1865. Stuntz opened the Soudan Iron Mine (originally named the Breitung Mine) in 1875 and began shipping ore in August 1884. Mining began with fifteen major open pits and shafts, and twenty other, smaller workings. By 1890, it became evident that underground mining was necessary to reach ore. From its opening until its closing in 1962, the mine produced over 17.9 million tons of ore. By the time all of the mines on the Vermilion Range closed in the 1960s, they had shipped 104 million tons. U.S. Steel Corporation donated the mine and the surrounding lands to the state in 1963. That same year, the Minnesota legislature created the Tower-Soudan State Park (now called the Soudan Underground Mine State Park). In 1966, the Soudan mine was designated a National Historic Landmark.

Known locally as "the range," the **Mesabi** was named after the Ojibwa red giant *Mesabe*, who slept in the earth. The Mesabi is a ridge of red ore lying in a lightning-bolt-like shape, 120 miles long, from Hoyt Lake to Grand Rapids. It is one of the largest bodies of ore in the world. The mineral here proved so rich, soft, and shallow that it could be dug from the earth in large open pits. The first ore was shipped from the Mesabi in 1892, and the range has yielded more than three billion tons in total. During the twentieth century, the Mesabi was the source of most of the nation's iron ore.

Farther south, near Crosby, lies the **Cuyuna Range.** Covered by glacial drift, ore was suspected here only when prospectors noticed their compass needles being deflected. In 1904, settler Cuyler Adams found ore. At his wife's suggestion, Adams named the range using part of his name and part of his dog's, Una. The first mine in the range was the Kennedy Mine, which opened in 1911. Cuyuna Range ore contains a high percentage of manganese, which is scarce in the United States. Ninety percent of the manganese the United States needed during World War II came from this range. Mining ceased by 1977, by which time the Cuyuna had given up about one hundred million tons of ore.

In 2001, Minnesota still ranked first nationally in iron ore, accounting for 70 percent of all domestic shipments to U.S. steel manufacturers.

Some Hull-Rust-Mahoning Mine Facts

The Mesabi Range's Hull-Rust-Mahoning Mine in Hibbing, Minnesota, is the largest open pit iron mine in the world. At three miles long, two miles wide, 535 feet deep, and covering 1,600 acres, the mine is visible from outer space. More than a billion gross tons of earth were extracted from the mine—more than from the Panama Canal.

The mine supplied as much as one-fourth of all the iron ore mined in the United States during World War I and World War II.

The mine was listed as a National Historic Landmark and added to the National Register of Historic Places on November 13, 1966. The mine is still operated today by the Hibbing Taconite Company, which extracts taconite pellets at the rate of 8.2 million tons annually.

MARK YOUR CALENDAR

Mark Your

AUGUST
C A L E N D A R

Uptown Art Fair, Minneapolis
www.uptownminneapolis.com

White Oak Rendezvous, Deer River
www.whiteoak.org

Tall Timber Days, Grand Rapids
www.visitgrandrapids.com

Bayfront Blues Festival, Duluth
www.bayfrontblues.com

Minnesota Bluegrass and Old-Time Music Festival, Richmond
www.minnesotabluegrass.org

WE Fest, Detroit Lakes **www.wefest.com**

Ox Cart Days, Crookston
www.visitcrookston.com

Minnesota Renaissance Festival, Shakopee **www.renaissancefest.com**

Minnesota State Fair, St. Paul
www.mnstatefair.org

Potato Days, Barnesville
www.potatodays.com

A State of Contention

No one can say that Minnesota is a state that takes things lying down. In fact, when civic pride is at stake, things can get quite spirited and downright dirty—sometimes literally!

Superior, Wisconsin, has a natural entrance into St. Louis Bay through a long, narrow sand spit in Lake Superior called "Minnesota Point." Of course, **Duluth** thought it should have one, too. So, in 1871, Duluthians began to build their own canal through the spit. Wanting to protect their advantage, Superior got a legal injunction to make the Duluth residents stop. When those in Duluth heard that the injunction was coming, they dug all day and night to finish the canal before the legal papers arrived. Regular, everyday citizens attacked the spit with shovels—and opened the passage before Superior could stop them in court.

Some say that the name of the 1851 town of **Manton, Minnesota,** was changed to "La Crescent" by a land speculation group called the Kentucky Land Company. They wanted a more romantic-sounding name to attract settlers, and took inspiration from the crescent-shaped bend of the Mississippi River around the town.

But there's another explanation for the name. Manton, Minnesota, was located on the opposite side of the Mississippi River from **La Crosse, Wisconsin.** La Crosse was named for the bat used in a Native American game, which had often been played on the city's site. Those in the Minnesota town across the river confused the name with "La Croix," French for "the cross." In reference to the Crusaders and Turks who would raise the Cross and the Crescent when fighting to recapture the Holy Sepulchre, they challenged La Crosse by renaming their city "La Crescent."

Around 1857, the town of **Austin,** located on the Cedar River, had a hankering to become the county seat. The honor belonged to the little nearby settlement of **Frankfort** where, with no official government building, a small tin box served as the county's file cabinet and safe. It was assumed that wherever the box was, there was the county seat. Two members of the county commission from Austin thus got the idea to abscond with the box. They rode as fast as they could for Austin, with Frankforters—and the sheriff—in hot pursuit. Halfway to Austin, the two stopped at the hotel in High Forest and paid the bartender to hide the box in a snowbank.

After the two were arrested, it seemed time for an election to determine once and for all where the county seat would be. Austin was voted in.

In 1887 at the end of baseball season, the local **Dassel** team won the first game of a doubleheader against the town of **Hutchinson.** Hutchinson soon discovered that Dassel had hired professionals to bring about the easily won victory.

To retaliate, Hutchinson secretly hired its own professional players for the second game against Dassel. They also hired an umpire, Jack Bennett from Minneapolis. Bennett arrived in Dassel on the pretense of advertising a Minneapolis exposition. Dassel's pros recognized Bennett, as Hutchinson knew they would. They asked Bennett to ump the upcoming game—also, just as Hutchinson knew they would.

Odds were running 4 to 1 against Hutchinson. At the bottom of the ninth inning, the score was 6-3 in favor of Dassel. But suddenly, Bennett seemed to go a bit blind as Hutchinson went to bat. He didn't call a single strike against the team, and Hutchinson was able to nab the lead. The final score was 9 to 6. Since the Dassel people had hired Bennett, no one ever suspected him of any ulterior motive. It was sweet revenge.

In the late nineteenth century, the rivalry between **Minneapolis** and **St. Paul** reached scandalous proportions. During the 1890 census, the two cities kidnapped each other's census takers in an effort to prove that it was the biggest. At the end of the process, the government demanded a recount of both cities.

The second census count found that fictitious children and boarders and nonexistent residences had bolstered both cities' numbers. Minneapolis was afforded ten thousand less people than its own figures showed, while the St. Paul number was readjusted by a figure just a little less than ten thousand. Once the count was officially declared, amity between the two cities was soon reestablished.

Short Geography Lesson

The 1972 movie *The Heartbreak Kid* was set in Minnesota. Apparently, writer Neil Simon and director Elaine May were not familiar with the geography of the state. The two main characters talk about running off to a "summer cabin in the mountains." There are no mountains in Minnesota.

One Big Rodent

In 1938, construction workers found the skeleton of a giant Pleistocene beaver in St. Paul. About the size of a black bear (eight feet long and weighing 480 pounds), it is the largest rodent to have inhabited North America.

Minnesota's Amphibians and Reptiles

Most of Minnesota's amphibians and reptiles live in the southeastern part of the state, perhaps because of its warmer temperatures. Secretive and shy, they are drawn to places inaccessible to humans, making researching them difficult. Below is a list of amphibians and reptiles known to inhabit the state.

Frogs and Toads
American toad
Canadian toad
Great plains toad
Treefrogs:
Cope's gray treefrog
Gray treefrog
Northern cricket frog
Spring peeper
Wester chorus/
   Boreal chorus frog
True frogs:
Bullfrog
Green frog
Mink frog
Northern leopard frog
Pickerel frog
Wood frog

Salamanders
Blue-spotted salamander
Eastern red-backed
   salamander
Four-toed salamander

Spotted salamander
Tiger salamander

Snakes
Black rat snake
Blue racer
Brown snake
Bullsnake
Common garter snake
Eastern hognose snake
Fox snake
Massasauga
   (venomous; rarely found)
Milk snake
Northern water snake
Plains garter snake

Redbelly snake
Ringneck snake
Smooth green snake
Timber rattlesnake
   (venomous; rarely found)

Turtles
Blanding's turtle
False map turtle
Northern map turtle
Ouachita map turtle
Painted turtle
Smooth softshell turtle
Snapping turtle
Spiny softshell turtle
Wood turtle

Source: Minnesota Department of Natural Resources

Game Called for Gunfire *The Minnesota/Cuba Connection*

A huge baseball fan, Fidel Castro often attended Havana Sugar Kings games at Gran Stadium in Cuba. He had once been a pitcher at the University of Havana. On July 24, 1959, in an exhibition game between his own pickup team, Los Barbudos ("The Bearded Ones"), and a military police team prior to a game between the Sugar Kings and the Rochester Red Wings, Castro pitched two innings while striking out two batters.

The following day in Havana, another game between the Red Wings and Sugar Kings began late in the evening. The game was exciting: the Sugar Kings started off a run in the bottom of the first, and the Red Wings scored two in the second. The Wings added another in the third to take a 3-1 lead until the bottom of the ninth inning, when the Sugar Kings scored twice to tie it.

As if Castro's presence and the tie weren't enough, when midnight arrived, it became the sixth anniversary of the storming of the Moncada Barracks by Castro and his supporters. Castro's organization, which took over Cuba in 1958, was called the "26th of July Movement." Fans started to celebrate by firing guns into the air, inside and outside the stadium.

In the top of the twelfth inning, Red Wing third-base coach Frank Verdi was struck on his helmet liner by a bullet. Havana shortstop Leo Cardenas was also grazed by a bullet, after which the umpires called the game. It is the only baseball game ever called on account of gunfire.

Red Wings President Frank Horton thought it best to call the U.S. Ambassador to Cuba to get the Red Wings out of the country as soon as possible.

August Recipe Wild Surf and Turf

This month's recipe is both land- and water-based, combining surf and turf with some fresh dill from your summer garden.

Wild Surf and Turf

4 (6–8 oz. each) center-cut
beef tenderloin medallions
4 teaspoons canola oil
Seasoned salt
2 tablespoons butter
4 cloves garlic, crushed

1 tablespoon chopped fresh dill weed
2 cups cooked wild rice
1/2 cup Alfredo sauce
16 medium shrimp, cooked
4 teaspoons Alfredo sauce to garnish
4 sprigs fresh dill to garnish

Preheat oven to 375°F. Coat beef with oil and seasoned salt. In a large skillet, sear the beef two minutes; remove from pan. In the same skillet, melt the butter. Sauté garlic; remove from heat. Stir in dill, wild rice, and the 1/2 cup of Alfredo sauce. Slit each tenderloin; stuff with 1/2 cup of wild rice mixture and four shrimp (with tails visible). Bake twenty-five minutes or until beef reaches desired doneness. Garnish each with one teaspoon of Alfredo sauce and one sprig of dill. Four servings.

Printed with permission from the Minnesota Cultivated Wild Rice Council

AUGUST WEATHER

August Normals for Duluth

Day	High	Low	Mean	Precip.	Snowfall
1	77	56	66	0.13	0
2	76	56	66	0.13	0
3	76	55	66	0.13	0
4	76	55	66	0.13	0
5	76	55	66	0.13	0
6	76	55	66	0.13	0
7	76	55	66	0.13	0
8	76	55	65	0.13	0
9	76	55	65	0.13	0
10	75	55	65	0.13	0
11	75	55	65	0.13	0
12	75	55	65	0.13	0
13	75	54	65	0.13	0
14	75	54	64	0.13	0
15	74	54	64	0.14	0
16	74	54	64	0.14	0
17	74	54	64	0.14	0
18	74	54	64	0.14	0
19	74	53	63	0.14	0
20	73	53	63	0.14	0
21	73	53	63	0.14	0
22	73	53	63	0.14	0
23	73	52	62	0.14	0
24	72	52	62	0.14	0
25	72	52	62	0.14	0
26	72	52	62	0.14	0
27	71	51	61	0.14	0
28	71	51	61	0.14	0
29	71	51	61	0.14	0
30	70	50	60	0.15	0
31	70	50	60	0.15	0

"What dreadful hot weather we have!
It keeps me in a continual state of inelegance."

— JANE AUSTEN

AUGUST WEATHER

August Normals for International Falls

Day	High	Low	Mean	Precip.	Snowfall
1	79	54	66	0.1	0
2	79	54	66	0.1	0
3	79	54	66	0.1	0
4	79	54	66	0.1	0
5	79	54	66	0.1	0
6	79	53	66	0.1	0
7	79	53	66	0.1	0
8	78	53	66	0.1	0
9	78	53	66	0.1	0
10	78	53	66	0.1	0
11	78	53	65	0.1	0
12	78	53	65	0.1	0
13	78	52	65	0.1	0
14	77	52	65	0.1	0
15	77	52	65	0.1	0
16	77	52	64	0.1	0
17	77	51	64	0.1	0
18	76	51	64	0.1	0
19	76	51	64	0.1	0
20	76	51	63	0.1	0
21	75	50	63	0.1	0
22	75	50	63	0.1	0
23	75	50	62	0.1	0
24	74	50	62	0.1	0
25	74	49	62	0.1	0
26	74	49	61	0.1	0
27	73	49	61	0.1	0
28	73	48	61	0.11	0
29	72	48	60	0.11	0
30	72	47	60	0.11	0
31	71	47	59	0.11	0

Source: National Oceanic and Atmospheric Administration (NOAA)'s National Weather Service

These climate normals are an average of thirty years of data between 1971 and 2000. Every ten years, the National Weather Service recalculates the normals using the next interval of thirty years. In 2010, the new normals will be recalculated using the period of 1981 to 2010.

AUGUST WEATHER HISTORY

On This Day in August

Day	Year	Weather
1	1955	A thunderstorm in Becker County dumps a foot of rain at Callaway.
2	1831	Cold outbreak across state with light frost reported at Ft. Snelling.
3	1896	Violent hailstorm destroys two-thirds of crops in Swift County.
4	1898	Storms dump 4.5 inches of rain on Montevideo.
5	1904	Detroit Lakes woman is hit by lightning. It melts her hairpins and the steel in her corset, but does not kill her.
6	1969	Tornadoes sweep across the north, hitting Ely, Backus, Outing, and Dark Lake. Damage could still be seen twenty years later in the Boundary Waters Canoe Area Wilderness.
7	1955	The climate record of George Richards of Maple Plain ends. He recorded weather data with lively notations on phenology and weather events. He began taking observations when he was eleven years old in 1883 and continued for seventy-two years.
8	1882	Snowstorm on Lake Michigan. Six inches of slush on ship decks.
9	1948	Mankato receives 7.72 inches of rain.
10	2004	Cool Canadian air is ushered in on strong northwest winds. International Falls has its coldest high temperature ever for August with 49 degrees. The Twin Cities only sees a high of 59.
11	1945	Downpour over Red Wing. Nearly 8 inches of rain.
12	2000	Record-setting dew points in Minnesota. The Twin Cities see a dew point of 76, with a rare 80-degree dew point at Faribault.
13	1964	A taste of fall over the area, with 26 in Bigfork and 30 in Campbell.
14	1978	Boundary Waters area hit by a tornado. Some of the damage could still be seen ten years later.
15	1936	St. Paul swelters with a high of 108.
16	1981	Chilly across the state with Tower reporting a low of 33 degrees.
17	1946	A tornado kills eleven people in the Mankato area. A 27-ton road grader is hurled about 100 feet. Another tornado an hour later destroys downtown Wells.
18	1953	Four heifers near St. Martin get lucky: A tornado picks them up and sets them back down again, unharmed.
19	1980	Strong winds at Belle Plaine severely damage five planes.
20	1904	Both downtown Minneapolis and St. Paul hit by tornadoes. This remains the highest official wind ever recorded in Minnesota over one minute (110 mph in St. Paul).
21	1883	Fourth deadliest tornado in Minnesota history hits Rochester. The tornado kills 31 residents and injures 100 more. Appalled by the lack of medical care received by the tornado's victims, Mother Alfred Moes, founder of the Sisters of St. Francis, proposes to build and staff a hospital if Dr. W. W. Mayo will run it.
22	1910	Daylight is dimmed in Duluth due to smoke from Rocky Mountain forest fires.

AUGUST WEATHER HISTORY

On This Day in August

Day	Year	Weather
23	1955	Hail in Houston County, with piles to a foot deep at Rushmore.
24	1934	Early Arctic blast over the state. Rochester and Fairmont have lows of 34 degrees.
25	1976	Roy Lake Fire. During the drought, 2,600 acres burn.
26	1915	Surprising cold and killing frosts across Minnesota, with 23 degrees at Roseau.
27	1992	A chilly night in Embarrass. The temperature dips to 28 degrees.
28	1989	Baseball-sized hail pummels Pequot Lakes.
29	1863	A devastating frost affects most of Minnesota, killing vines and damaging corn.
30	1977	Flooding on the southwest side of the Twin Cities, with the international airport getting 7.28 inches of rain in 4.5 hours.
31	1949	Earliest snowfall known for Minnesota. A trace of snow falls at the new Duluth Airport.

Source: Minnesota State Climatology Office: DNR Waters

Minnesota's One-of-a-Kind Lake

In a land of more than ten thousand lakes, there's one that stands out: This one contains saltwater.

Appropriately named Salt Lake, it is at most only four feet deep and is one-third as salty as an ocean. It sits on the border of Minnesota and South Dakota, near the town of Marietta. Salt Lake is well-known among Minnesota bird-watchers as a great place to see prairie and saltwater birds found nowhere else in the state. It's also home to a variety of unusual plants that have adapted to the saline environment, such as the salt grasses growing on the shore.

It's rare to find a salt lake as far east as Minnesota. Some have used the existence of Salt Lake to declare the state "The Gateway to the West."

The Sheriff Was a Heavyweight

Born in 1891 in St. Paul, Minnesota, heavyweight Tommy Gibbons was the first boxer to go an entire fifteen rounds with Jack Dempsey. It occurred during the World Championship Fight in Shelby, Montana, in 1923. Gibbons lost the decision.

Gibbons hung up his gloves after being knocked out, for the first and only time, by Gene Tunney in 1925. At the end of his boxing career, Tommy Gibbons's record was 56-4-1 with forty-four no-decisions and one no-contest. He scored forty-eight knockouts. Following his retirement, Tommy Gibbons was elected Sheriff of Ramsey County four times.

August in the Garden

August Gardening To-Do List • Summer Beans • Caring for Surface Tree Roots

August Gardening To-Do List

The August garden requires three important tasks: Water, weed, and watch.

Water. It's important to keep your garden and lawn—and the birds—watered. But contrary to popular belief, a brown lawn isn't necessarily a dead lawn. Grasses do go dormant in times of drought, but will recover quickly when the rains fall. If a green lawn is important to you, water regularly. If a water shortage is expected, however, or you don't like to spend your time tending to grass, you may choose to let your lawn go dormant, watering it as little as once a month.

Remember to keep the birdbath filled and change the water regularly. Standing water is less healthy for birds.

Weed. Keep the weeds in your garden pulled, before they have a chance to flower and go to seed again. Weeds rob plants of water and nutrients, harbor insects and diseases, and can grow tall enough to shade and kill your flowers and plants.

Watch. Keep an eye out for insects, slugs, and snails in your garden and the damage they can cause, and look for any evidence of disease throughout the garden. Take the necessary steps to control the problem.

Summer Beans

The Valley of the Jolly Green Giant," where the mega-man grew his famous corn, peas, and beans, refers to the Minnesota River Valley around Le Sueur. Here are some tips for keeping your own summer green bean crop in tip-top shape:

- **Plant beans every two weeks** for a continual, staggered supply. Bush beans will be ready to harvest in fifty to fifty-five days. Pole beans may take fifty to sixty days.

- **Beans like a loose, moist, moderately rich soil** with a slightly acidic pH of about 6.0 to 6.2. They will grow well in ordinary garden soil.

- **Plant bush beans in rows or blocks,** with four to six inches between each seed. Plant the seeds one to two inches deep. Pole beans need some type of support to grow on. Be sure the trellis or teepee is in place before you seed. Plant six to eight seeds per teepee or every six inches apart. They may need some initial help in climbing.

- **Water the soil immediately** and keep the plants well watered, at least one inch of water at a time. Four-inch deep mulch will help keep their shallow roots moist.

- **Pick beans while young and tender** (about as thick as a pencil). When they begin to firm up, they can be gently pulled from the vine or snapped off at the stem end.

- **The more you pick, the more beans you get.**

Caring for Surface Tree Roots

It can be hard to mow under a tree if its roots have grown slightly above the soil surface. It might be tempting to bury the roots under a raised bed or chop them away, but if you do, you'll risk losing the whole tree. Try one of the following methods instead to save the mower, the tree, and your sanity!

- Apply a two- to three-inch layer of mulch under the tree canopy. It will keep the surface roots under cover and provide a good environment for the tree.

- Plant perennial groundcovers under the tree. They will insulate the roots without depriving the tree of water and nutrients:

- First, select plants suitable to the growing conditions under your tree.

- Space the plants throughout the area.

- Dig holes for the plants that are slightly larger than the groundcover's root system.

- Amend the holes with compost, peat, or other organic matter.

- Plant, mulch, and water.

"In the parching August wind, Cornfields bow the head,

Sheltered in round valley depths, On low hills outspread."

— CHRISTINA GEORGINA ROSSETTI

Softball Began with Kittens

In 1895, Minneapolis fireman Lewis Rober was looking for a way to fill the time between fires during his twenty-four hour shifts. His eye caught sight of the vacant lot next to the station, and he got the idea for a game that was similar to baseball, but scaled down to fit the empty lot. The diamond was smaller, the ball was a bit bigger, and the pitching was done underhand.

Rober tried the game out with his fellow firefighters assigned to Engine 11 at Second and Bank streets. They named the game "kitten ball" after the name of their team, the Kittens. Their games soon got the attention of the neighborhood, and people came to watch.

In the fall of 1895, Rober transferred to Minneapolis's Engine House No. 19 and started a team there. By 1900, other fire-station teams had gotten together, and a league was formed. By 1906, more than twenty teams played every evening during the summer. Kitten ball quickly spread

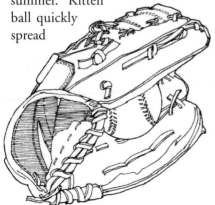

to firehouses and their neighborhoods throughout the country.

Illinois does have some claim to being the inventor of softball, however. On September 16, 1887, Chicagoan George Hancock developed a similar game as a way for baseball players to keep in practice during the winter. Hancock took a boxing glove and tied it into a ball. He used a broom handle as a bat, and the "soft ball" was fielded barehanded rather than with a glove. Hancock's game was called "Indoor Baseball."

In 1934, with games like Rober's and Hancock's being played across the United States (and moving into Canada), a national organization came up with official rules and called the game "softball."

Softball has become the most popular participant sport in the United States. Forty million Americans play at least one game of softball during a year. And while Hancock's game may have preceded Rober's by a slight margin, Rober's idea of co-workers and neighbors getting together to play in open lots more closely resembles the spirit of the neighborhood softball game we know today.

Gladys's

August Household Tips

August brings fresh vegetables to the table; and we all hope everyone eats them, as mother advised. But some ends of asparagus and pockets of pea pods have been known to remain on the plates after the family has gone back outdoors. Here are some tips to prevent your kitchen drain from clogging and for keeping your garbage disposal smelling fresh.

Preventing Drains from Clogging

- Use a metal or plastic trap (that looks like a strainer) over the drain to catch sizable debris before it gets sucked down and possibly caught.

- Never pour liquids that can harden down the drain. Glue, wax, paint, or grease should never be run down the drain. When you finish cooking, pour liquid grease into an empty jar or can. Let the rest of the grease harden in the pan and scoop out as much as you can into the garbage. For the residual grease, squirt the pan with dishwashing liquid and allow it to soak for a while so the fat breaks up into smaller particles.

- Do not dispose of coffee grounds or tea leaves in the sink.

- To retrieve metal items, such as flatware or pins that have fallen into the drain, attach a magnet to a piece of stiff twine or pipe cleaner and use it to fish the items out.

- To clear scum and build-up, pour some baking soda, followed by running hot water, into the drain about once a week. Alternatively, you may pour boiling water down the drain; or pour in one cup of vinegar and after thirty minutes, run very hot water through the drain.

- Avoid using chemical drain cleaners whenever possible. It's better to clear a clog mechanically than to use harsh chemicals that may corrode metal pipes.

Cleaning a Garbage Disposal

- If used properly, a garbage disposal will clean itself. But to keep odors at bay, run hot soapy water through it on a daily basis. Fill the sink with two or three inches of cold water. Turn on the disposal and allow this water to run through with no wastes added.

- To clear the unit of greasy food, throw a couple of ice cubes in and run the disposal. The ice works to congeal the fat, allowing the unit to grind it into disposable pieces.

- Put a slice of lemon into the disposer to make it smell sweeter.

- Caustic drain-cleaning chemicals may damage the unit; don't use them.

SEPTEMBER

"By all these lovely tokens

September days are here,

With summer's best of weather

And autumn's best of cheer."

— HELEN HUNT JACKSON

Fall in Minnesota is an incendiary time. The forest's leaves seem to start to catch fire, beginning their transformation from shades of green to saturated tints of orange, yellow, and red. Ripe vegetables and fruits bend their vines and consume the rich nutrients in their soils. The sun itself seems aglow in pale, evening skies.

But the month can be incendiary in other ways, as well. One of the nation's worst forest fires happened in Hinckley in September, and Chisholm had its own September battle with the blaze. Northfield was the scene of a different kind of fire: that from guns. It seems nature and human tempers run hot at this time of the year.

By the end of the month, however, a certain unique-to-Minnesota coolness comes that is comforting. Thousands of hawks beat their formidable wings in the air just over our heads; and if we're lucky, we can catch the breeze sweeping by our faces. If we're even more fortunate, we can be there to see and feel those rare acres of tallgrass prairies fanning themselves, waving a goodbye to summer and a greeting to the soon-arriving winter.

The Outlaw Jesse James

On September 7, 1876, the James-Younger Gang, made up of Confederate guerillas, attempted to hold up the Northfield First National Bank. In the unsuccessful endeavor, they killed cashier Joseph Lee Heywood, and fled with no money.

When merchants near the bank discovered the robbery in progress, they quickly armed themselves and fired through open windows, killing two members of the gang, Clel Miller and Bill Stiles. Bob Younger was wounded. He and the remaining five members disappeared into the surrounding woods, with a posse gathering up stream behind them.

In the next few days, one thousand men joined in the pursuit of the outlaws. Frank and Jesse James managed to elude capture, but Bob, Cole, and Jim Younger and Charlie Pitts were caught near the town of Madelia on September 21. Pitts was killed during the ensuing gunfight, while the Younger brothers were apprehended and later sentenced to life in prison. Bob Younger died in prison of tuberculosis on September 16, 1889.

Cole and Jim Younger were paroled on July 14, 1901. Cole went to Missouri and joined the Frank James Wild West Show. Jim Younger committed suicide in St. Paul on October 19, 1902.

Northfield holds a "Defeat of Jesse James Days" celebration every year.

Minnesota's September Fires

One of the state's most notorious disasters—and one of the country's greatest forest fires—occurred on September 1, 1894, in Hinckley. The fire consumed 320,000 acres of land and killed 418 people.

From May 1 to September 1, less than two inches of rain had fallen in the forests that surrounded the town of Hinckley. All summer, lightning and sparks from passing trains had ignited patches of "slash" left by loggers, and small fires were not an uncommon sight.

September 1 dawned hot and dry, just like the previous days. But after lunch, a wind kicked up, and a big fire began to build in the southwest. Volunteers quickly built breaks around town, but by 3:00 p.m., they had collapsed. Hinckley caught fire, and within an hour, the townspeople were mobbing the train station, hoping to catch the 4:00 p.m. *Limited* out.

James Root, the engineer of the *Limited*, drove the fastest train on the St. Paul & Duluth line. Root had left Duluth early that afternoon, bound for St. Paul. En route, the train stopped in Carlton. As he pulled from the station, Root turned on the headlight because of the smoke and darkness. Slowed to a crawl by the reduced visibility, the train was running about ten minutes late. Shortly after 4:00 p.m., about a mile from Hinckley, Root saw people running up the track toward the train. He helped the fifty or so frantic people onboard and started to back out of the burning area.

After only a quarter mile, a wall of flame struck the train and took out every window on its west side. The explosion sprayed Root's neck and head with glass. Severely bleeding, he continued to back the train, hoping to make Skunk Lake, about four miles away.

As the train crested Hinckley Hill, Root passed out. A fireman noticed the train was slowing and found Root slumped over, his hand still on the throttle. He splashed Root with water. As the engineer came to, he jumped to the task of speeding up the train—despite the fact that his hand was seared to the metal throttle.

Skunk Lake was barely a mud hole. The passengers nonetheless took shelter in the shallow water. By 6:00 p.m., the big fire had broken into smaller fires that died out in the cool evening. Today, the Hinckley Fire Museum stands in dedication to the worst single-day disaster ever to befall Minnesota.

Fourteen years later, on Saturday, September 5, 1908, a fire engulfed Chisholm. Its six thousand residents ran from the town and watched it burn from a nearby hill. Luckily, no one was killed.

The Hinckley and Chisholm fires inspired the state to establish a ranger service for spotting blazes before they spread.

All That Glitters Is Not Gold ... Or Diamonds

Although most of us have heard of the great California Gold Rush of 1848, few of us know about Minnesota's "Gold Rush," which began in 1865. Henry James, the state geologist, was prospecting in the Vermilion Lake area and had discovered iron ore. But one piece of rock he found particularly caught his fancy. He took it to St. Paul and delivered it to the governor, who sent it to the mint in Philadelphia to be tested.

The rumor of gold quickly spread, and by 1866, three hundred people were prospecting on the northeast side of Lake Vermilion. When the long-awaited U.S. Mint report finally arrived, it stated that the three-pound piece of quartz that James picked up was estimated to contain $25.63 in gold and $4.42 in silver to the ton. But when speculators pointed out that gold mining was profitable at only $6–$8 per ton, the gold rush died down as quickly as it began.

In the summer of 1893, however, gold was discovered on the U.S.-Canadian border on Little American Island in Rainy Lake. Miners dreaming of making it rich flocked to northern Minnesota, leading to the settlement of many communities, including International Falls. The Little American Mine has been the only productive gold mine ever to operate in Minnesota. But despite all of the efforts to make gold mining profitable in the Rainy Lake area, low production resulted in a gold-bust by 1898. By 1901, Rainy Lake City was a ghost town.

At just about the same time, another Minnesotan thought he had found a rare and shiny treasure. One summer day in 1894, a homesteader near present-day Lake Bemidji was strolling along the west shore of the lake. His boot kicked up some pebbles, which he saw sparkling in the sun. He was sure he had discovered a diamond field.

He sent a sample of the rocks off to an expert in New York. In the meantime, he and a few friends quickly secured options on all the land in the vicinity. Again, a rumor of riches quickly spread; by 1897, hopeful people poured in, and the city began to rapidly grow.

Today, Diamond Point Park sits on the shores of Lake Bemdji. The results of the homesteader's mineral test, though, showed that the pebbles contained simple quartzite.

Dreams, however, die hard. Today, a number of companies are actively exploring for gold in Minnesota.

A Span of Time

The Stone Arch Bridge below St. Anthony Falls in Minneapolis is the only one of its kind ever constructed over the mighty Mississippi River. Built in 1883 of native granite and limestone, it is 2,176 feet long by twenty-eight feet wide. The bridge, which resembles a Roman viaduct, is graced with twenty-three arches.

Big Balloons and Big Sticks
The Minnesota State Fair

Since the first "Territorial Fair" in 1854, Minnesota has held an agricultural festival annually—with the exception of five different years when the celebrations were called off due to scheduling issues, wartimes, or a polio outbreak. In 1885, the fair's location settled on its current site in St. Paul. In addition to showing off the state's crops, entertainment was always a staple of fair fare.

In 1925, the U.S. Navy dirigible *Shenandoah* was scheduled to appear. However, during the early morning hours, *Shenandoah* hit a thunderstorm over Noble County, Ohio. Because maintenance funds had never been approved, some of the craft's structures were weak, and the ship began to break up. Bit by bit, over three hours, the dirigible fell apart. The pilot, along with thirteen of his forty-man crew, died.

The scheduled appearance of another notable guest had a happier ending. On September 2, 1901, Vice President Theodore Roosevelt visited and first uttered the famous phrase, "Speak softly and carry a big stick."

The oldest ride on the fairgrounds is "Ye Old Mill," built in 1913.

The Age of the Iron Horse

Minnesota's first locomotive was the *William Crooks*. Built in 1861, it was put in service in 1862 for the St. Paul & Pacific Railroad, which later became part of the Great Northern Railway. The classic 4-4-0-configured vehicle is one of the only locomotives from the age of the American Civil War to survive to the present day. The *William Crooks* now rests at the Lake Superior Railroad Museum in Duluth.

The former Owatonna train depot now houses the famous Old 201. This 1880 locomotive was once driven by the famous engineer, Casey Jones.

Hey, Hey, It's the Monkees

Peter Tork of The Monkees—a four-member pop band created in 1965 for a NBC television series that ran from 1966 to 1968—was an English major at Carleton College in Northfield for three years. He flunked out twice, after which he decided to pursue music full-time.

The University of Minnesota

Chartered in 1851, seven years before Minnesota became a state, the University of Minnesota is a land-grant university with a strong tradition of academic excellence and public service. It is noted for its research in several fields, and its important breakthroughs and "firsts":

- Maria Sanford, professor of rhetoric and elocution from 1880 to 1909, was one of the first women in America ever to rise to the rank of full professorship.

- A legend in the surgical world, Dr. Owen Wangensteen, head of the department of surgery at the university, developed a suction device in 1945 to prevent post-operative intestinal blockage. It dramatically reduced mortality from abdominal surgery.

- Alumnus Seymour Cray designed the world's first supercomputer in the 1950s. His ERA 1103 was the first commercially successful scientific computer. It was a successor to UNIVAC 1101, the first stored-program computer in the United States.

- Medical school surgeons F. John Lewis and C. Walton Lillehei performed the world's first successful open-heart surgery in 1952. The patient was a five-year-old girl.

- Dr. Richard DeWall, physician and scientist in the Medical School Department of Surgery, developed the first successful heart-lung machine in 1955. The device extends operative time, allowing for more complex procedures.

- Engineering graduate Earl Bakken developed the first wearable pacemaker in 1957 with C. Walton Lillehei.

- In 1958, C. Walton Lillehei became the first person to successfully replace a heart valve with an artificial valve.

- After World War II, Donald Kent "Deke" Slayton earned a Bachelor of Science degree in aeronautical engineering from the University of Minnesota. He was one of the original Mercury Seven NASA astronauts selected in 1959.

- Richard Lillehei and William Kelly performed the world's first successful pancreas transplant in 1966.

- Dr. Christiaan Barnard learned surgery at the University of Minnesota. He performed the world's first human heart transplant in 1967 in South Africa.

- In 1968, Dr. Robert Good performed the world's first successful human bone marrow transplant.

- In 1975, the first implantable infusion pump was invented by University of Minnesota surgeons Henry Buchwald, Richard Varco, mechanical engineers Frank Dorman and Perry Blackshear, Jr., and physiologist Perry J. Blackshear.

- The first total-body computed to-mography (CT) scanner was developed at the University of Minnesota in 1977–1978.

- Dr. Stuart Jamieson, professor and head of cardiothoracic surgery, performed Minnesota's first heart-lung transplant in 1986 and the Midwest's first double-lung transplant in 1988.

- In 1988, Russell Johnson, a professor in the department of microbiology, identified the organism that causes Lyme disease and patented a vaccine for it.

- In 2000, a team led by Vivek Kapur at the College of Veterinary Medicine sequenced the genome that causes disease and death in poultry, cattle, and swine.

- In 2000, the gene that causes a common form of muscular dystrophy in adults, called myotonic dystrophy Type 2, was discovered.

- In 2005, memory loss was reversed in mice with Alzheimer's-type symptoms for the first time.

- Fifty-six varieties of soybeans have been developed by the University of Minnesota since 1922.

Tallgrass Prairies

When the pioneers of Minnesota first saw the eighteen million acres of big bluestem and Indian Grass waving and shivering in the wind, they were mesmerized. Now, about two hundred years later, virgin tallgrass prairie is the rarest of all major North American biomes. Minnesota has less than one percent of its tallgrass prairies left.

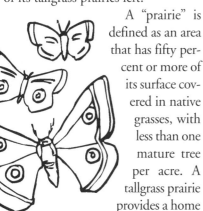

A "prairie" is defined as an area that has fifty percent or more of its surface covered in native grasses, with less than one mature tree per acre. A tallgrass prairie provides a home for rare birds, such as prairie chickens, chestnut-collared longspurs, marbled godwits, and Sprague's pipits. Three hundred or more species of flowers and grasses draw rare butterflies.

A true prairie is also made of herds of buffalo and bouts of fire. Fire converts grasses into readily available nutrients and stops the spread of shrubs and trees, which constantly threaten to take over and thus end the prairie. With their grazing, buffalo reduce the buildup of dead grasses.

The Minnesota Department of Natural Resources and the Minnesota Nature Conservancy are dedicated to preserving what's left of the state's prairie lands and bringing back what they can. Once, pioneering Minnesotans worked to renovate prairie lands into farmland. Today, their descendants are working to restore them.

What's in a Name? *Foods in the Supreme Court*

Former Chief Justice of the United States Supreme Court Warren Earl Burger was born in St. Paul on September 17, 1907. Burger was one of seven children born to parents of Swiss-German descent. He grew up on the family farm at the edge of St. Paul and attended John A. Johnson High School, where he was president of the student council. He graduated from St. Paul College of Law (now known as the William Mitchell College of Law) in 1931. He was an assistant U.S. attorney general from 1953 to 1956 and then served as judge of the United States Court of Appeals for the District of Columbia until he became chief justice.

In 1925, the year he graduated from high school, Burger worked in St. Paul with a crew building the Robert Street Bridge over the Mississippi River. Concerned about the number of deaths on the project, he requested that a net be installed to catch anyone who fell. The manager of the project rebuffed him. In later years, Burger made a point of visiting the bridge whenever he came back to town.

Although early in his career on the U.S. Supreme Court (1969–1986) he joined a number of decisions that the court of his predecessor, liberal Chief Justice Earl Warren, had made, Burger's court took a much more conservative turn in later years.

In 1971, for example, he wrote the unanimous decision supporting school busing to end "all vestiges of state-imposed segregation." And in the most controversial ruling of his term, Roe vs. Wade (1973), Burger voted with the majority to recognize a broad right to privacy that prohibited states from banning all abortions. In later years, however, the Burger Court allowed local governments to become more fully involved in supporting religious activities and it upheld the use of capital punishment.

Warren Burger died in 1995. He is one of three Supreme Court justices to share a first or last name with a food item (the other two are Felix Frankfurter and Salmon P. Chase), a fact that was once featured on two TV programs: a segment of *The Tonight Show* and in an episode of *The Simpsons.*

Goat Prairies

The magnificent Mississippi River Valley, between Red Wing and Winona, is characterized by towering bluffs that are home to several varieties of vegetation found nowhere else but here in southeastern Minnesota.

Known as "goat prairies," these variants of tallgrass prairies are seen on south-southwest-facing slopes. The special prairie grass that grows here absorbs the considerable winter sun like a solar collector, yet can withstand strong freezes at night.

The term "goat prairie" refers to the steep angle of the slopes "that only a goat could graze."

September Recipe

Minnesota Honeycrisp Apple Praline Cake

The Minnesota state fruit is the Honeycrisp apple, which was produced from a cross of a Macoun and a Honeygold apple as part of the University of Minnesota's 1960 breeding program. The goal was to create an apple that could withstand harsh winters without losing its quality.

The skin of a Honeycrisp is mostly red with a yellow background, while the surface has shallow dimples and dots. The flesh is coarse and cream-colored, and the taste ranges from mild to strongly aromatic. The Honeycrisp is a great eating and baking apple; try yours in the recipe below.

Minnesota Honeycrisp Apple Praline Cake

Cake
3 cups all-purpose flour
$2^1/_4$ cups granulated sugar, divided use
1 tablespoon baking powder
$^1/_2$ teaspoon salt
4 large eggs, beaten
1 cup vegetable oil

$^1/_2$ cup orange juice
$2^1/_2$ teaspoons vanilla extract
7 medium Honeycrisp baking apples, peeled and chopped
2 teaspoons ground cinnamon
18-ounce package cream cheese

Topping
$^1/_2$ cup butter or margarine
$^3/_4$ cup packed brown sugar

$^1/_3$ cup whipping cream
$1^1/_2$ cups chopped pecans

Preheat oven to 350°F. Grease and flour a ten-inch tube pan. To make the cake, combine the flour, 2 cups of the granulated sugar, the baking powder, and the salt in a mixing bowl. Set the flour mixture aside.

In a second bowl, combine the beaten eggs, oil, orange juice, and vanilla. Pour this egg mixture into flour mixture and mix well, but just until combined, with an electric mixer. Do not overmix.

In a third bowl, toss the chopped apples, cinnamon, and remaining $^1/_4$ cup of granulated sugar. Separately, cube the cream cheese and divide into thirds.

Spread $^1/_3$ of the batter in a prepared tube pan. Sprinkle with $^1/_3$ of the apples and $^1/_3$ of the cream cheese. Repeat until all the batter, apples, and cream cheese are used; a layer of apples and cream cheese should be on top, not covered by batter. Bake fifty to fifty-five minutes, at which point the cake will be not quite done.

While the cake is baking, make the topping. Place the butter, brown sugar, whipping cream, and pecans in a small saucepan. Stirring constantly, bring the mixture to a boil. Remove the mixture from the heat and pour over the almost-done cake. Bake five to ten minutes more until a wooden toothpick or skewer inserted in the cake comes out clean. Cool cake in the pan fifteen to twenty minutes; then remove from the pan and cool on a wire rack.

Printed with permission from Minnesota.gov

SEPTEMBER WEATHER

September Normals for Duluth

Day	High	Low	Mean	Precip.	Snowfall
1	70	50	60	0.14	0
2	69	49	59	0.15	0
3	69	49	59	0.15	0
4	68	49	59	0.15	0
5	68	48	58	0.15	0
6	68	48	58	0.15	0
7	67	48	58	0.15	0
8	67	47	57	0.15	0
9	67	47	57	0.15	0
10	66	47	57	0.15	0
11	66	46	56	0.15	0
12	66	46	56	0.15	0
13	65	46	55	0.14	0
14	65	45	55	0.14	0
15	65	45	55	0.14	0
16	64	45	54	0.14	0
17	64	44	54	0.14	0
18	64	44	54	0.14	0
19	63	44	53	0.14	0
20	63	43	53	0.14	0
21	63	43	53	0.13	0
22	62	43	52	0.13	0
23	62	42	52	0.13	0
24	62	42	52	0.13	0
25	61	42	52	0.12	0
26	61	41	51	0.12	0
27	61	41	51	0.12	0
28	60	41	51	0.12	0
29	60	40	50	0.11	Trace Amt.
30	59	40	50	0.11	0.1

"September blow soft till the fruit's in the loft."

— PROVERB

SEPTEMBER WEATHER

September Normals for International Falls

Day	High	Low	Mean	Precip.	Snowfall
1	71	47	59	0.11	0
2	70	46	58	0.11	0
3	70	46	58	0.11	0
4	69	46	58	0.11	0
5	69	45	57	0.11	0
6	69	45	57	0.11	0
7	68	44	56	0.11	0
8	68	44	56	0.11	0
9	67	44	56	0.11	0
10	67	43	55	0.11	0
11	66	43	55	0.11	0
12	66	43	54	0.1	0
13	66	42	54	0.1	0
14	65	42	54	0.1	0
15	65	42	53	0.1	0
16	64	41	53	0.1	0
17	64	41	53	0.1	0
18	64	41	52	0.1	0
19	63	40	52	0.1	0
20	63	40	51	0.1	0
21	62	40	51	0.1	0
22	62	39	51	0.1	0
23	62	39	50	0.1	0
24	61	39	50	0.09	0
25	61	38	50	0.09	0
26	61	38	49	0.09	0
27	60	38	49	0.09	0
28	60	38	49	0.09	0
29	59	37	48	0.09	0
30	59	37	48	0.08	0.1

Source: National Oceanic and Atmospheric Administration (NOAA)'s National Weather Service

These climate normals are an average of thirty years of data between 1971 and 2000. Every ten years, the National Weather Service recalculates the normals using the next interval of thirty years. In 2010, the new normals will be recalculated using the period of 1981 to 2010.

SEPTEMBER WEATHER HISTORY

On This Day in September

Day	Year	Weather
1	1894	"The Great Hinckley Fire." Drought conditions are responsible for a massive fire that starts near Mille Lacs and spreads to the east. Smoke from the fires brings shipping on Lake Superior to a standstill.
2	1937	Severe thunderstorms over northern Minnesota, with 4.61 inches of rain dumped on Pokegama. Flooding reported in Duluth.
3	1970	The record-setting hailstone falls, making Coffeyville famous. It had a circumference of 17.5 inches and weighed 1.67 pounds.
4	1941	A late batch of tornadoes hits Minneapolis, New Brighton, and White Bear Lake, killing six people.
5	1990	Nine inches of rain fall over the next two days in Duluth, washing out a million dollars worth in roads.
6	1922	Heat wave over Minnesota with highs over 100 in southwest Minnesota. One of the hot spots is New Ulm, with 105 degrees.
7	1986	A touch of winter over the north, with 20 degrees at Embarrass and 30 at Duluth.
8	1900	The most deadly hurricane in U.S. history hits Galveston, Texas. Almost six thousand people die. This same storm brings heavy rain to southeast Minnesota days later.
9	1917	Very chilly air, with 17 degrees at Roseau.
10	1910	Duluth has the shortest growing season ever with frost-free days from June 14 to September 10 (87 days). Normally, the frost-free season is 143 days.
11	1900	The soggy remains of the Galveston Hurricane brings 6.65 inches of rain to St. Paul over two days.
12	1869	A hailstorm breaks windows and causes considerable damage to late vegetables at Madilia in Watonwan County.
13	1834	Smoky skies at Ft. Snelling due to fires burning nearby.
14	2099	The next total solar eclipse will be visible in the Twin Cites, depending on the weather.
15	1916	St. Paul's earliest snow ever.
16	1992	New Market hit with nearly a foot of rain. A bridge collapses from floodwater in northern Le Sueur County.
17	1911	Pipestone is hit with baseball-sized hail that smashes numerous windows at the Calumet Hotel and high school. One local observer measures hail three inches deep.
18	1991	Duluth gets a 2.5-inch summer snowstorm, with fall still five days away.
19	1980	Golf-ball-size to baseball-size hail hits St. Paul. One company has 75 to 95 percent of the glass in their greenhouses smashed.
20	1972	Downpour in Duluth, with 5.5 inches in ten hours.
21	1924	Windstorm with a peak gust of 64 mph in Duluth.
22	1936	Summerlike heat continues with 101 at Ada, Beardsley, and Moorhead.
23	1937	From summer to winter. The temperature begins at 101 in Wheaton, and tumbles to below freezing as the cold front passes through.

SEPTEMBER WEATHER HISTORY

On This Day in September

Day	Year	Weather
24	1869	Heavy rain dumps nearly 10 inches on the White Earth Reservation.
25	1929	Willmar experiences a deluge that drops 5.22 inches of rain in 24 hours.
26	1980	Cold morning across the state, with a low of 20 degrees at Tower and 16 at Embarrass.
27	1898	Heat wave with 91 degrees at Beardsley and 90 at Moorhead.
28	1983	Late summer with 91 degrees at Montevideo and 90 degrees at Elbow Lake.
29	1876	Cold day over the region with a high of 45 in the Twin Cities (normally the high should be 65).
30	1985	Four inches of snow fall in Ely, with just a trace at the Twin Cities.

Source: Minnesota State Climatology Office: DNR Waters

Sighting Hawks at Hawk Ridge

What may be the best autumn hawk-watching in North America occurs at Duluth's Hawk Ridge Nature Reserve. From mid-August through November, a seasonal average of over ninety-four thousand raptors migrate past Hawk Ridge. The "big days" for hawk watching generally run from September 10 to September 25. The record number of raptors counted in one day at Hawk Ridge was 102,321 on September 15, 2003.

MARK YOUR CALENDAR

Mark Your SEPTEMBER CALENDAR

Western Minnesota Steam Threshers Reunion, Rollag
www.rollag.com

Hay Days Grass Drags, Forest Lake
www.snobarons.com/haydays

Defeat of Jesse James Days, Northfield
www.defeatofjessejamesdays.org

King Turkey Day and The Great Gobbler Gallop, Worthington
www.kingturkeyday.com

Dozinky, a Czech Fall Harvest Festival, New Prague www.newprague.com

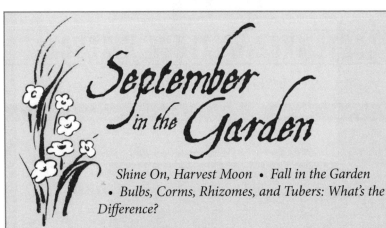

September in the Garden

Shine On, Harvest Moon • Fall in the Garden
• Bulbs, Corms, Rhizomes, and Tubers: What's the
Difference?

Shine On, Harvest Moon

In the Midwest, during the full moon phase nearest to the autumnal equinox, there are several days when the moon rises soon after sunset. This yearly phenomenon gives gardeners and farmers extra daylight hours in which they can complete harvesting.

Fall in the Garden

A snowfall, a thunderstorm, a heat wave. They are all typical of a Midwest fall. Despite the weather or the calendar, there's one sure sign that the season has truly arrived: the leaves begin to show their first hints of oranges, reds, and yellows. Here are some things to do to keep your garden enjoyable and lively until winter sets in:

- Sow meadows and prairies with wildflower seeds.
- Hardy bulbs can be planted until the ground is frozen. Mulch heavily until February.
- Seed bare spots in lawn.
- Plant trees and shrubs.
- Wrap or set up barriers around young tree trunks to protect them from rabbits and deer (see "Protecting Trees and Shrubs from Rodents in Winter," November chapter).
- Shield evergreens with burlap to prevent winter sunburn (see "Winter Burn," February chapter).
- Mix shredded leaves with grass clippings to mulch around flowers. Mulch up to the plant crowns—where the roots meet the stems—but not over the top of the crown.
- Save a bag of shredded leaves for touching up mulch in February.
- Put high-energy foods like suet and peanut butter in bird feeders and watch for unusual birds as they drop in for some quick refreshment on their way south (see "Peanut Butter Suet Cookies," December chapter).
- Take note of the wildlife changing into their winter coats.

Bulbs, Corms, Rhizomes, and Tubers: What's the Difference?

"Bulb" is a generic term for most spring-blooming and summer-blooming flowers that are planted in the fall. What many call "bulb" flowers are not produced from bulbs at all: crocuses grow from corms, irises grow from rhizomes, and dahlias grow from tubers. Whichever term is used, however, all four are underground storage units containing large amounts of carbohydrates.

Here are some other distinguishing traits:

- **Bulb:** generally teardrop-shaped, with a pointed top and a round bottom. The outer skin is paperlike and dark brown. Bulbs are layered like an artichoke; onions, lilies, tulips, and narcissus are true bulbs.

- **Corm:** thick, underground, enlarged stems that produce new roots, leaves, and flowers during each growing season. The bulb of a corm is shorter and rounder than that on true bulbs, with a concave bottom and a flat top. The outer skin is hard and brown. It does not separate easily from the rest of the bulb. Anemones, crocuses, and gladioli are three such plants.

- **Rhizome:** plants with a rootlike stem. They grow horizontally under the surface of the soil. They send up leaves and flowers at intervals. Irises and some lawn grasses are rhizomatous plants.

- **Tuber:** this term is applied to any plant with underground storage parts that does not fit the above categories. Tubers are similar to rhizomes, except they are true roots. Common tubers include potatoes and dahlias.

Versatility, Plus!

On September 22, 1968, Minnesota Twins baseball player Cesar Tovar played all nine positions against the Oakland A's. He was the second player ever to do so: Bert Campaneris of the Kansas City A's was the first in 1965. The Twins won the game 2–1.

"Autumn arrives, array'd

in splendid mein;

Vines, cluster'd full,

add to the beauteous scene,

And fruit-trees cloth'd

profusely laden, nod,

Complaint bowing to the fertile sod."

— *FARMER'S ALMANAC* (1818)

September Household Tips

The timber rattlesnake and the massasauga rattlesnake are the only two types of poisonous snakes in Minnesota (see "Minnesota's Amphibians and Reptiles," August chapter). But you should take precautions to avoid any snake bite; and if you are bitten, treat it seriously until you know for certain whether or not you have been injected with venom. Here are some general tips on how to recognize poisonous snakes and how to treat snakebite.

Identifying Poisonous and Nonpoisonous Snakes

Most of the poisonous snakes in North America are pit vipers. They include rattlesnakes, cottonmouths, and copperheads. Poisonous snakes can usually be identified by their arrow-shaped, flat heads. A rattlesnake, of course, has the famous rattle at the tip of the tail.

The coral snake is the deadliest snake in the United States. It has wide bands of red and black separated by narrow rings of bright yellow encircling its body. (Keep this rhyme in mind: "Red touches yellow, you're a dead fellow; red touches black, it's a friendly Jack.") Coral snakes have blunt heads, black snouts, and round eyes; and they do have nonvenomous imitators. Here are some tips for telling the two types of snakes apart:

- Nonvenomous snakes usually have a spoon-shaped, round head with round pupils.
- Nonvenomous snakes usually have only one color.
- If the snake has stripes all the way from its head to its tail, it's probably a nonvenomous snake.
- Venomous snakes have a small depression between the eye and the nostril called a "pit," which is used to sense heat in their prey.
- All venomous snakes in the U.S. (except for the coral snake) have an elliptical pupil (like a cat's eye). The pupil looks like a small slit in the middle of the eye.
- Venomous rattlesnakes have a rattle on their tails, but some nonvenomous snakes will also rattle their tails. They lack the typical "rattle" sound, however.

Be sure to familiarize yourself with what the snakes in your area look like. A search on the Internet is a good way to learn about them. If you know you'll be in an area with snakes, wear boots, thick socks, and heavy slacks, and don't put your hands and feet in positions where you cannot see them—many climbers have been bitten that way.

As with all animals, treat snakes with respect. Do not harass them or try to get too close. Most snakes would prefer to avoid you.

How to Treat a Snake Bite

- Get the victim and yourself away from the snake so no one is bitten again.
- Keep the victim calm and still, either sitting or lying down.
- Elevate the site of the bite at or below the level of the heart.
- Remove all constricting clothing, bracelets, and rings close to the bite.
- Wash with warm water and soap (or run water over the bite).
- Immobilize the bitten area by splinting it. To splint, secure the injured part to a firm object. The ends of the splint should extend beyond the injured area, to immobilize the joints above and below the injury.
- Keep the victim well hydrated, but do not offer any alcoholic beverages.
- Call the emergency medical service (EMS) or get the victim to a hospital immediately.
- If you think that it may be a couple of hours before you can get to professional medical help, wrap a band of cloth two inches above (or closer to the heart than) the fang mark, or two inches above the swelling if it has begun. Do not make the band tight; you should be able to slip one finger between it and the skin. If the flesh swells, keep moving the band so that it stays two inches above the swelling. If there is no swelling, loosen and retighten the band every fifteen to thirty minutes.
- Remember: never cut into the wound or try to suck the venom out. Piercing the wound may cause infection.

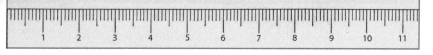

Metric Football First—and Last?

Two Northfield colleges share a "nation's-only" claim to fame. On September 17, 1977, St. Olaf College beat Carleton College 43–0 in the only NCAA-sanctioned metric football game in history. In "metric football," all field measurements are—you guessed it—metric.

OCTOBER

"There is no season

when such pleasant and sunny spots

may be lighted on,

and produce so pleasant an effect

on the feelings,

as now in October."

— NATHANIEL HAWTHORNE

The month of October certainly has its fans. The peaking colors of the trees and the sense that it will not last long seems to bring out an appreciation for art in everyone. Poet Edna St. Vincent Millay once wrote that the autumn trees "ache and sag and all but cry with color. They bend and blow and burn against an October sky."

Nature does put on quite the show this month, and state residents do enjoy the theater of it all. The Minnesota Department of Natural Resources faithfully makes weekly updates on where to get the best seat for the season's colors.

But there are other works of art concurrently being exhibited in the state, too, natural and otherwise: the Jeffers Petroglyphs carved into ancient rocks are a national treasure, the state's theatrical tradition is world-renowned, and tall tales about a certain colossal lumberjack make the very young to the very old smile.

Now, sit back and enjoy the show.

An Evening at the Theater

- Founded in 1914, the **Duluth Playhouse** is one of the oldest community theaters in the United States.

- Minnesota's oldest professional theater is the **Old Log Theatre** in Excelsior, Minnesota, which first opened its doors in 1940.

- Bucking the standard Broadway model, Sir (William) Tyrone Guthrie wanted a playhouse that would thrust the stage into the audience, enabling actors and theatergoers to interact. He also wanted to establish a repertory theater where a group of actors could master a series of plays—from Greek classics to modern drama—without the need for smash hits to survive. In May 1960, Guthrie, fellow producer Oliver Rea, and director Peter Zeisler selected Minneapolis as the site for their new endeavor. The **Guthrie Theater** opened in 1963 with a production of *Hamlet* directed by Guthrie himself.

Average Precipitation and High and Low Temperatures in October

Place	Avg. Precip. (Inches)	Avg. High Temp.	Avg. Low Temp.
Bemidji	1.9	66	44
Duluth	2.4	53	35
Int'l Falls	1.9	52	32
Minneapolis	1.9	60	40
Moorhead	1.5	58	35
Rochester	2.1	60	38
St. Cloud	2.0	58	36
Windom	1.4	61	37

Source: Minnesota State Climatology Office: DNR Waters

Paul Bunyan Tall Tales

It may come as a shock to some Minnesotans who like their legends to be grassroots and living, but Paul Bunyan did not come from the minds of lonely lumberjacks. He was born out of the imaginations of a journalist and an ad man. On July 24, 1910, James McGillivray wrote a story for the *Detroit News-Tribune* about a lumberjack of immense proportions and strength. Then in 1914, when a man named W. B. Laughead was given the job of developing an advertising campaign for the Red River Lumber Company, he happened to remember the story of the huge lumberjack. He wrote his copy around big Paul Bunyan. The campaign was so popular that the company had to publish a promotional booklet describing Paul's adventures. By the 1920s, the legendary Paul Bunyan and his blue pet ox, Babe, were the subjects of books, articles, and short stories.

Today, Brainerd calls itself the "Home of Paul Bunyan and Babe, the Blue Ox;" and in downtown Bemidji, a 1937 statue of Paul stands eighteen feet tall and weighs more than two tons. You can even watch the "Paul and Babe Web cam" on the Bemidji Area Chamber of Commerce Web page.

While other states tell of their own Paul Bunyan escapades, certainly Minnesota has claimed Paul Bunyan as its very own. Here are just a few Minnesota tall tales of the big man:

- Paul Bunyan was born on the shores of Lake Bemidji. Five storks were needed to deliver the baby giant, and a herd of cows worked around the clock to feed him.

- When baby Paul tossed in his crib, he knocked down four square miles of standing Minnesota timber.

- By the time he was a year old, Paul had to use wagon wheels for buttons.

- Not only did Paul grow fast, but Babe grew so fast that wherever she stepped, a lake was formed. That's why Bemidji has hundreds of "footprint" lakes.

- Babe became so big that she measured forty-two ax handles between the eyes. The Great Lakes were scooped out to provide drinking water for her, and she "snacked" on thirty bales of hay.

- Babe helped form the Mississippi. When a huge tank wagon she was towing sprung a leak, the rushing water formed Lakes Bemidji and Itasca, while the overflow trickled down to New Orleans to form the Mississippi River.

- The Pequot Lakes water tower seems to resemble a large fishing bobber. That's because it belonged to Paul Bunyan, who lost the bobber during a fight with a forty-foot northern pike.

The County Line

The state of Minnesota has 87 counties. Cook County extends the farthest east and is composed of about 91 percent government land. Mahnomen County takes its name from the Ojibwa word meaning "wild rice." Here are some more county facts:

- **Largest by population:** Hennepin, population 1,116,200
- **Smallest by population:** Cook, population 5,168

- **Largest by area:** St. Louis, 6,225 square miles
- **Smallest by area:** Ramsey, 155 square miles
- **First county established:** nine counties were established by the territorial legislature on October 27, 1849. Only Benton, Dakota, Itasca, Ramsey, Wabasha, and Washington remain.
- **Last county established:** Lake of the Woods, in 1922

County	Population	Square Miles	County Seat	Founded
Aitkin	15,301	1,819	Aitkin	1857
Anoka	298,084	424	Anoka	1857
Becker	30,000	1,310	Detroit Lakes	1858
Beltrami	39,650	2,505	Bemidji	1866
Benton	34,226	408	Foley	1849
Big Stone	5,820	497	Ortonville	1862
Blue Earth	55,941	752	Mankato	1853
Brown	26,911	611	New Ulm	1855
Carlton	31,671	860	Carlton	1857
Carver	70,205	357	Chaska	1855
Cass	27,150	2,018	Walker	1851
Chippewa	13,088	583	Montevideo	1870
Chisago	41,101	418	Center City	1851
Clay	51,229	1,045	Moorhead	1862
Clearwater	8,423	995	Bagley	1902
Cook	5,168	1,451	Grand Marais	1874
Cottonwood	12,167	640	Windom	1857
Crow Wing	55,099	997	Brainerd	1857
Dakota	355,904	570	Hastings	1849
Dodge	17,731	440	Mantorville	1855
Douglas	32,821	634	Alexandria	1858
Faribault	16,181	714	Blue Earth	1855
Fillmore	21,122	861	Preston	1853
Freeborn	32,584	708	Albert Lea	1855
Goodhue	44,127	759	Red Wing	1853
Grant	6,289	546	Elbow Lake	1868
Hennepin	1,116,200	557	Minneapolis	1852
Houston	19,718	558	Caledonia	1854
Hubbard	18,376	923	Park Rapids	1883
Isanti	31,287	439	Cambridge	1857
Itasca	43,992	2,665	Grand Rapids	1850
Jackson	11,268	702	Jackson	1857

County	Population	Square Miles	County Seat	Founded
Kanabec	14,996	525	Mora	1858
Kandiyohi	41,203	796	Willmar	1858
Kittson	5,285	1,097	Hallock	1879
Koochiching	14,355	3,102	International Falls	1906
Lac Qui Parle	8,067	765	Madison	1863
Lake County	11,058	2,099	Two Harbors	1856
Lake of the Woods	4,522	1,297	Baudette	1923
Le Sueur	25,426	448	Le Center	1853
Lincoln	6,429	537	Ivanhoe	1873
Lyon	25,425	714	Marshall	1871
Mahnomen	5,190	556	Mahnomen	1906
Marshall	10,155	1,772	Warren	1879
Martin	21,802	709	Fairmont	1857
McLeod	34,898	492	Glencoe	1856
Meeker	22,644	609	Litchfield	1856
Mille Lacs	22,330	574	Milaca	1857
Morrison	31,712	1,124	Little Falls	1856
Mower	38,603	712	Austin	1855
Murray	9,165	704	Slayton	1875
Nicollet	29,771	452	Saint Peter	1853
Nobles	20,832	716	Worthington	1857
Norman	7,442	876	Ada	1881
Olmsted	124,277	653	Rochester	1855
Otter Tail	57,159	1,980	Fergus Falls	1858
Pennington	13,584	617	Thief River Falls	1910
Pine	26,530	1,411	Pine City	1856
Pipestone	9,895	466	Pipestone	1857
Polk	31,369	1,970	Crookston	1858
Pope	11,236	670	Glenwood	1862
Ramsey	511,035	155	Saint Paul	1849
Red Lake	4,299	432	Red Lake Falls	1896
Redwood	16,815	880	Redwood Falls	1862
Renville	17,154	983	Olivia	1855
Rice	56,665	498	Faribault	1853
Rock	9,721	483	Luverne	1857
Roseau	16,338	1,663	Roseau	1894
Scott	89,498	357	Shakopee	1853
Sherburne	64,417	437	Elk River	1856
Sibley	15,356	589	Gaylord	1853
St. Louis	200,528	6,225	Duluth	1855
Stearns	133,166	1,345	Saint Cloud	1855
Steele	33,680	430	Owatonna	1855
Stevens	10,053	562	Morris	1862
Swift	11,956	744	Benson	1870
Todd	24,426	942	Long Prairie	1855
Traverse	4,134	574	Wheaton	1862
Wabasha	21,610	525	Wabasha	1849
Wadena	13,713	536	Wadena	1858
Waseca	19,526	423	Waseca	1857
Washington	201,130	392	Stillwater	1849
Watonwan	11,876	434	Saint James	1860
Wilkin	7,138	752	Breckenridge	1858
Winona	49,985	626	Winona	1854
Wright	89,986	661	Buffalo	1855
Yellow Medicine	11,080	758	Granite Falls	1871

Source: the 2000 United States Census

It's Cereal

Puffed Wheat was the invention of Minnesota scientist Alexander Anderson. In 1902, he created a steam-injected drum that would explode whole-grain kernels under high pressure. This swelling enhanced their nutritional value and rendered them more readily digestible. His "puffing canon" gave rise to Puffed Wheat's "shot from guns to give you trigger-fast food energy" ad campaign, which was rated one of the Top 100 of the twentieth century by *Advertising Age* magazine. But Anderson has yet another claim to fame. According to a Minnesota Public Radio interview with his grandson, Robert Hedin, Alexander Anderson was the young man who gave directions to the Jesse James gang about how to get to Northfield, Minnesota (see "The Outlaw Jesse James," September chapter).

Wheaties was born in 1924 when a Minneapolis health clinician accidentally spilled some wheat bran mixture on a hot stove, creating "wheat flakes" that were tasty. The association between Wheaties and sports began in 1933, when the cereal first sponsored Minneapolis Millers minor league baseball broadcasts on radio station WCCO. A sign on the left-field wall at old Nicollet Park in south Minneapolis read, "Wheaties, The Breakfast of Champions," after the phrase had been coined by Minneapolis ad man Knox Reeves.

"Cheerioats" (later Cheerios) debuted on June 19, 1941. The cereal was created by General Mills in Golden Valley, Minnesota. It claimed to be "the first oat-based, ready-to-eat, cold cereal."

The Cloquet Fire *The Worst in Minnesota History*

On October 12, 1918, the worst natural disaster in Minnesota history occurred, in terms of lives lost in a single day.

Since 1916, northern Minnesota had seen relentless drought conditions, and the summer of 1918 was very hot and dry. The slash of past logging, the brush from second-growth forests, and sparks from passing trains had transformed the region into a tinderbox.

Approximately seventy-five separate fires, driven by sixty-mph winds, merged and destroyed an area forty miles long and twenty miles wide. Two thousand square miles of timberland north of Duluth were consumed. Cloquet lost its entire residential and business districts. As it rebuilt, Cloquet called itself the "Modern Phoenix."

A separate Moose Lake-Kettle River fire destroyed an area thirty-one miles long and fourteen miles wide. In total, 453 lives were lost, 52,000 people were injured or displaced, 38 communities were leveled, 250,000 acres were burned, and $7.3 million in property damage was suffered.

Leave the Driving to Us

When Frank Hibbing discovered iron ore in the Mesabi Iron Range in 1893, he settled a town right over the mineral-rich spot. But by 1910, with the mining operation now surrounding the town, it became clear that it would have to be moved so that the ore deposits beneath it could be accessed.

Two men in the area, Carl Wickman and Andrew Anderson, owned a Hupmobile, which they had purchased hoping to start a dealership. But as Hibbing was being moved about a mile to the south to a small village known as Alice, the two began making a profit from carrying miners between the two towns, for 15 cents a ride. With their new transportation business going well, Wickman and Anderson left behind the car dealership idea and merged with an in-town taxi service to form the Mesaba Transportation Company. Wickman then ordered a vehicle especially made to carry multiple people—quite possibly the world's first bus.

In the 1920s, a company in Oakland, California, started manufacturing a "safety coach" —also known as a "Grey-hound"— with seven rows of seats each holding four people. Wickman bought and acquired numerous smaller bus lines, and in 1930, he organized his holdings under "The Greyhound Corporation."

The Wild and Scenic St. Croix River

On October 2, 1968, President Lyndon Johnson signed into law the Wild and Scenic Rivers Act, which recognizes the importance of free-flowing waters and seeks to protect them for future generations.

The Upper St. Croix—and its major tributary, the Namekagon—was among the first eight rivers in the country to be protected under the act. The Lower St. Croix was added in 1972. Together, the two portions of this National Scenic Riverway provide 227 miles of clean water on which to canoe, fish, and camp.

St. Croix (Upper) River: Designation: October 2, 1968. The segment between the dam near Taylors Falls, Minnesota, and the dam near Gordon, Wisconsin, is preserved. This includes the Namekagon River from Lake Namekagon downstream to its confluence with the St. Croix River.

Classification/Mileage:

Scenic — 181.0 miles

Recreational — 19.0 miles

Total — 200.0 miles

St. Croix (Lower) River: Designation: October 25, 1972. The segment from the dam near Taylors Falls, Minnesota, downstream 27 miles, is preserved.

Classification/Mileage:

Scenic — 12.0 miles

Recreational — 15.0 miles

Total — 27.0 miles.

According to the National Park Service of the U.S. Department of the Interior, winged maple leaf mussels were thought to be extinct until some were rediscovered in the St. Croix River in 1987. To help prevent future extinction, scientists are now helping to raise the young mussels and are reintroducing them into their former range, which includes the St. Croix National Scenic Riverway.

Halfback Joe Guyon

Born in Mahnomen, Minnesota, in 1892 at the White Earth Indian Reservation, Joseph Napoleon Guyon was a full-blooded Chippewa. He attended Carlisle Indian School and then took Georgia Tech to the National College Championship in 1917.

He played professional football with the Canton Bulldogs, Cleveland Indians, Oorang Indians, Rock Island Independents, Kansas City Cowboys, and New York Giants.

For most of his career, Joe Guyon was overshadowed by another outstanding Native American halfback, Jim Thorpe. Both were talented athletes, but the better-known Thorpe received most of the headlines. Guyon once said, "It was hard trying to make something of yourself. Sports were one of the few ways a youngster could pull himself up."

Joe Guyon was inducted into the Pro Football Hall of Fame in 1966.

Football Hero

Called the "greatest football player of the first half of the twentieth century," Bronislau "Bronko" Nagurski, it is said, usually just closed his eyes and charged. Born on November 3, 1908, in Rainy River, Ontario, Canada, Nagurski played high school football in International Falls and Bemidji. In 1927, he moved on to play with the University of Minnesota Gophers, where he was an All-American tackle and fullback.

Nagurski turned professional when he joined the Chicago Bears in 1930, staying with the organization until 1937. His often flawless blocking helped the Bears achieve the first perfect record in NFL history in 1934 (13–0). He could play equally well in the positions of end, tackle, and fullback. He was the first person inducted into both the College Football Hall of Fame and the Professional Football Hall of Fame.

Bronko didn't just play football. He was named to the Minnesota Sports Hall of Fame for wrestling, a sport in which he participated from 1935 until 1958. He became a three-time world heavyweight champion. In 1941, the International Falls high school chose the nickname "Broncos" for their sports teams in honor of Nagurski.

Sports Illustrated named Nagurski one of the three greatest athletes in Minnesota history (the other two were Dave Winfield and Kevin McHale). Bronko Nagurski died in International Falls on January 7, 1990.

In 1993, the Football Writers Association of America created the annual Bronko Nagurski Trophy, an award for the best defensive player in college football. And after his death, International Falls opened the Bronko Nagurski Museum in Smokey Bear Park. It is the only museum dedicated to a single football player.

History of Pro Football Teams in Minnesota

Minneapolis
Minnesota Vikings, 1961–present (NFL)

Duluth
Kelleys, 1923–25 (NFL)
Eskimos, 1926–27 (NFL)

Twin Cities
Minneapolis Marines, 1921–24 (NFL)
Minneapolis Red Jackets, 1929–30 (NFL)

"Delicious autumn!

My very soul is wedded to it,

and if I were a bird

I would fly about the earth

seeking the successive autumns."

— GEORGE ELIOT

If You Want Your Little Brown Jug, *You'll Have to Win It*

The Little Brown Jug trophy is awarded to the winner of each college football game between Minnesota and Michigan. It is the second oldest trophy in college football history (the oldest is the Territorial Cup, fought for by the Arizona State University Sun Devils and the University of Arizona Wildcats).

On October 31, 1903, the Michigan Wolverines came to Minnesota to play the Gophers. The Wolverines' student manager was instructed to purchase something in which to carry water. The manager bought a five-gallon jug for thirty cents from a local store.

On Northrup Field in front of twenty thousand fans, the teams were tied 6–6 late in the second half. But as snowstorm clouds gathered overhead, Minnesota fans stormed the field in celebration. The game had to be called with two minutes remaining. The Wolverines walked off the field, leaving the jug behind.

The next day, Minnesota's custodian Oscar Munson found the jug. He took it to the head of the Minnesota athletics department, L. J. Cooke. They painted the jug brown and wrote on the side of it "Michigan Jug—Captured by Oscar, October 31, 1903" and "Michigan 6, Minnesota 6." Of course, the Minnesota "6" was written much larger than the Michigan "6."

When Michigan coach Fielding Yost wrote a letter asking for the jug back, Cooke wrote in response: "We have your little brown jug; if you want it, you'll have to win it."

The two teams have fought for possession of the Little Brown Jug every year since.

The Northernmost Point Is the Northwest Angle

Sitting amid low-lying spruce forests along the Canadian border is the Northwest Angle, a jut of land that extends into Lake of the Woods. It is the northernmost point of Minnesota, as well as the northernmost point of land in the contiguous United States. It is located across the lake, connected to the Canadian province of Manitoba. It is one of two places in the lower forty-eight that you can drive to only by way of a foreign country.

The Red Lake Indian Reservation owns the boggy interior of the Northwest Angle. And Lake of the Woods itself is an amazing expanse of water: it covers nearly one million acres; it is ninety miles long and fifty-five miles wide. The lake has sixty-five thousand miles of shoreline and contains fourteen thousand islands.

Jeffers Petroglyphs

Unlike the early rock paintings that have been found around the world, Minnesota possesses pictures that are carved into the rock instead of painted on it.

Near Jeffers, rising out of the prairie, is a dome of lichen-encrusted quartzite that has been exposed for thousands of years. Throughout that time, various Paleo-Indian groups have chiseled nearly two thousand pictures into the rock. Dating from 1750 A.D. back to 3,000 B.C., each of the pictures was pecked into the hard surface with a pointed rock and a hammerstone.

These prehistoric carvings, or "petroglyphs," depict animals such as bison, bears, wolves, turtles, and elk, as well as thunderbirds, atlatls, and arrows. Human forms, sometimes wearing horned headdresses, imply that some of the petroglyphs held a spiritual significance. Others are simple geometric designs, handprints, or footprints.

The Jeffers Petroglyphs Historic Site is a holy place for the Native Americans who come to visit and pray. The site's staff works to make sure that the petroglyphs are treated with respect and reverence. The site was added to the National Register of Historic Places in 1970.

October Recipe
Salmon Fillets with Morel Mushrooms

This month, combine salmon fillets from the fall run with the state mushroom, and you've got a tasty dinner to warm up a cool night.

Salmon Fillets with Morel Mushrooms

3 tablespoons butter
5 shallots, minced
18 ounces morels, trimmed, cleaned, and sliced
¾ cup bottled clam juice
¾ cup dry white wine
3 tablespoons whipped cream
2 teaspoons chopped fresh tarragon (or ½ teaspoon dried)
6 eight-ounce salmon fillets
fresh lemon juice
2 tablespoons butter, melted

Melt three tablespoons of butter in a large, heavy skillet over medium heat. Add shallots and sauté for two minutes. Increase heat to medium-high. Add morels; sauté until beginning to brown, about eight minutes. Add clam juice and wine; boil until liquids have almost evaporated (about twenty minutes).

Add the cream to mushrooms; boil until thickened (about one minute). Mix in the chopped tarragon. Season with salt and pepper.

Preheat broiler. Arrange the salmon fillets skin side down on the broiler pan. Brush with lemon juice; then the two tablespoons of butter. Broil until just cooked through, without turning (about six minutes). Sprinkle with salt and pepper. Transfer the fillets to plates and spoon the morels over the top. Serves six.

Printed with permission from Minnesota.gov

OCTOBER WEATHER

October Normals for Duluth

Day	High	Low	Mean	Precip.	Snowfall
1	59	40	50	0.11	0
2	59	40	49	0.10	0
3	59	39	49	0.10	0
4	58	39	49	0.10	0
5	58	39	48	0.10	0
6	57	38	48	0.09	0
7	57	38	47	0.09	0
8	57	38	47	0.09	0
9	56	37	47	0.09	0
10	56	37	46	0.08	0
11	55	37	46	0.08	0
12	55	36	46	0.08	0
13	54	36	45	0.08	0
14	54	35	45	0.08	Trace Amt.
15	53	35	44	0.07	Trace Amt.
16	53	35	44	0.07	Trace Amt.
17	52	34	43	0.07	Trace Amt.
18	52	34	43	0.07	Trace Amt.
19	51	34	42	0.07	0.1
20	51	33	42	0.07	0.1
21	50	33	42	0.07	0.1
22	50	32	41	0.07	0.1
23	49	32	41	0.07	0.1
24	49	31	40	0.07	0.1
25	48	31	40	0.07	0.1
26	47	31	39	0.07	0.1
27	47	30	38	0.07	0.1
28	46	30	38	0.07	0.1
29	46	29	37	0.07	0.2
30	45	29	37	0.07	0.2
31	44	28	36	0.07	0.2

OCTOBER WEATHER

October Normals for International Falls

Day	High	Low	Mean	Precip.	Snowfall
1	59	37	48	0.08	0
2	58	36	47	0.08	0
3	58	36	47	0.08	0
4	58	36	47	0.08	0
5	57	36	47	0.08	0
6	57	35	46	0.07	0
7	57	35	46	0.07	0
8	56	35	45	0.07	0
9	56	34	45	0.07	0
10	55	34	45	0.07	0
11	55	34	44	0.07	0
12	54	33	44	0.07	0.1
13	54	33	43	0.07	0.1
14	53	33	43	0.06	0.1
15	53	32	42	0.06	0.1
16	52	32	42	0.06	0.1
17	52	31	42	0.06	0.1
18	51	31	41	0.06	0.1
19	51	31	41	0.06	0.1
20	50	30	40	0.06	0.1
21	49	30	40	0.06	0.1
22	49	29	39	0.06	0.1
23	48	29	38	0.06	0.1
24	47	28	38	0.06	0.1
25	47	28	37	0.06	0.1
26	46	28	37	0.05	0.1
27	46	27	36	0.05	0.1
28	45	27	36	0.05	0.1
29	44	26	35	0.05	0.2
30	43	26	34	0.05	0.2
31	43	25	34	0.05	0.2

Source: National Oceanic and Atmospheric Administration (NOAA)'s National Weather Service

These climate normals are an average of thirty years of data between 1971 and 2000. Every ten years, the National Weather Service recalculates the normals using the next interval of thirty years. In 2010, the new normals will be recalculated using the period of 1981 to 2010.

OCTOBER WEATHER HISTORY

On This Day in October

Day	Year	Weather
1	1989	Temperatures across central and southern Minnesota begin in the 80s. A cold front comes through and drops the mercury to the 40s.
2	1849	Persistent rain at Ft. Snelling leaves 4 inches in a day and a half.
3	1999	Earliest-ever single-digit temperature for fall in Minnesota. Embarrass has a low of 9 degrees.
4	1939	Storm dumps 2.16 inches of rain at Fairmont.
5	1963	Heat wave across area with 98 at Beardsley, 96 at Madison, and 94 at Elbow Lake.
6	1987	Snow falls over Arrowhead region.
7	1980	Summerlike heat over the state with 92 at Montevideo and 84 at the Twin Cities.
8	1871	"Great Chicago Fire." Severe drought caused dry conditions in the city that was mostly built of wood.
9	1938	Forest fires claim twenty-one lives in northern Minnesota.
10	1949	Bizarre storm brings hurricane-force winds across Minnesota. Possibly the strongest non-thunderstorm wind seen in the state. Top winds are clocked at 100 mph at Rochester, with a gust of 89 mph at the Twin Cities International Airport. The top ten floors of the Foshay building evacuated; tenants feeling seasick from the swaying building.
11	1909	Snowstorm hits the state with temperatures dropping to 7 degrees in the north.
12	1918	Dry fall weather sets the stage for a dangerous fire threat. Several fires roar through large area of Carlton and St. Louis counties. Hardest hit are the towns of Cloquet, Moose Lake, and Brookston. The Carlton County *Vidette* calls it a "hurricane of burning leaves and smoke." At least 453 people are killed, possibly as many as 1,000. More than 11,000 people become homeless.
13	1820	Snowstorm at Ft. Snelling dumps 11 inches.
14	1966	An enormous hailstone crashes through the windshield of a truck near Claremont in Dodge County. It is reported to be 16 inches in circumference.
15	1968	Short-sleeve weather across central and southern Minnesota. The Twin Cities see a high of 85.
16	1880	Earliest blizzard in Minnesota. Over a foot of snow in the western counties. Railroads blocked; damage done to Great Lakes shipping. Huge drifts exceeding 20 feet form in the Canby area and last until spring, when flooding occurs across the Minnesota River valley.
17	1971	Heavy rains in northwestern Minnesota. Georgetown gets 4.02 inches.
18	1916	Blizzard over Minnesota. Hallock's temperature is in the 60s; drops to 2 degrees by the 20th.
19	2000	Warmest October 19 in Minnesota history. Many cities see highs in the 80s with the Twin Cities hitting 84. Appleton in Swift County reports 90 degrees.
20	2002	Heavy snow across central Minnesota. It falls in a ten-to-twenty-mile-wide band from southeast North Dakota to around Grantsburg, Wisconsin. Little Falls picks up 9 inches.

OCTOBER WEATHER HISTORY

On This Day in October

Day	Year	Weather
21	1916	Three-day blizzard ends. Bird Island falls from 65 degrees to 13 degrees.
22	1938	Sleet and wind causes damage along Minnesota-Wisconsin border.
23	1899	Warm day in the Twin Cities with a high of 82.
24	1922	Storm over Minnesota brings 55 mph winds at Collegeville.
25	1830	Heat wave at Ft. Snelling. Temperature reaches 80.
26	1985	Indian summer across the state. Twin Cities hit 70.
27	1943	One of the worst Twin Cities fogs in memory. With an average of 75 feet in thickness, a very dense fog blankets the area. At the worst, streetlights cannot be seen 25 yards away. Drivers refuse to cross unmarked railroad crossings, and traffic is brought to a standstill.
28	1971	Blizzard over the Rockies. Twenty-seven inches at Lander, Wyoming.
29	2004	Exceptionally muggy for October. Dew points surge into the middle to upper 60s over central and southern Minnesota. Ladybugs are extremely active.
30	1936	Gale dust storm causes damage in central Minnesota. Heavy wind damage in Stearns County.
31	1991	"Great Halloween Blizzard" begins. Trick-or-treating is memorable for the few who venture out.

Source: Minnesota State Climatology Office: DNR Waters

Bar Closed *The Volstead Act, October 28, 1919*

It was a Minnesotan, Representative Andrew Volstead, who introduced the congressional measure that put the Eighteenth Amendment to the federal constitution into effect. "Prohibition," or "the Volstead Act," was passed over President Woodrow Wilson's veto and banned the manufacture, transport, export, sale, or possession of alcoholic beverages—anything that contained more than one-half percent of alcohol.

At first, the public seemed to adhere to the law, but support began to wane as crime increased. Volstead did not get reelected in 1922, but low farm prices, rather than prohibition legislation, may have been the reason for his defeat.

In early 1933, in anticipation of the Eighteenth Amendment's repeal, the Volstead Act was revised to allow the manufacture and sale of 3.2 percent beer. It was too little too late. The act was voided later that year with the adoption of the Twenty-First Amendment.

October in the Garden

A Minnesota Tip on Roses • Add Value—and Fall Color—to Your Home • A Tour of Fall Color

A Minnesota Tip on Roses

Minnesota is wild about roses. Lyndale Park Rose Garden on the northeast shore of Lake Harriet in Minneapolis is the second oldest public rose garden in the United States. There are more than two thousand roses in more than two hundred varieties in the Rohrer Rose Garden in Winona.

In fact, a successful procedure for protecting roses against early freezes in the fall, the cold of winter, and thaw-freeze cycles in the spring was developed in the state and called the "Minnesota Tip Method." Beginning in mid-October, follow the steps below to safeguard your roses:

- Loosely tie together the rose canes with a rot-resistant twine.
- Dig a trench from the base of the plant outward. The trench must be as long as the plant is tall. With a spading fork, loosen the soil around the base of the plant.
- Gradually tip the plant over and lay it in the trench. Bend the roots, not the stem.
- Cover the plant with soil removed when digging. Once complete, the soil should be level.
- Mark the base of the plant with a stake. Tip all the plants in a bed in the same direction; this will make it easier to lift the plants the following spring.
- Once the soil freezes, mulch with a layer of straw at least six inches deep. Use chicken wire, boards, or hardware cloth to keep the mulch from blowing away. If mice are a problem, put down some mothballs before applying the mulch.
- Remove the mulch about the first of April. As soon as the soil dries in mid-April, lift the roses by using a spading fork.

Add Value—and Fall Color—to Your Home

Landscaping can increase your home's value by 15 percent. But beyond its monetary worth, colorful autumn foliage is an investment in beauty that you can enjoy for years. Create a burst of fall color in your yard by planting some of the following shrubs:

Red to Orange Fall Color	Barberry	Purple Fall Color
Amelanchier	(Emerald Carousel)	Dogwood
(Regent Serviceberry)	Euonymus (Burning Bush)	
Amur Maple	Rhododendron (P.J.M.)	**Yellow Fall Color**
(Bailey Compact)	Rhus (Sumac)	Witch Hazel
Aronia (Glossy Black	Spirea (Goldflame)	
Chokeberry)	Viburnum (Cranberry)	

A Tour of Fall Color

The annual transformation of the deciduous forest from a monochromatic scheme of summer greens to a full-color-scale tapestry of reds, oranges, purples, and golds turns almost all of us into "leaf peepers" at this time of year.

Although fall color tends to begin in the Upper Midwest during September or October and generally sweeps south with the shorter days and longer nights, specific weather conditions can influence the timing of the change. An early frost can kill leaf cells before they have time to change color, and heavy rains or very strong winds can denude trees of their leaves too soon. Fall colors are best viewed when the weather has been clear, dry, and cool.

When planning leaf-viewing excursions, keep an eye on local weather forecasts and call ahead to chambers of commerce to see when peak colors are expected. The Minnesota Department of Natural Resources provides weekly updates.

Fall Colors of Minnesota Trees

Ash, Black — yellow to brown
Ash, Green — yellow
Ash, White — purple
Aspen — yellow to golden-orange
Aspen, Quaking or Trembling — yellow
Basswood or American Linden —
    yellow to brown
Beech, Blue — yellow to orange
Birch, Paper — yellow
Birch, River — yellow
Box Elder — yellow
Butternut — yellow
Cedar, Red — purplish
Cherry, Black — yellow
Chokecherry — often red
Coffeetree, Kentucky — yellow
Cottonwood — yellow
Hackberry — yellow
Hawthorn or Thornapple —
    usually yellow
Hickory, Bitternut — yellow

Hickory, Shagbark — yellow
Ironwood — yellow-brown; holds some
    leaves into winter
Juneberry, Alleghany — red
Maple, Black — yellow to orange, and
    occasionally red
Maple, Red — yellow or red
Maple, Silver — yellow
Maple, Sugar — yellow to orange, and
    occasionally red
Mountain Ash, American — yellow to red
Oak, Bur — yellow-brown
Oak, Northern Pin — red
Oak, Red — bronze
Oak, Swamp White — yellow to brown
Oak, White — purple-red to violet-purple
Pincherry — red
Pine, Jack — yellow-green
Tamarack — yellow
Walnut, Black — yellow

Gladys's

October Household Tips

Minnesota's allergy season begins in March or April and can go through October. The season starts with the blooming of trees such as ashes and oaks, followed by the growing of grasses in May through July, and ending with the rising of the weeds from mid-August through October. Dust mites, however, can affect us year-round, as can the dander from our pets.

Since October means you'll probably be spending a bit more time indoors, here are a few tips for reigning in the dust inside your home and, as you look forward into winter, keeping your water pipes running free.

Household Tips for Dust-Sensitive People

- Don't use brooms, feather dusters, or strong cleaning chemicals that release potentially health-threatening vapors. Instead, use mops and cloths moistened with water. This will keep most of the dust confined to the article until it can be rinsed out.

- Eliminate as many knickknacks and odd-shaped items that you can so that your dust rag can make a clean and smooth pass over surfaces.

- Eliminate larger dust-attracting items, such as Venetian blinds, bed canopies, heavily upholstered furniture, and carpeting, if you can. Every time someone walks across a carpet, dust is stirred up.

- Change the vacuum cleaner's bag outdoors. Clean the area around the bag with a moist cloth before installing a fresh bag and replace it when only half full. Run the machine for at least thirty seconds before returning it to the house so any loose dust will be expelled.

How to Thaw a Frozen Water Pipe

- First, check to make sure the pipe hasn't cracked. Frozen water in the pipe may have expanded enough to cause the pipe to break, in which case the pipe will need to be repaired.

- If the pipe hasn't split, turn off the water leading to the pipe. Shut off the main water supply coming into your house, or the intermediate water-shut-off valves that may have been installed if you have a newer home.

- Open all the faucets connected to the frozen pipe to get rid of the cold water in the pipe and to minimize pressure.

- Thaw the frozen pipe by wrapping it with bath towels or cloths. Secure the towels around the pipe with duct tape, if desired. Pour hot water from a teakettle over the towels. Repeat until the water has thawed and runs through the faucet. (Or wrap the pipe in a heating pad or place a heat lamp next to it until the water thaws.)

- **Remember:** Don't use any electrical appliances if there is standing water. Boiling water, open flames, or propane torches should not be used for thawing pipes. Pipes may explode if they're heated excessively or too quickly.

- **Prevention:** Wrap thermostat-controlled heat tape or cable around pipes that tend to freeze. If you plan on taking a long winter vacation, consult a plumber about the possibility of draining the plumbing system to prevent frozen pipes and water damage.

Hunting Minnesota Moose

Is a Once-in-a-Lifetime Experience

"Moose," an Algonquin word meaning "twig-eater," is the largest member of the deer family. Averaging 950 to 1,200 pounds, a moose eats a massive amount of browse. Minnesota is estimated to have a total moose population of five to eight thousand.

Mature moose are characterized by a front shoulder hump and a flap of skin hanging below the throat (called a "bell"). Bulls carry flat, palmated antlers, which start to grow in April and are usually shed in December or January.

Although moose have poor eyesight, their senses of smell and hearing are acute. Their long legs and splayed hooves enable them to move easily through marshy areas and along northern Minnesota streams and lakes. They can dive to the bottom of shallow ponds, where they rip up bottom-growing vegetation.

Contrary to popular opinion, moose are seldom aggressive; typically only when a cow feels her calf is in danger or a bull is in rut do their gentle demeanors change. Mating season occurs from mid-September to mid-October; calves (usually twins) are born in May or June.

Hunting moose was prohibited in Minnesota from 1922 until 1972, when a limited hunt was initiated. Beginning in 1991, the moose permit officially became a "once in a lifetime" license. Licensees from 1991 to present are not eligible to apply for future moose hunts.

"The thinnest yellow light of November

is more warming and exhilarating

than any wine they tell of.

The mite which November contributes

becomes equal in value

to the bounty of July."

— HENRY DAVID THOREAU

November is National Beard Month and Talk Like a Robot Month. On a state level, however, November is when Minnesotans get their last taste of fall and their first gulp of winter.

Occasionally, a 70- or 80-degree day manages to squeeze through the shorter daylight hours and lower sun angles, but temperatures can also drop well below zero, such as they did on November 30, 1896, when -45 degrees Fahrenheit was measured at Pokegama Dam in Itasca County. Indian summer days are interrupted by frequent polar air masses that often settle in for two weeks at a time, reminding Minnesotans to prepare for what's ahead. Now's the time to mulch the garden, pack away the patio furniture, and make sure the snowblower is filled with oil.

But while November does tend to make us look to the near future, it's also a time that invites us to glance back at the close past. At the end of the month, Thanksgiving reminds us to be grateful for having another year to enjoy.

And if the company of family, friends, and good thoughts isn't enough to keep you warm, November just might be the right time to grow a beard—if only to keep you from talking like a robot when those icy winds blow.

To Long Life!

Minnesota has long been at the forefront of healthy living, as evidenced by the story of the Mayo family (see "Rochester's Famed Mayo Clinic," this chapter). During November 1918, in fact, movies, churches, and other places that attracted crowds were closed to prevent the spread of an influenza epidemic that struck the Twin Cities.

More recently, in 1987, Minnesota became the first state to establish a publicly subsidized health insurance program for children who had no access to private systems. Later legislation provided state-subsidized coverage for almost a half-million low-income residents. In 2004, 92.6 percent of Minnesota citizens were covered (the national average for other states was 84 percent).

The investment in health has paid off. In 2006, Minnesotans were found to live longer (78.8 years), on average, than residents of any other state except Hawaii (80.0 years). Data from the year 2000 show that Minnesota women fare even better, with an average of 81.5 years.

Bald Eagles and The Raptor Center

In 1983 at the Sherburne National Wildlife Refuge, the first successful nesting of bald eagles in central Minnesota in over thirty years took place. Today, Minnesota has the most breeding pairs of bald eagles in the lower forty-eight states (behind only Alaska), with an estimated 1,310. Florida has 1,133 breeding pairs, and Wisconsin has 1,065. The bald eagle was removed from the endangered species list on July 9, 2007. Today, there are nearly 9,789 pairs of bald eagles in the contiguous United States.

Eagles mate for life. They return to the same nests each year and lay their eggs in March. The eggs incubate for about thirty-five days, and by late June or July, the young are ready to fly. Bald eagles like to winter in the Wabasha area of the Mississippi, where the water remains unfrozen.

In addition to repopulating the wilderness areas, bald eagles are becoming somewhat common in urban locations, such as the Twin Cities, where several dozen pairs make their living amid freeways, bridges, boats, and human activities.

The University of Minnesota College of Veterinary Medicine in St. Paul is the home of The Raptor Center, a rehabilitation center for eagles, hawks, owls, falcons, and other birds of prey. The center was founded in 1974 by Dr. Gary Duke and Dr. Patrick Redig—along with four baby great horned owls. In the early 1970s, Dr. Duke was conducting research on the digestive efficiency of grain-eating turkeys, and Dr. Redig was a sophomore veterinary student. The owls were brought to Dr. Duke by another of his veterinary students, providing an opportunity for Duke to expand his research to include avian meat eaters.

Dr. Duke sought additional owls for his study through the Minnesota Department of Natural Resources. An avid falconer, Dr. Redig offered to care for the owls as well as other birds not needed for research. Over time, he began to repair their injuries and return them to the wild.

Today, The Raptor Center treats more than eight hundred birds a year and reaches more than 250,000 people annually through its education programs. Dr. Redig pioneered the avian orthopedic and anesthetic techniques that are used by avian veterinarians today.

Some Very Large Deer

Minnesota is home to the northern woodland white-tailed deer, the largest of seventeen known subspecies of white-tailed deer in the U.S.

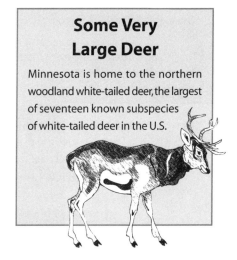

Rochester's Famed Mayo Clinic

It sounds like the plot of a Jacqueline Susann romance novel. In a little Midwest river valley town, one family works together to build a successful medical practice and winds up helping the world.

The story unwinds like this: In 1845, a young English chemist named William Worrall Mayo immigrates to New York. Nine years later, he earns his medical degree in Indiana. In 1855, he moves to Le Sueur, Minnesota, where he sets up a medical practice. In 1861, he and his wife give birth to their first son, William James Mayo. After a stint as a surgeon in the Civil War, William Worrall Mayo moves his family to Rochester; and in 1865, their second son, Charles Horace, is born.

Father Mayo soon gains a reputation throughout southern Min-nesota for his medical and surgical skills. He teaches his sons a hands-on knowledge of human anatomy with the help of a Dakota Sioux skeleton. The boys are also encouraged to experiment with the microscope, and little nine-year-old Charles, standing on a box, begins administering ether while his father operates. They even learn to tie off blood vessels and assist at autopsies. By the time they enter medical schools—William James at the University of Michigan and Charles at Northwestern University in Chicago—both are comfortable in the medical world.

In August 1883, a tornado hits Rochester. Along with the Mayo doctors, the Sisters of St. Francis Convent are called in to help treat the injured at the temporary hospital that is set

---

Here's a look at just some of the clinic's "firsts" and achievements:

- The first graduate school of medicine, established in 1915, was the Mayo Graduate School of Medicine in Rochester.
- The first post-operative recovery room in a hospital was established at the Mayo Clinic.
- In 1950, Mayo Clinic doctors Philip Hench and Edward Kendall shared the Nobel Prize in Medicine (along with a Swiss doctor) for their work on ACTH (adrenocorticotropic hormone) and cortisone.

- The world's first blood bank was established at the Mayo Clinic in 1933.
- In 1973, the Mayo Clinic was the first medical center in the country to use CT (computed tomography) scanning.
- Research at the clinic led to cortisone treatment for arthritis sufferers, the design of a mask and an anti-blackout suit for high-altitude test pilots, technology for open-heart surgery, an advancement in the use of lasers to destroy brain tumors, and the use of chemicals to dissolve gallstones without surgery.

up in the town's dance hall. After the crisis, the sisters offer to build a hospital in Rochester if Dr. Mayo and his sons will direct its operations. In 1889, St. Mary's Hospital becomes a reality, with fourteen hundred beds. While Dr. Mayo has pioneered the use of the microscope to diagnose diseases, his sons become known as daring physicians and surgeons in their own right. People from all over the world begin to seek them out, often as their last hope.

In 1892, it becomes clear that the surgical practice at St. Mary's is growing to the point that the Mayos need more help. Gradually, more surgeons, physicians, and laboratory and research workers are added to the team. In 1929, a new, larger clinic is opened.

Today, the Mayo Clinic is affiliated with the University of Minnesota and is one of the planet's largest and most renowned medical centers. Currently more than fifty-two thousand people work for the Mayo Medical Center (which includes the clinic and two affiliate hospitals), treating 521,000 patients in 2006.

"Over the River and Through the Woods"

Various versions of this song have appeared over the years. The words are based on the poem by Lydia Maria Child.

Over the river, and through the wood,
to Grandfather's house we go;
the horse knows the way to carry the
    sleigh
through the white and drifted snow.

Over the river, and through the wood,
trot fast my dapple gray!
Spring over the ground like a
    hunting hound!
For 'tis Thanksgiving Day.

Over the river and through the wood,
now Grandmother's cap I spy!
Hurrah for the fun! Is the pudding
    done?
Hurrah for the pumpkin pie!

November at the HHH Metrodome

On November 19, 1981, after partially collapsing the day prior, the roof of the Hubert H. Humphrey Metrodome completely deflated due to a 10.2-inch snowfall. The deflation was blamed on a large rip in the roof, caused by a bolt that snapped and bent a piece of steel, which then punctured the fabric roof. The roof was repaired four days later.

The Metrodome's roof is made of two layers of Teflon-coated, fiberglass fabric, said to be the largest application of Teflon on Earth. Air pressure, six pounds per square foot, from twenty fans inside the stadium, keep the roof in place.

Minnesota Vote

for President Since 1860

Key to Party Abbreviations

AC: Anderson Coalition
AM: American Party of Minnesota
Am: American
AP: American Populist
BL: Better Life
C: Communist
Cit: Citizens
CF: Christian Freedom
CP: Constitution
D: Democratic
DFL: Democratic-Farmer-Labor
D-Peo: Democratic People's
DSF: Democratic Southern Faction
FL: Farmer-Labor
G: Greenback
GL: Greenback Labor
GPM: Green Party Minnesota
GRP: Grassroots
I: Independent

IDB: International Development Bank
IER: Independents for Economic Recovery
IG: Independent Grassroots
In: Industrial
InG: Industrial Government
InL: Industrial Labor
IR: Independent-Republican
L: Libertarian
MCP: McCarthy '76 Principle
M-Pop: Midroad-Populist
MnPeo: Minnesota People's
MnProg: Minnesota Progressive
MnT: Minnesota Taxpayers
NA: New Alliance
NER: National Economic Recovery
NGD: National Gold Democratic
NL: Natural Law
P&F: Peace and Freedom

Peo: People's
PO: Public Ownership
Pro: Prohibition
Prog: Progressive
R: Republican
RP: Reform
RPM: Reform Party Minnesota
S: Socialist
SD: Socialist Democrat
SE: Socialist Equality
SIn: Socialist Industrial
SL: Socialist Labor
SW: Socialist Workers
U: Union
UL: Union Labor
UST: U.S. Taxpayers
WC: Workers Communist
WL: Workers League
WW: Workers World

Source: Minnesota Legislative Manual (Blue Book)
2005–2006

1860
Abraham Lincoln (R) 22,069
Stephen A. Douglas (D) 11,920
John C. Breckenridge (DSF)................748

1864
Abraham Lincoln (R) 25,055
George B. McClellan (D).................17,367

1868
Ulysses S. Grant (R) 43,722
Horatio Seymour (D) 28,096

1872
Ulysses S. Grant (R) 55,708
Horace Greeley (D) 35,211

1876
Rutherford B. Hayes (R) 72,955
Samuel J. Tilden (D)......................48,587

Peter Cooper (G)............................2,389
Green Clay Smith (Pro) 144

1880
James A. Garfield (R)..................... 93,902
Winfield S. Hancock (D).................53,315
James B. Weaver (GL) 3,267
Neal Dow (Pro)................................286

1884
James G. Blaine (R) 111,685
S. Grover Cleveland (D) 70,065
John P. St. John (Pro) 4,684
Benjamin F. Butler (G).....................3,583

1888
Benjamin H. Harrison (R) 142,492
S. Grover Cleveland (D)................104,385
Clinton B. Fisk (Pro) 15,311
Alson J. Streeter (UL)......................1,097

1892

Benjamin H. Harrison (R) 122,823
James B. Weaver (Fusion Electors) ... 107,077
S. Grover Cleveland (D) 100,920
James B. Weaver (Peo) 29,313
John Bidwell (Pro) 14,182

1896

William McKinley (R) 193,503
William J. Bryan (D-Peo) 130,735
Joshua Levering (Pro) 4,339
John M. Palmer (NGD) 3,222
Charles H. Machett (SL) 954

1900

William McKinley (R) 190,461
William J. Bryan (D-Peo) 112,901
John G. Wooley (Pro) 8,555
Eugene V. Debs (SD) 3,065
Joseph R. Maloney (SL) 1,329

1904

Theodore Roosevelt (R) 216,651
Alton B. Parker (D) 55,187
Eugene V. Debs (PO) 11,692
Silas C. Swallow (Pro) 6,253
Thomas E. Watson (Peo) 2,103
Charles H. Corregan (SL) 974

1908

William H. Taft (R) 195,843
William J. Bryan (D) 109,401
Eugene V. Debs (PO) 14,527
Eugene W. Chafin (Pro) 11,107
Thomas L. Hisgen (L) 426

1912

Theodore Roosevelt (Prog) 125,856
Woodrow Wilson (D) 106,426
William H. Taft (R) 64,334
Eugene V. Debs (PO) 27,505
Eugene W. Chafin (Pro) 7,886
Elmer Reimer (SL) 2,212

1916

Charles E. Hughes (R) 179,544
Woodrow Wilson (D) 179,152
Allan L. Benson (S) 20,117
J. Frank Hanly (Pro) 7,793
Elmer Reimer (InL) 468
Edward J. Meier (Prog) 290

1920

Warren G. Harding (R) 519,421
James M. Cox (D) 142,994
Eugene V. Debs (S) 56,106
W. W. Watkins (Pro) 11,489
William W. Cox (In) 5,828

1924

Calvin Coolidge (R) 420,759
Robert M. LaFollette (I) 339,192
John W. Davis (D) 55,913
William Z. Foster (WC) 4,427
Frank F. Johns (SIn) 1,855

1928

Herbert Hoover (R) 560,977
Alfred E. Smith (D) 396,451
Norman M. Thomas (S) 6,774
William Z. Foster (WC) 4,853
Verne L. Reynolds (In) 1,921

1932

Franklin D. Roosevelt (D) 600,806
Herbert Hoover (R) 363,959
Norman M. Thomas (S) 25,476
William Z. Foster (C) 6,101
Jacob S. Coxey (FL) 5,731

1936

Franklin D. Roosevelt (D) 698,811
Alfred M. Landon (R) 350,461
William Lemke (U) 74,296
Norman M. Thomas (S) 2,872
Earl R. Browder (C) 2,711
John W. Aiken (In) 961

1940

Franklin D. Roosevelt (D) 644,196
Wendell L. Wilkie (R) 596,274
Norman M. Thomas (S) 5,454
Earl R. Browder (C) 2,711
John W. Aiken (In) 2,553

1944

Franklin D. Roosevelt (D) 589,864
Thomas E. Dewey (R) 527,416
Norman M. Thomas (S) 5,073
Edward A. Teichert (InG) 3,176

1948

Harry S. Truman (DFL) 692,966
Thomas E. Dewey (R) 483,617

Continued next page

1948 (continued)

Henry A. Wallace (Prog) 27,866
Norman M. Thomas (S) 4,646
Edward A. Teichert (InG) 2,525
Farrell Dobbs (SW) 606

1952

Dwight D. Eisenhower (R) 763,211
Adlai E. Stevenson (DFL) 608,458
Vincent Hallinan (Prog) 2,666
Eric Hass (InG) 2,383
Stuart Hamblen (Pro) 2,147
Farrell Dobbs (SW) 618

1956

Dwight D. Eisenhower (R) 719,302
Adlai E. Stevenson (DFL) 617,525
Eric Hass (InG) 2,080
Farrell Dobbs (SW) 1,098

1960

John F. Kennedy (DFL) 779,933
Richard M. Nixon (R) 757,915
Farrell Dobbs (SW) 3,077
Eric Hass (InG) 962

1964

Lyndon B. Johnson (DFL) 991,117
Barry M. Goldwater (R) 559,624
Eric Hass (InG) 2,544
Clifton DeBerry (SW) 1,177

1968

Hubert H. Humphrey (DFL) 857,738
Richard M. Nixon (R) 658,643
George C. Wallace (Am) 68,931
Leroy Eldridge Cleaver (P&F) 935
Fred Halstead (SW) 808
Eugene J. McCarthy (write-in votes) 585
Charlene Mitchell (C) 415
Henning A. Blomen (InG) 285

1972

Richard M. Nixon (R) 898,269
George S. McGovern (DFL) 802,346
John G. Schmitz (Am) 31,407
Louis Fisher (InG) 4,261
Benjamin M. Spock (MnPeo) 2,805
Linda Jenness (SW) 940
Gus Hall (C) 662

1976

Jimmy Carter (DFL) 1,070,440
Gerald Ford (IR) 819,395
Eugene J. McCarthy (MCP) 35,490
Peter Camejo (SW) 4,149
Thomas J. Anderson (Am) 3,592
Gus Hall (C) 1,092
Margaret Wright (Peo) 635
Lyndon H. LaRouche (IDB) 543
Roger L. McBride (L) 529
Jules Levin (InG) 370
Frank P. Zeidler (S) 354

1980

Jimmy Carter (DFL) 954,174
Ronald Reagan (IR) 873,241
John B. Anderson (AC) 174,990
Ed Clark (L) 31,593
Barry Commoner (Cit) 8,407
No candidates specified (Am) 6,139
Gus Hall (C) 1,184
Clifton DeBerry (SW) 711
Deidre Griswold (WW) 698
David McReynolds (S) 536

1984

Walter Mondale (DFL) 1,036,364
Ronald Reagan (IR) 1,032,603
Lyndon H. LaRouche (I) 3,865
Mel Mason (SW) 3,180
David Bergland (L) 2,996
Robert Bob Richards (AP) 2,377
Sonia Johnson (Cit) 1,219
Gus Hall (C) 630
Ed Winn (WL) 260
Dennis Serette (NA) 232

1988

Michael Dukakis (DFL) 1,109,471
George Bush (IR) 962,337
Eugene J. McCarthy (MnProg) 5,403
Ron Paul (L) 5,109
James Warren (SW) 2,155
Jack Herer (GRP) 1,949
Lenora B. Fulani (NA) 1,734
Lyndon H. LaRouche (NER) 1,702
David Duke (AP) 1,529
Delmar Dennis (AM) 1,298
Ed Winn (WL) 489

1992

Bill Clinton (DFL) 1,020,997
George Bush (IR) 747,841
Ross Perot (I) 562,506
Andre Marrou (L) 3,373
James "Bo" Gritz (CP) 3,363
Jack Herer (GRP) 2,659
John Hagelin (NL) 1,406
James Warren (SW) 990
Lenora B. Fulani (NA) 958
Howard Phillips (MnT) 733
Lyndon H. LaRouche, Jr. (IER) 622

1996

Bill Clinton (DFL) 1,120,438
Bob Dole (R) 766,476
Ross Perot (RP) 257,704
Ralph Nader (GPM) 24,908
Harry Browne (L) 8,271
Dennis Peron (GRP) 4,898
Howard Phillips (UST) 3,416
John Hagelin (NL) 1,808
John Birrenbach (IG) 787

James Harris (SW) 684
Jerry White (SE) 347

2000

Albert Gore (DFL) 1,168,266
George W. Bush (R) 1,109,659
Ralph Nader (GPM) 126,696
Patrick Buchanan (RPM) 22,166
Harry Browne (L) 5,282
Howard Phillips (CP) 3,272
John Hagelin (RP) 2,294
James Harris, Jr. (SW) 1,022

2004

John F. Kerry (DFL) 1,445,014
George W. Bush (R) 1,346,695
Ralph Nader (BL) 18,683
Michael Badnarik (L) 4,639
David Cobb (GPM) 4,408
Michael Peroutka (CP) 3,074
Thomas J. Harens (CF) 2,387
Bill Van Auken (SE) 539
Roger Calero (SW) 416

Minnesota vs. Turkey

In 1909, a disgusted suffragist stated that the women of Turkey would get to vote before Minnesota's women did. In 1910, Turkish women voted in their country's elections. It took nine more years, when the Nineteenth Amendment was finally ratified in 1919, for Minnesota women to get the same right as those in Turkey.

Significant Moments in Minnesota's Political History

• The first Minnesota United States senators were Henry Rice and General James Shields. Shields, a Democrat, is the only person in United States history to serve as a U.S. senator for three different states.

• The election of 1936 brought a dramatic victory to the Farmer-Labor party.

• Beloved Minnesota political figure Hubert Humphrey served as vice president under Lyndon Johnson from 1965 to 1969.

• The majority opinion of the U.S. Supreme Court in the landmark case of Roe vs. Wade (1973) was written by Harry Blackmun, who grew up in St. Paul.

• From 1977 to 1981, Minnesota's Walter Mondale was the U.S. vice president under Jimmy Carter.

• In 1993, Minneapolis elected its first African-American mayor, Democrat Sharon Sayles Belton.

The Big Blizzard

For Minnesotans, November 11, 1940, will always be remembered as the "Armistice Day Blizzard." A mild morning metamorphosed into a rapidly approaching, strong winter storm by the afternoon. When the storm hit Duluth, winds reached 63 mph and the temperature dropped forty-one degrees in twenty-four hours. Across the state, ice took down power lines. Snowfall measured 16.8 inches in the Twin Cities.

Many duck hunters were out on the Mississippi, and it was reported that one hunter died while standing in the river bottom holding a willow branch, frozen with his feet anchored in the ice. In all, forty-nine people lost their lives.

Stunt pilot Max Conrad of Winona became a hero that day. Using a small yellow Piper Cub airplane, he braved fifty-knot winds to search for dead or trapped hunters; he dropped matches, whiskey, and five-gallon pails of food to the survivors he found.

Weather (Or Not) to Dance …

The Chippewa (Ojibwa) Indians marked the year's first snowfall by participating in "The Snowshoe Dance." Many Native American ceremonies revolved around seasonal changes and weather conditions, such as the Sun and Thunder Dances.

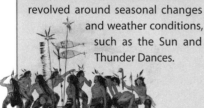

The Great Lakes Storm of 1913

In 1913, a blizzard with hurricane-force winds hit the Great Lakes area for four days, from November 7 to 11. Dubbed the "White Hurricane" or the "Big Blow," the storm stretched from Lake Huron to the shores of Lake Superior in Duluth.

Two major storm fronts converged to create the storm, fuelled by the relatively warm waters of the lakes—a phenomenon called a "November gale." It produced 90 mph winds, waves over thirty-five feet high, and whiteout snow squalls.

The storm hit its peak on November 9, overturning ships on four of the five Great Lakes. Twelve ships sank in the storm, eight of them on Lake Huron. More than 250 people died. It was the deadliest and most destructive natural disaster to ever hit the Great Lakes.

Intermittent lulls in the storm and the slow pace of the weather reports contributed to the storm's destructiveness. In the midst of the tragedy, however, some good did arise. Analysis of the storm and its impact led to improved forecasting, faster responses to storm warnings, and stronger construction of marine vessels.

Thanksgiving Goes National

In 1621, under Governor William Bradford, the settlers at Plymouth in the Massachusetts colony first celebrated Thanksgiving. George Washington and James Madison each issued a Thanksgiving proclamation once during their presidencies, but it wasn't until 1863 when President Lincoln issued his Thanksgiving Day Proclamation that the holiday became a national annual event, to occur on the last Thursday of November.

"The sky breathed autumn,

sombre, shrouded;

Shorter and shorter grew the days;

Sad murmurs filled the woodland ways

As the dark coverts were denuded;

Now southward swept the caravan

Of the wild geese, a noisy clan;

And mists above the meadows brooded;

A tedious season they await

Who hear November at the gate."

— FROM *EUGENE ONEGIN* BY
ALEKSANDR SERGEYEVICH PUSHKIN, 1833
(TRANSLATED BY BABETTE DEUTSCH)

November Recipe
Indian Wild Rice Corn Pudding

Minnesota is the nation's biggest turkey producer, raising an estimated forty-six million of the birds in 2007. With the total estimate of turkeys raised in the United States in 2007 at 272 million, Minnesota produces almost one of every six turkeys sold in the country. Along with your feast of turkey, stuffing, and pumpkin pie this November, try this delectable vegetable side dish.

Indian Wild Rice Corn Pudding

¹/₃ cup uncooked wild rice
1¹/₂ cups whole kernel corn, drained
3 eggs, well beaten
1 small onion, minced
¹/₄ cup all-purpose flour
1¹/₂ teaspoon salt

Dash pepper
1 teaspoon sugar
Dash nutmeg
1 tablespoon melted butter
2 cups light cream
1 jar pimientos, drained and chopped

Cook wild rice according to package directions. Combine the cooked wild rice, corn, eggs, and onion. Separately, combine flour, salt, pepper, sugar, and nutmeg and stir into corn mixture. Add butter, cream, and pimientos and mix well. Pour into a buttered, two-quart, shallow baking dish. Set dish in larger pan and pour hot water to one-inch depth around inner dish. Bake at 325°F uncovered for one hour or until pudding is firm and a knife inserted in center comes out clean. Cut into squares and serve hot. Makes four to six servings. *from North Woods Cottage Cookbook by Jerry Minnich*

NOVEMBER WEATHER

November Normals for Duluth

Day	High	Low	Mean	Precip.	Snowfall
1	44	28	36	0.07	0.3
2	43	27	35	0.07	0.3
3	42	27	35	0.07	0.4
4	42	26	34	0.08	0.4
5	41	26	34	0.08	0.4
6	40	26	33	0.08	0.4
7	40	25	32	0.08	0.4
8	39	25	32	0.08	0.5
9	39	24	31	0.08	0.5
10	38	24	31	0.08	0.5
11	37	23	30	0.08	0.5
12	37	23	30	0.08	0.5
13	36	22	29	0.08	0.5
14	36	22	29	0.08	0.5
15	35	21	28	0.07	0.5
16	35	21	28	0.07	0.6
17	34	20	27	0.07	0.6
18	34	19	27	0.07	0.6
19	33	19	26	0.07	0.6
20	32	19	26	0.07	0.6
21	32	18	25	0.07	0.6
22	31	17	24	0.07	0.6
23	31	17	24	0.07	0.6
24	31	16	24	0.06	0.6
25	30	16	23	0.06	0.6
26	30	15	22	0.06	0.6
27	29	15	22	0.06	0.5
28	29	14	21	0.06	0.5
29	28	14	21	0.05	0.5
30	28	13	20	0.05	0.5

NOVEMBER WEATHER

November Normals for International Falls

Day	High	Low	Mean	Precip.	Snowfall
1	42	25	33	0.05	0.3
2	41	24	33	0.05	0.3
3	41	24	32	0.05	0.3
4	40	23	31	0.05	0.3
5	39	22	31	0.05	0.3
6	38	22	30	0.05	0.4
7	38	21	30	0.05	0.4
8	37	21	29	0.05	0.4
9	36	20	28	0.05	0.4
10	36	20	28	0.05	0.4
11	35	19	27	0.05	0.4
12	34	19	26	0.05	0.4
13	34	18	26	0.05	0.5
14	33	17	25	0.05	0.5
15	32	17	25	0.05	0.5
16	32	16	24	0.05	0.5
17	31	16	23	0.05	0.5
18	31	15	23	0.05	0.5
19	30	15	22	0.04	0.5
20	30	14	22	0.04	0.5
21	29	13	21	0.04	0.5
22	28	13	20	0.04	0.5
23	28	12	20	0.04	0.5
24	27	11	19	0.04	0.5
25	27	11	19	0.04	0.5
26	26	10	18	0.04	0.5
27	26	9	18	0.04	0.5
28	25	9	17	0.04	0.5
29	25	8	16	0.03	0.5
30	24	8	16	0.03	0.5

Source: National Oceanic and Atmospheric Administration (NOAA)'s National Weather Service

These climate normals are an average of thirty years of data between 1971 and 2000. Every ten years, the National Weather Service recalculates the normals using the next interval of thirty years. In 2010, the new normals will be recalculated using the period of 1981 to 2010.

NOVEMBER WEATHER HISTORY

On This Day in November

1	1991	Classes are canceled across the state due to the "Great Halloween Blizzard." Three-foot drifts across I-94 from the Twin Cities to St. Cloud.
2	1842	Warm spell at Ft. Snelling. Temperature gets up to 60 degrees.
3	1991	"Great Halloween Blizzard" ends with a total of 28.4 inches of snow at the Twin Cities.
4	1727	The first outdoor celebration at the chapel of Fort Beauharnois on Lake Pepin was postponed due to "variableness of the weather."
5	1941	Snowstorm hits southern Minnesota. Heaviest snow at Fairmont.
6	1947	Snowstorm moves through the state with high winds, causing $1 million in damages.
7	1844	Large prairie fire at Ft. Snelling. More fires later on in the week.
8	1999	November heat wave. Temperatures in the 70s and 80s with records shattered in many places. The Twin Cites hits 73 degrees; Canby sees 82.
9	1850	Sky darkened at Ft. Snelling due to prairie fires.
10	1975	The SS *Edmund Fitzgerald* sinks off Whitefish Bay. All twenty-nine members of the crew perish.
11	1940	"Great Armistice Day Blizzard" (see "The Big Blizzard," this chapter). Barometer falls to 28.66 inches at Duluth. Some roads so badly blocked with snow they aren't reopened until November 22.
12	1933	Dust storm hits southwest Minnesota, while a blizzard rages in the northwest.
13	1938	Snowstorm across northern Minnesota. Barometer falls to 29.31 in Duluth.
14	2002	A magnitude 7.9 earthquake in Alaska turns water black in some wells in southeast Minnesota due to magnesium particles that have been shaken loose.
15	1976	So far this year, there have been more than three thousand forest fires.
16	1931	Tornado near Maple Plain in Hennepin County. The path of the storm totals 5 miles long.
17	1835	Strange night at Ft. Snelling: northern lights seen over prairie fires.
18	1979	Heat wave continues in southwest Minnesota. Temperature hits 70 degrees at Browns Valley.
19	1957	Snowstorm in southeast Minnesota. A foot is dumped at Winona. Heavy crop losses.
20	1953	Freezing rain hits parts of Minnesota. Three inches of ice on telephone wires at Lake Benton.
21	1980	Around this time, about 28,000 Canada geese spend their nights on Silver Lake in Rochester.
22	1970	Gale-driven snow across Minnesota. Winds more than 45 mph over Rochester and Duluth.
23	1954	Gale over Minnesota. Considerable damage in downtown Wadena.
24	1825	Warm spell begins at Ft. Snelling. Temperature rises up to 70 degrees over the week.
25	1820	Ft. Snelling in the midst of a three-day blizzard that dumps 9 inches of snow.

NOVEMBER WEATHER HISTORY

On This Day in November

Day	Year	Weather
26	1965	Snowstorm across the north. Duluth gets 14.7 inches; 13.6 inches at Grand Rapids.
27	1985	Cold hits the north. Crookston is at -30 degrees.
28	1960	Storm produces near hurricane-force winds on Lake Superior; 20- to 40-foot waves on the lake. Erosion and damage on the North Shore.
29	1835	Ft. Snelling is at -11 degrees.
30	1896	Chilly across Minnesota. Temperatures at the Pokegama Dam measure -45 degrees.

Source: Minnesota State Climatology Office: DNR Waters

Mark Your NOVEMBER CALENDAR

Tundra Swan Watch, Winona
www.visitwinona.com

Lighting Festival, Taylors Falls
www.taylorsfallschamber.org

Niagara Underground

The farmer was merely searching for his lost pigs. But he found something much taller: Niagara Cave, one of the largest caves in the Midwest, with an underground waterfall tumbling down for sixty feet.

Carved out by underground streams, the limestone cavern's ceiling reaches up more than a hundred feet, with deep canyons and gorges below.

Fun Facts about Winona

• Winona's newspaper, the *Daily Republican* (later the *Republican Herald*), claims to be the first daily newspaper published after Minnesota's admission into the Union in 1858.

• Dr. Thomas Welch, the dentist who came up with the formula for concentrated grape juice, lived in Winona from 1858 to 1868.

• William Windom of Winona was a congressman, senator, secretary of the treasury twice, and a leading contender for the Republican nomination for president in 1880. He is the only person from Minnesota to have appeared on U.S. currency—briefly, on two-dollar bills.

• Winona Laura Horowitz was born on October 29, 1971, in Winona and later became actress Winona Ryder.

• Winona is the only place in Minnesota where you face north when looking at Wisconsin. A jog in the Mississippi River, which normally flows north to south, causes the waterway to flow briefly from west to east, and thus the geographic anomaly.

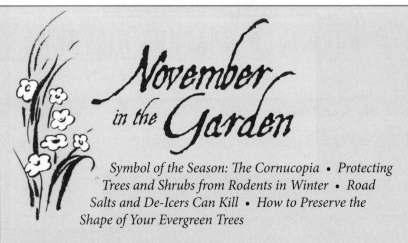

November in the Garden

Symbol of the Season: The Cornucopia • Protecting Trees and Shrubs from Rodents in Winter • Road Salts and De-Icers Can Kill • How to Preserve the Shape of Your Evergreen Trees

Symbol of the Season: The Cornucopia

Perhaps no symbol better represents November and the season of harvest than the cornucopia, the traditional horn-shaped basket that is a frequent centerpiece on Thanksgiving tables. This icon of food and abundance dates to the fifth century B.C. and Greek mythology. Amalthea, the nymph who raised Zeus, fed him goat's milk. In return, Zeus gave Amalthea the goat's horn, which had the power to give to its possessor whatever he or she wished for. This gave rise to the legend; original depictions showed the goat's horn filled with fruits and flowers.

And no matter how much you ate or took from the horn, it always replenished itself; thus, the "Horn of Plenty" was born.

Protecting Trees and Shrubs from Rodents in Winter

Winter can make finding food difficult for animals in the wild. Mice often feed on bark during the winter, girdling pines and other woody species. If the bark of your trees becomes chewed all the way around the trunk and through the cambium to the wood, the tree will gradually die from starvation, since food manufactured by the leaves moves downward to the roots through the inner bark. And since mice work under the snow, you may not know of the damage they're doing until spring.

To protect your trees and shrubs from mouse damage, place a cylinder of one-quarter-inch, mesh hardware cloth around the trunk of the tree. The cylinder should extend two to three inches below the ground line for mice and eighteen to twenty-four inches above the anticipated snow line for protection against rabbits. When snow becomes deep, tramping it down around the base of the tree will keep the top of the cylinder above the snow line. The cloth can be left on year-round, but make sure it's larger than the trunk to allow for growth.

Rabbits feed on bark above the snow line and may cut off entire branches. As an alternative to the mesh hardware cloth, a cylinder of chicken wire can be used instead to ward off rabbits. However, check such a fenced-in area frequently to ensure that a rabbit has not gained entrance and is trapped inside. Dried blood in mesh bags hung from the tree's branches is also said to repel rabbits.

For the best control over rodents of all kinds, make sure you encourage and protect their natural predators: foxes, owls, and hawks.

Road Salts and De-Icers Can Kill

While de-icing products can be almost indispensable when trying to clear a slippery sidewalk or driveway, they can be hard on landscape plants. Salts sprinkled by hand can wash into the soil, and road salts sprayed from trucks can cause damage to twigs and needles on trees. Stunted growth, poor or nonexistent flowering and fruiting, leaf burn, premature fall color—and even death—may result. Here are a few tips to help manage this year's snow and ice on your plants:

- Shovel first and salt last. Use a shovel or snowblower to remove the majority of snow.

- Avoid dumping the snow on shrubs and small trees. Heavy snow can break branches.

- Once most of the snow is removed, use sand to de-slick walkways. If you must use a de-icer, choose an environmentally friendly one, such as magnesium chloride or calcium magnesium acetate.

- Protect plants from roadway salts with a physical barrier, such as burlap, decorative fencing, or other structures.

- In spring, thoroughly water areas exposed to road and sidewalk salt. Heavy spring rains or a soaking watering will leach the salt through the soil and away from plant roots.

How to Preserve the Shape of Your Evergreen Trees

Winter, with its biting winds, heavy snows, and ice storms, has the potential to destroy the central leader (trunk) of evergreen trees. Such a loss can cause a spruce or other evergreen tree to lose its characteristic, pyramidal shape. You can help restore this outline by creating a new central leader:

- Cut off the damaged leader, leaving a 1.5-inch stub.

- Choose one of the shorter side shoots to serve as the new leader.

- Tie the new leader you've selected to the damaged leader's stub. Over time, this side shoot will start to grow upright.

- Remove the tie after one year.

- If several other side shoots begin to grow upward, prune out all but the new leader you've trained to be an upright-growing stem.

Gladys's

November Household Tips

While a Thanksgiving dinner is always a welcome respite from the workweek, it comes with its own required chores, including carving the turkey and washing all those dishes. Here's help for both:

Sharpening Knives

- When sharpening knives on a steel or stone, hold the blade at a shallow angle (about ten to fifteen degrees).

- Draw the knife toward you and across the stone (or draw the knife blade down the steel). Repeat the process on the opposite side of the blade.

- If using a rotary grinder or commercial knife sharpener with little wheels, pull the blades through several times in the same direction so that you don't damage the blade. (This is not recommended for fine knives.) Knives with serrated edges do not need to be sharpened.

- Using a mug. You can sharpen knives on the unglazed base of a mug. Hold the blade at a slight angle to the mug and slide the blade in one direction.

The most effective way to get a good cutting edge on a knife is to use a whetstone saturated with vegetable oil. Whetstones come with both a coarse and a fine side. Sharpen a very dull knife first on the coarse side of the stone, then on the fine side. Holding the knife firmly, place the blade at an angle to the stone. Slide the knife firmly across the stone away from you, from its heel to its tip. Repeat four times. Then turn the knife over and reverse the procedure, working toward you and repeating four times.

If a blade is only slightly dull, sharpen only using the fine side of the stone. Afterward, wash the stone thoroughly and wrap it in a cloth to store it.

How to Load a Dishwasher

- Scrape off bones and large quantities or chunks of food. Empty glasses and cups. Don't rinse; most dishwashers can clean away food particles (but not burnt-on food; wash these dishes by hand).

- Put pots and baking dishes with the most residues in the lower rack facing down toward the spray arm. Make sure pot handles are secure and won't interfere with or block the spray arm.

- Put plates and bowls in the bottom rack.

- Position large platters or cookie sheets along the sides so they don't prevent the water from reaching the detergent dispenser and the silverware basket.
- Use the top rack for smaller and lighter items, including plastics labeled "dishwasher-safe." Place cups and glasses between prongs or snugly over two prongs to hold them securely. Never wash glasses or fragile glassware on the bottom rack.
- Silverware (meaning "stainless steel") cleans best when you put it in the basket with the handles downward. For safety, however, place sharp knives blade down. Be careful not to let a thin knife stick through the basket bottom and stop the spray arm. (Most silver manufacturers recommend that you not wash silver in a dishwasher.)
- Remember to choose the air-dry option, and always wash full loads. A dishwasher uses the same amount of hot water and energy whether it's half-filled or fully loaded.

Giant Geese Found!

In the 1950s, the giant Canada goose, a subspecies of the Canada goose, was believed to be extinct until, in the winter of 1962, Harold Hanson of the Illinois Natural History Survey spotted a small flock in Rochester, Minnesota.

Of Unsticky Tape and Sticky Notes

In 1925, 3M (Minnesota Mining and Manufacturing) invented a tape that could be applied and removed without damaging painted surfaces. The "masking tape" was used by the auto industry to paint two-tone cars.

One legendary 3M tale tells of a customer who told a company salesman in 1930 to "take this tape back to your stingy Scotch bosses and tell them to put more adhesive on it." That complaint supposedly inspired 3M's famous cellophane "Scotch tape."

In 1974, another 3M employee named Art Fry, who sang in a church choir in St. Paul, was fond of using scraps of paper to mark his place in his hymnal. But the scraps had a tendency to fall out. His frustration led him to remember an adhesive that had been invented years before by 3M scientist Dr. Spencer Silver. It held, but could be removed easily. A year and a half later, Fry took his "sticky" notes idea to the 3M marketing department.

When a citywide giveaway in Boise, Idaho revealed that 90 percent of people trying the sticky notes would buy them again, the company went into production of "Post-It Notes" in 1980. They are now one of the five top-selling office products in the United States.

DECEMBER

"Full knee-deep lies the winter snow,

And the winter winds are wearily sighing:

Toll ye the church bell sad and slow,

And tread softly and speak low,

For the old year lies a-dying.

Old year you must not die;

You came to us so readily,

You lived with us so steadily,

Old year you shall not die."

— ALFRED LORD TENNYSON

Mark Twain once said that the coldest winter he ever spent was a summer in Duluth. And ever since, the jokes about a Minnesota winter have abounded.

As do the Minnesota snows. In northeastern Minnesota, you can count on the white stuff to last from December into late March. In the south, you can keep the cross-country skis and snowshoes in use from late December to late February.

But whether north or south, Minnesotans take a certain amount of pride in their ability to withstand their state's cold temperatures and even revel in their winters. There are at least twenty thousand miles of groomed snowmobile trails in the state, and the two largest curling clubs in the country are located in Minnesota. The St. Olaf Christmas Festival is a nationally anticipated and broadcast event, and in Minnesota you can do all your Christmas shopping in one of the world's grandest malls.

Duluthians have even come up with their own antidote—and anecdote—to Mark Twain. It goes like this: One of their city's cab drivers was asked by a visitor, "Well, what's summer in Duluth like?" The driver replied, "I don't know yet. I've only lived here for fourteen months."

Granite Falls *Blue Devils and the World's Oldest Rock*

Granite Falls claims to have two of Minnesota's most exotic environmental features: the world's oldest rock and an endangered lizard called the "blue devil."

Near the Yellow Medicine County Historical Museum, at the junction of Minnesota Highways 67 and 23, is a sign that states, "World's Oldest Rock." Below it is a lichen-covered piece of granitic gneiss that is 3.8 billion years old.

Just west across the highway is the Blue Devil Valley Preserve, a thirty-five-acre parcel of land set aside by the Minnesota Department of Natural Resources as one of the state's five natural habitats for the endangered blue devil lizard (also known as the five-lined skink).

The blue devil, a lizard indigenous to Minnesota, usually reaches five to eight-and-a-half inches in length. Adults are brown or black, and have five light, narrow stripes down their backs and sides. The head of the lizard is marked with a "V." Males who are older may become a gold-brown or olive color with only faint traces of striping. Young devils have bright blue tails that will eventually fade in males but remain a blue-gray color in females.

In fall and winter, the quick and serpentine lizards burrow in rock crevices and tunnels. They usually begin hibernating in September. In spring and summer, they may bask atop rocks and actively forage for food. During the hottest parts of the day, though, they tend to prefer the coolness of rotten logs and humus.

Minnesota Wolves

and the Ely International Wolf Center

Minnesota has more timber wolves (3,020, according to the Minnesota Department of Natural Resources' winter 2004-2005 estimate) than any other state except Alaska. Only seven states in the lower forty-eight have viable wolf packs: Minnesota, Wisconsin, Michigan, Washington, Montana, Idaho, and Wyoming. The huge national forests and parks in the northeastern corner of the state, especially the Superior National Forest and the Boundary Waters Canoe Area Wilderness, provide excellent, protected wolf habitat. And with Ontario across the border, Minnesota's wolf numbers can be continually replenished. Packs are found in northwestern Minnesota as well.

The track of the wolf is much larger than those of coyotes. The average pad size in a wolf is 4.5 inches long and 3.5 inches wide. A coyote's pad measures 2.75 inches long and a little less than 1.5 inches wide. Wolves stand 2.5 feet at the shoulder and weigh fifty to one hundred pounds; coyotes stand 1.5 feet and average twenty-five to forty pounds. Distinguishing a wolf's tracks from those of a large dog, however, can be difficult. A variety of measures taken on a series of tracks is required to verify a wolf's presence.

In 1990, the Minnesota legislature granted $1.2 million for the construction of a center to honor the wolf and educate people about an animal surrounded by myth and misunderstanding. The result was Ely's International Wolf Center, which opened on June 26, 1993. The complex includes a captive wolf pack, interactive videos, art, literature, and exhibits that educate and challenge our thinking about wolves. Other displays detail the biology of the gray wolf, its pack structure and behavior, and its struggle to survive as its habitats are increasingly logged or settled.

The center sponsors hikes to an abandoned wolf den, "howling weekends," and excursions into wolf country by dog sled.

You're the Boss

Nearly one-fourth (approximately twelve million acres) of Minnesota's land is in public ownership. The federal government owns about 3.4 million acres (7 percent of the land area) and the state government owns about 8.4 million acres (17 percent of the land area).

Northfield's St. Olaf College

When a large number of Norwegian immigrants settled in Rice County, Minnesota, in the late nineteenth century, they desired a post-secondary school for their young people that would not only offer classes in both Norwegian and English, but also keep true to their Lutheran traditions. In the 1870s, Rev. Bernt Julius Muus, with the help of the Rev. N. A. Quammen and

H. Thorson, petitioned parishioners and farmers for money to buy a plot of land on which to build such a school. The three men received about $10,000 in pledges, which provided them with enough funds to buy land and four old Northfield schoolhouse buildings. St. Olaf's opened on January 8, 1875, and by 1886, the school had expanded into a college.

Today, St. Olaf College is the only undergraduate liberal arts college in the United States accredited in the four fine arts of art, dance, music, and theater. In 1924, it broadcast the first radio drama in U.S. history (*As You Like It*). Its music program, founded by F. Melius Christiansen in 1903, is world-renowned. The St. Olaf Band became the first American college musical organization to conduct a concert tour abroad

when it traveled to Norway in 1906.

The St. Olaf Choir was founded by Christiansen in 1907 as the St. John's Lutheran Church Choir in Northfield, and it was the first to perform a cappella choral singing in the United States. The choir influenced not only the music of the Lutheran Church in Minnesota, but also choral singing in many other states. It has produced over a dozen recordings and toured Europe, China, Korea, and Australia. The choir performs annually in the nationally broadcast "St. Olaf Christmas Festival" (est. 1912), along with the St. Olaf Orchestra and four of the college's other choirs.

In 2005 the St. Olaf Band, St.

"Um! Yah! Yah!"

We come from St. Olaf,
we sure are the real stuff.
Our team is the cream of the
colleges great.
We fight fast and furious,
our team is injurious.
Tonight Carleton College
will sure meet its fate.

Um! Yah! Yah!, Um! Yah! Yah!
Um! Yah! Yah!, Um! Yah! Yah!
Um! Yah! Yah!, Um! Yah! Yah!
Um! Yah! Yah! Yah!

Um! Yah! Yah!, Um! Yah! Yah!
Um! Yah! Yah!, Um! Yah! Yah!
Um! Yah! Yah!, Um! Yah! Yah!
Um! Yah! Yah! Yah!

Olaf Orchestra, and St. Olaf Choir toured Norway to celebrate that country's centennial of independence from Sweden. The choir was also invited to perform at the White House for President George W. Bush and guests to commemorate The National Day of Prayer.

The school's fight song, based on a Norwegian folk tune and titled "Um! Yah! Yah!" is the only one in the United States in three-quarter (waltz) meter. It is one of the few college songs to mention another college, Carleton, in its lyrics. (However, the respective opposing school's name is inserted when sung at athletic competitions.)

Before graduating, St. Olaf students must complete approximately twenty courses in "foundation studies" (such as writing, a second language, oral communication, mathematical reasoning, and physical activity) and "core and integrative studies" that include human behavior and society, natural science, Western culture, and biblical theology. St. Olaf offers forty-one majors for the bachelor of arts degree and four for the bachelor of music degree.

In 1949, St. Olaf was the first Lutheran college to house the academic honor society Phi Beta Kappa. And Minnesota author F. Scott Fitzgerald wrote of the school in his novel *The Great Gatsby*. His main character, Jay Gatsby, attended St. Olaf briefly and worked as a janitor.

Long Underwear and Union Suits: The Munsingwear Story

Wool underwear was itchy until George Munsing of Minneapolis came up with the idea of covering wool thread with silk in the late 1800s. In 1887, along with Frank Page and Edward Tuttle, Munsing created a business called the Northwestern Knitting Company to manufacture the knit underwear. By 1891, the company had also patented the "union suit," an undergarment that combined an undershirt and underdrawers in a single piece of clothing.

Munsing is also reported to be the originator of the classic golf shirt. In 1919, his business was renamed "Munsingwear Corporation."

Miami, Florida-based Supreme International, a supplier of mens' and boys' casual apparel, acquired Munsingwear in 1996.

MARK YOUR CALENDAR

Mark Your DECEMBER CALENDAR

Holidazzle, Minneapolis
www.macysholidazzle.com

St. Olaf Christmas Festival, Northfield
www.stolaf.edu/christmasfest

A Strange Claim to Fame

"Lutefisk Capital of the United States"

Ahh! Christmas Eve. Nothing brings me happier childhood memories of Christmases past than the traditional holiday meal of lutefisk and lefse. But that's probably because my maternal grandmother emigrated from Norway.

Two Minnesota cities deserve a Norwegian nod in December, as they both claim to be lutefisk centers: Madison boasts itself as the "Lutefisk Capital of the United States," and Glenwood claims the title "Lutefisk Capital of the World." Madison, however, put its money where its mouth is. In 1983, the Madison Chamber of Commerce ponied up $8,000 and dedicated a twenty-five-foot-long, fiberglass fish—named "Lou T. Fisk" —and set him permanently on his pedestal in Jacobson Park.

Real lutefisk is made from air-dried whitefish—usually cod—that is prepared in a sequence of alternate soakings between cold water and lye, and then boiled. Lefse is a traditional Norwegian potato flatbread.

Minnesotan Garrison Keillor once wrote of lutefisk:

"Every Advent we entered the purgatory of lutefisk, a repulsive gelatinous fishlike dish that tasted of soap and gave off an odor that would gag a goat. We did this in honor of Norwegian ancestors, much as if survivors of a famine might celebrate their deliverance by feasting on elm bark. I always felt the cold creeps as Advent approached, knowing that this dread delicacy would be put before me and I'd be told, 'Just have a little.' Eating a little was like vomiting a little, just as bad as a lot."

And, as those famous Midwesterners Ole and Lena have reported, "Well, we tried the lutefisk trick and the raccoons went away, but now we've got a family of Norwegians living under our house!"

Actually, according to a survey conducted by the National Information Office for Meat in Norway, today only two percent of Norwegians eat lutefisk on Christmas Eve. It is far more popular with Norwegian-Americans and Norwegian-Canadians.

For me and many Minnesotans, Christmas Eve will always smell like lutefisk.

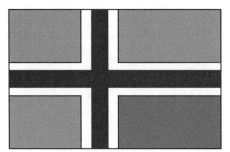

'Tis the Shopping Season

St. Paul's first store opened in 1842, and it seems it was an augur of bigger things to come for the state. A little over one hundred years later, the nation's first enclosed shopping mall, Southdale, opened in Edina. The two-story mall was built by Dayton's in 1956.

But in 1992, the state claimed a shopping title on the global level. The Mall of America, the world's largest enclosed mall, opened in Bloomington.

Since the early 1990s, the Mall of America has become the most popular tourist attraction in the state, with forty million visitors annually. The mall's 4.2 million square feet include the largest indoor theme park in the country, more than five hundred stores, fifty restaurants, and fourteen movie screens. It even has a mega-aquarium. At Underwater Adventures, visitors walk down a three-hundred-foot-long acrylic tunnel surrounded by more than a million gallons of water and 4,500 sea creatures, including tropical fish, sharks, octopi, and stingrays.

Oh, and what would Mall of America's hanging price tag read? $650 million.

December Recipe Fattigmand

My great-grandparents emigrated from Oslo, Norway, to Canby, Minnesota, where my grandmother was born in 1895. Her Christmastime fattigmand cookies were greatly anticipated, rich treats. My aunt tells me fattigmand roughly translates to "poor man." It could be that the cookies were so named because, whether rich or poor, most people could make these cookies out of ingredients they already had in the house.

Fattigmand

4 egg yolks
4 tablespoons sugar
4 tablespoons sweet (heavy) cream
Dash of vanilla

Enough flour to make a soft dough and roll out (approximately 1 to 2 cups)
Lard (or melted Crisco) for frying
Powdered (or regular) sugar

In a large bowl, beat the egg yolks; then add the sugar, cream, and vanilla. Mix together thoroughly. Slowly add only enough flour to make a soft but manageable dough. Too much flour and too much handling will make the cookies tough.

Dust the rolling surface with flour and sugar. Roll the dough out thinly (⅛ inch) and cut into diamond shapes, approximately three to four inches long by two inches wide. Cut a one-inch slit in the middle of each fattigmand. This will keep the cookie from puffing out in the middle.

Heat the lard in a deep fryer or a deep, heavy, cast iron skillet to 375°F. Fry small batches of cookies (if they are overcrowded, they will take longer to fry) until very lightly browned (look for a light gold color; one to two minutes).

Drain on absorbent paper (brown paper grocery bags or paper towels) until cool. Sprinkle with powdered sugar.

from Grandma Alma Foss Gruenenwald

DECEMBER WEATHER

December Normals for Duluth

Day	High	Low	Mean	Precip.	Snowfall
1	27	13	20	0.05	0.5
2	27	12	20	0.05	0.5
3	27	11	19	0.04	0.5
4	26	11	19	0.04	0.5
5	26	10	18	0.04	0.5
6	25	10	18	0.04	0.5
7	25	9	17	0.04	0.5
8	25	9	17	0.04	0.5
9	24	8	16	0.03	0.5
10	24	8	16	0.03	0.5
11	24	7	16	0.03	0.4
12	23	7	15	0.03	0.4
13	23	7	15	0.03	0.4
14	23	6	14	0.03	0.4
15	22	6	14	0.03	0.4
16	22	5	14	0.03	0.4
17	22	5	13	0.03	0.4
18	21	4	13	0.02	0.5
19	21	4	13	0.02	0.5
20	21	4	12	0.02	0.5
21	21	3	12	0.02	0.5
22	20	3	12	0.02	0.5
23	20	3	11	0.02	0.5
24	20	2	11	0.02	0.5
25	20	2	11	0.02	0.5
26	19	2	10	0.02	0.5
27	19	1	10	0.03	0.5
28	19	1	10	0.03	0.5
29	19	1	10	0.03	0.5
30	18	0	9	0.03	0.5
31	18	0	9	0.03	0.6

DECEMBER WEATHER

December Normals for International Falls

Day	High	Low	Mean	Precip.	Snowfall
1	24	7	15	0.03	0.5
2	23	6	15	0.03	0.5
3	23	6	14	0.03	0.5
4	22	5	14	0.03	0.5
5	22	4	13	0.03	0.5
6	22	4	13	0.03	0.5
7	21	3	12	0.03	0.5
8	21	3	12	0.03	0.5
9	20	2	11	0.02	0.5
10	20	2	11	0.02	0.4
11	20	1	10	0.02	0.4
12	19	0	10	0.02	0.4
13	19	0	9	0.02	0.4
14	18	-1	9	0.02	0.4
15	18	-1	8	0.02	0.4
16	18	-2	8	0.02	0.4
17	17	-2	8	0.02	0.4
18	17	-3	7	0.02	0.4
19	17	-3	7	0.02	0.4
20	16	-3	7	0.02	0.4
21	16	-4	6	0.02	0.4
22	16	-4	6	0.02	0.4
23	16	-5	6	0.02	0.4
24	15	-5	5	0.02	0.4
25	15	-5	5	0.02	0.4
26	15	-6	5	0.02	0.5
27	15	-6	4	0.02	0.5
28	14	-6	4	0.02	0.5
29	14	-7	4	0.02	0.5
30	14	-7	3	0.02	0.5
31	14	-7	3	0.02	0.5

Source: National Oceanic and Atmospheric Administration (NOAA)'s National Weather Service

These climate normals are an average of thirty years of data between 1971 and 2000. Every ten years, the National Weather Service recalculates the normals using the next interval of thirty years. In 2010, the new normals will be recalculated using the period of 1981 to 2010.

DECEMBER WEATHER HISTORY

On This Day in December

Day	Year	Weather
1	1998	The warmest December day ever in the Twin Cities with 68 degrees. St. Cloud rises to 61.
2	1982	Warm-up over southern Minnesota. Record high of 63 degrees at Twin Cities.
3	1856	Severe Blizzard in Iowa lasts for three days.
4	1953	Ice storm in the southeast. Two inches of ice on telephone wires.
5	2001	Warm December day with a high of 63 degrees at the Twin Cities. Summerlike thunderstorms develop and drop quarter-size hail at the Eyota Post Office in Olmsted County.
6	1950	Snowstorm hits Duluth with 23.2 inches of snow in twenty-four hours. Total snowfall is 35.2 inches.
7	1982	A farmer near St. Bonifacius bails his fourth crop of alfalfa hay today.
8	1804	John Sayer at the Snake River Fur Trading Post near present-day Pine City mentions: "Cold day. Thermometer ten degrees below freezing." On this day in 1876 the term "blizzard" is first used, appearing in the government publication *Monthly Weather Review.*
9	1961	Mora gets about a foot of snow.
10	1889	Late season thunderstorm observed at Maple Plain.
11	1983	Nine cars fall through the ice at the same time on Buffalo Lake in central Minnesota. There were only 5 to 6 inches of ice on the lake.
12	1939	December gale at the North Shore; winds clocked at 48 mph in Duluth.
13	1821	Cold snap begins at Ft. Snelling. Except for one day, below zero temperature for nineteen days.
14	1933	Severe ice storm hits southeast and central Minnesota.
15	1939	Lilacs budding at New London due to an extended warm spell. Highs in the 50s were common for the first half of December.
16	1940	Snowstorm hits the state. Water equivalent of the snow reaches 1.27 inches at Winona.
17	1946	Heavy snow with wind across northern Minnesota. Duluth has winds up to 62 mph.
18	1922	Heat wave across the south. Temperature rises into the 60s at New Ulm and St. Peter.
19	1922	Heat wave across Minnesota. New Ulm reaches the 60s.
20	1989	Hard-pressed to find snow cover in Minnesota. Only good place to cross-country ski is at Grand Marais and along the Gunflint Trail.
21	1939	Latest date for Lake Minnewaska to freeze over at Glenwood.
22		Every year, the amount of sunlight on this day can vary from nearly nine hours along the Iowa border to eight hours and fifteen minutes at International Falls.
23	1833	Warm spell at Ft. Snelling. Temperature reaches 45 degrees.

DECEMBER WEATHER HISTORY

On This Day in December

Day	Year	Weather
24	1982	Heavy rain over the state with slushy snow over southwest Minnesota. Twin Cities see 2.61 inches of precipitation through Christmas.
25	1922	People golfing in the Twin Cities as temperatures reach the 50s.
26	1985	Hurricane-force winds over the Dakotas as gale moves across the Upper Midwest.
27	1982	Snowstorm starts across state and dumps 16 inches in the Twin Cities.
28	1927	Temperature falls from 41 to -15 at Farmington.
29	1830	Snowstorm across the upper Midwest dumps 36 inches in Kansas City.
30	1980	Heat wave across the state. Redwood Falls hits 51.
31	1937	Damage done by a flood at Grand Marais. Eighteen inches of snow is dumped on Grand Portage.

Source: Minnesota State Climatology Office: DNR Waters

The State of Snowmobiling

You could say the state is snowmobile crazy. Minnesota has more than twenty thousand miles of groomed snowmobile trails and is said to have the most snowmobiles per capita: one for every twenty Minnesotans.

It all began in Roseau in 1955. Three entrepreneurs of Polaris Industries, Inc., Edgar and Allan Heteen and David Johnson, were busy making farm equipment, such as elevators, straw choppers, and corncribs. But then Allan and David got a bright idea. Tired of using skis to get to their favorite winter hunting locations, they "borrowed" parts from the company and built a machine that could carry them across the snow.

Edgar, angry with the other two for wasting time and company materials on a frivolity, sold the machine to the lumberyard owner for $465 to help pay the company's bills. Never one to be kept down, Allan started building a second machine, which Edgar promptly sold as well. That first year, Edgar sold six of the so-called "iron dogs."

Edgar left the company in June 1960 and started a competing business called Polar Manufacturing in Thief River Falls, Minnesota. The company's name was later changed to Arctic Cat. Today, Polaris and Arctic Cat are two of the world's largest snowmobile manufacturers, employing thousands of people.

Feeding Birds • Peanut Butter Suet Cookies •
A Living Christmas Tree

Feeding Birds

In the winter, birds need high-energy foods, and lots of them. In the season's shorter days, they must eat about fifty percent of their body weight just to keep warm. That's the same as a 150-pound person eating seventy-five pounds of food per day.

It will take about two weeks for your neighborhood birds to discover and add your bird feeder to their daily feeding routes. To attract them, place some feeders close to the house and some farther away. Try a variety of feeders: hanging feeders, tray feeders with a roof, suet feeders, and feeders with suction cups that can stick to your windows. For fun, keep a Web cam trained on your feeder and try to identify your yard's winged residents.

Feeding wild birds, however, is not without controversy and does carry some potential risks. Birds may contract and spread disease by gathering at poorly maintained feeders and watering stations. Birds at feeders are more prone to attack by cats and other predators, or may accidentally fly into windows. Regular disinfecting of feeders, however, can reduce risks. Once a month, all feeders and watering stations should be washed in mild dish soap and weak bleach solution and allowed to air-dry before being refilled. Check to make sure your feed has not become moldy or rancid. Position feeders to reduce overcrowding.

To encourage winter birds to visit your yard, try the recipe below for your hanging suet feeder.

Peanut Butter Suet Cookies

1 cup lard	2 cups cornmeal
1 cup crunchy peanut butter	1 cup whole wheat, soy, or white flour
2 cups oats	$\frac{1}{2}$ cup crushed eggshells

Optional: walnuts, pecans, sunflower seeds, shelled peanuts, dehydrated blueberries or cranberries, raisins, figs, dates, or mountain ash berries

Melt the lard and peanut butter in a pan. Stir in all the remaining ingredients. Fill small, plastic margarine containers about half full or form into individual patties and wrap in waxed paper; then freeze all in a large, plastic bag.

Remember to always add grit (such as the crushed eggshells used in the recipe above, fine chicken grit, or ground oyster shells). Birds have no teeth, so they eat sand or gravel (grit) to help grind up their food. In the winter, snow often covers up grit sources. Birds then have to look for grit along roadsides, where cars may hit them. Save birds from this scenario by providing grit in your suet.

A Living Christmas Tree

Every year, as we were taking down the Christmas tree and carefully putting the decorations away, my father would say, "It's like you're packing away all the memories." If you've ever felt that nostalgic ache in your heart while hauling your tree to the curbside after the holidays, you may want to consider having a live Christmas tree.

With a live tree, there's no throwing away of the good times. You can commemorate a special Christmas celebration by planting the tree that was an intimate part of it in your yard. Here's a guide to getting the most from your "live" Christmas tree:

- A few weeks before Christmas, start looking for a local nursery or Christmas tree farm that sells living Christmas trees.
- Find out if your tree will be balled and burlapped or container grown. You will need a large galvanized tub to display a balled-and-burlapped tree.
- Prepare the tree's outdoor site while temperatures are moderate. Dig a hole large enough to accommodate the tree and roughen the sides of the hole with a shovel. Cover the hole with a board or fill it with woodchips.
- Store the soil under a tarp or in a location where it will not freeze.
- Once you have purchased your tree, gradually introduce it from outside to inside over three or four days via a garage or an enclosed porch. A tree that is dormant and exposed to immediate warmth will start to grow, and you'll want to avoid any quick resumption of growth. If your tree is balled and burlapped (not container grown), place the tree in the large tub, stabilizing it in a straight, vertical position using rocks or bricks. Water often enough to keep the roots moist but not soggy. Fill the empty space around and on top of the ball with mulch to retain as much moisture as possible.
- While the tree is acclimatizing on the porch or in the garage, check it for animals and insect eggs. Purchase an antidesiccant or antiwilt spray at a garden supply store to minimize needle loss.
- Move the tree inside to a cool location (away from heating ducts) just prior to your holiday celebration. Place container-grown trees on a large saucer.
- Leave your tree inside no longer than four to seven days (some say you can leave the tree inside as long as ten days, but you don't want to initiate growth in a dormant tree). Move the tree back to the porch or garage for several weeks. This allows the tree to gradually adjust to the cold outdoor temperatures.
- Plant, water, and mulch—and always remember those special times.

Gladys's

December Household Tips

A snowy, winter Minnesota night calls for a warm, crackling fire. Whether you prefer to enjoy yours indoors in an overstuffed armchair along with a good book, or on the patio with neighbors and hot chocolates, here are some fire pointers:

Building a Fire in Your Indoor Fireplace

- Remove ashes and soot from an old fire. Keep large cinders and half-burned logs.

- Clear the hearth of anything flammable. Look up the chimney to make sure the damper is open.

- Place a few sheets of crumpled newspaper at the bottom of the fireplace grate. A grate enables fire to pull in the air it needs to keep a draft going up the chimney.

- Over the paper crisscross some short, dry kindling sticks that are one-half inch by ten inches. Or use "fatwood" for kindling. Fatwood is chemical-free pine, cut into sticks, that creates a one-match flame for fire starting.

- On top of the kindling, place eight or ten pieces of hardwood—such as oak, maple, cherry, or hickory—in a crisscross pattern, using pieces about one inch square by one foot long so the fire does not collapse.

- Crumple two more sheets of paper and light them. Hold them up inside the fireplace for a few seconds to warm the flue and establish an upward flow of air. Light the paper in the fireplace grate from each end.

- Once the paper lights the kindling, and the kindling lights the hardwood (approximately ten minutes), you may add two or three pieces of larger split, dry hardwood toward the rear of the fireplace. Hardwoods keep the fire burning at a constant temperature. The ideal firewood has dried for about one year.

- Place your fireplace screen in front of your fire as protection from stray sparks.

Building a Fire in Outdoor Bowls and Fireplaces

- First, never leave an outdoor fire unattended. Place the fireplace or bowl in a level spot. The location of the fire must not be close to trees, buildings, or any object that could get ignited due to a spark.

- Be sure to have a sand bucket, fire extinguisher, hose, or other water supply within easy reach when using your outdoor fireplace.
- To become familiar with how your outdoor fireplace draws air, responds to changes in the wind, and how long it burns before you need to add fuel, start with a small fire and use minimal fuel (wood, gel, or gas).
- Use a fatwood stick to light the fire.
- After the flames have died down a bit, use insulated safety gloves to place the mesh screen that comes with the outdoor fireplace in front of or over the fire. The screen keeps sparks and burning debris from escaping the fire area.
- Be sure your fire is completely out before leaving your outdoor fireplace at the end of the evening.

Throwing Stones *The Ice Sport of Curling*

In 1565, Holland artist Peter Breugel painted "Hunters in the Snow" and another work that pictured people playing a game resembling modern curling. These paintings support the theory that curling originated in continental Europe.

The Scots, however, are the undisputed developers of the modern game. By 1638, curling, played by sliding a heavy, round stone across the ice toward a target, was as popular in Scotland as golf and archery. By the nineteenth century, thousands were curling in almost every Scottish parish.

Using their wives' flatirons, settlers from Scotland introduced the game of curling to Minnesota in the 1850s. Today in the United States, there are more than thirteen thousand curlers in 135 clubs. Curling debuted as a medal sport in the 1998 Winter Olympic Games in Japan, after a retroactive decision was passed that made the curling competition from the 1924 Winter Olympics "official," as opposed to a "demonstration event."

Minnesota has continued to embrace the sport in a big way. The largest curling club in the country is the St. Paul Curling Club, founded in 1888, with almost eleven hundred dues-paying members. The Duluth Curling Club, organized in 1891, is the second largest in the U.S. The game is also popular in Bemidji, home of the 2006 United States men's and women's Olym-pic curling teams.

"Happy, happy Christmas, that can win us back to the delusions of our childhood days, recall to the old man the pleasures of his youth, and transport the traveler back to his own fireside and quiet home!"
—CHARLES DICKENS